# A Buddhist History of the West

# A Buddhist History of the West

## Studies in Lack

David R. Loy

STATE UNIVERSITY OF NEW YORK PRESS

Published by
STATE UNIVERSITY OF NEW YORK PRESS,
ALBANY

© 2002 State University of New York

For information, address
State University of New York Press
90 State Street, Suite 700, Albany, NY 12207

Production, Laurie Searl
Marketing, Fran Keneston

**Library of Congress Cataloging-in-Publication Data**

Loy, David R., 1947–
     A Buddhist history of the West : studies in lack / David R. Loy.
     p. cm. — (SUNY series in religious studies)
     Includes bibliographical references and index.
     ISBN 0-7914-5259-X (alk. paper) — (ISBN 0-7914-5260-3 (pbk. : alk. paper)
     1. Civilization, Western—Psychological aspects. 2. Civilization, Western—Philosophy.
3. Civilization, Western—Classical influences. 4. Philosophy, Buddhist. 5.
Buddhism—Doctrines. 6. Self (Philosophy) 7. Identity (Psychology) 8.
Self-consciousness. I. Title. II. Series.

CB245.R68 2002
909'.09821—dc21                                                        2001049415

10 9 8 7 6 5 4 3 2 1

# CONTENTS

ACKNOWLEDGMENTS     VII

INTRODUCTION: TOWARD A BUDDHIST PERSPECTIVE     1

ONE     THE LACK OF FREEDOM     17

TWO     THE LACK OF PROGRESS     41

THREE     THE RENAISSANCE OF LACK     65

FOUR     THE LACK OF MODERNITY     87

FIVE     THE LACK OF CIVIL SOCIETY     125

SIX     PREPARING FOR SOMETHING THAT NEVER HAPPENS     171

SEVEN     THE RELIGION OF THE MARKET     197

AFTERWORD: THE FUTURE OF LACK     211

NOTES     217

BIBLIOGRAPHY     223

INDEX     229

# ACKNOWLEDGMENTS

Earlier drafts of some of these chapters have been published previously. Permission from the following journals and publishers to reprint this material is gratefully acknowledged.

"Freedom: A Buddhist Critique" (a shortened version) in *Justice and Democracy: Cross-Cultural Perspectives,* ed. Ron Bontekoe and Maria Stepaniants. Honolulu: University of Hawaii Press, 1997. The full version was published under the same title in *International Studies in Philosophy* 32, no. 2 (2000).

"The Spiritual Origins of the West: A *Lack* Perspective," in *International Philosophical Quarterly* 40, no. 2 (June 2000).

"Trying to Become Real: A Buddhist Critique of Some Secular Heresies," *International Philosophical Quarterly* 32, no. 4 (December 1992).

Chapter 5: "Trying to Become Real," in David Loy, *Lack and Transcendence: The Problem of Death and Life in Psychotherapy, Existentialism, and Buddhism* (Atlantic Highlands, N.J.: Humanities Press, 1996; Amherst, N.Y.: Humanity Books, 1999).

"Preparing for Something that Never Happens: The Means/Ends Problem in Modern Culture," *International Studies in Philosophy* 26, 4 (1994). Also published in *Varieties of Ethical Reflection* Michael Barnhart, ed. (Lanham, MD: Lexington Books, 2001).

"The Religion of the Market," in *Journal of the American Academy of Religion* 65, no. 2 (Summer 1997). Also published in *Visions of a New Earth: Religious Perspectives on Population, Consumption and Ecology,* ed. Harold C. Coward and Dan Maguire. Albany, N.Y.: State University of New York Press, 1999).

Among the many people who have helped along the way, special thanks to Fred Dallmayr, Ruben Habito, Gary Snyder, and Eugene

Webb, along with a deep bow to Jon Watts and other members of the Think Sangha. I am also grateful to Harold Coward (editor, SUNY series in Religious Studies), Nancy Ellegate (editor, SUNY Press) and Laurie Searl (editor, SUNY Press) for their assistance and encouragement.

Last but certainly not least: thank you, Linda.

To all those working toward a
better understanding of our *lack*

History is the tragic record of heroism and expiation out of control and of man's efforts to earn expiation in new, frantically driven and contrived ways. The burden of guilt created by cumulative possessions, linear time, and secularization is assuredly greater than that experienced by primitive man; it has to come out some way.

—Ernest Becker, *Escape from Evil*

# TOWARD A BUDDHIST PERSPECTIVE

> If one looks with a cold eye at the mess man has made of his
> history, it is difficult to avoid the conclusion that he has been
> afflicted by some built-in mental disorder which drives him
> towards self-destruction.
>
> —Arthur Koestler

If our sense of self is a construct, as Buddhism and contemporary psychology agree, it is also ungrounded. This book is about the ways we have tried to ground ourselves, to make ourselves feel more real. To be self-conscious is to experience our ungroundedness as a sense of *lack,* but what we are lacking has been understood differently in different historical periods. The chapters that follow show how our understanding of this *lack* changed at crucial historical junctures; in fact, these new understandings of *lack* seem to be why those junctures were so crucial in the development of the West.

Traditionally, religion is the main way we try to ground our ungroundedness. From such a lack perspective, then, the history of the West is not a story of gradual secularization, for we can never escape the burden of our lack and the need to transcend it. Rather, our history becomes a tale of the increasingly this-worldly ways we have attempted to resolve this lack. Since it is due to our ungroundedness, which is basically a spiritual problem, these attempts have for the most part been unsuccessful. In psychotherapeutic terms: we have unconsciously projected and objectified our lack by trying to ground ourselves somewhere *in*

1

the world. Our inability to do that means we continue to be haunted by our own shadow.

What makes this a *Buddhist* history of the West? Reduced to its essentials, Buddhism teaches that, if we want to be happy, our greed, ill will, and delusion must be transformed into their more positive counterparts: generosity, compassion, and wisdom. Is this true collectively as well as personally? The history of the West, like all histories, has been plagued by the consequences of greed, ill will, and delusion. The first two are obvious enough. What is emphasized in the pages that follow is the third: the largely unconscious ways that we have tried to resolve our lack—ways that have often led to greater suffering.

It must be emphasized at the outset that this book offers a Buddhist perspective, not *the* Buddhist perspective. It is one contemporary interpretation of Buddhist teachings that attempts to develop those teachings in a particular direction, in order to understand what they can mean for us today, in a world very different from Shakyamuni's. In accordance with its own emphasis on impermanence and essencelessness, Buddhism has been adaptable as it has disseminated to other places and cultures. To what, then, is Buddhism adapting today, as it infiltrates Western consciousness? Buddhist-Christian dialogue continues to be a fruitful interreligious encounter; others might point more facetiously to Hollywood's fascination with Tibetan Buddhism. Yet it is becoming clearer that Buddhism's main point of entry into Western culture is now Western psychology, especially psychotherapy.

This interaction is all the more interesting because psychoanalysis and most of its offspring remain marked by an antagonism to religion that is a legacy of the Enlightenment, which defined itself in opposition to myth and superstition. In spite of that—or because of it?—this interaction between Buddhism and Western psychology is an opportunity for comparison in the best sense, in which we do not merely wrench two things out of context to notice their similarities, but benefit from the different light that each casts upon the other. While contemporary psychology brings to this encounter a more sophisticated understanding of the ways we make ourselves unhappy, it seems to me that Buddhist teachings provide a deeper insight into the source of the problem.

What is that problem? For the most part "I" experience my sense-of-self as stable and persistent, apparently immortal; yet there is also awareness of my impermanence, the fact that "I" am growing older and will die. The tension between them is essentially the same one that confronted Shakyamuni himself, when, as the myth has it, he ventured out of his father's palace to encounter for the first time an ill man, an aged man, and finally a corpse. Insofar as this problem often motivates the psychotherapeutic quest to understand ourselves and the meanings of our lives and our deaths, there is already a deep affinity between the two.

Most traditional religions resolve the contradiction by claiming that the soul is immortal. Buddhism does the opposite, not by simply accepting our mortality in the usual sense, but by offering a path that emphasizes realizing something hitherto unnoticed about the nature of that impermanence. Inasmuch as Western psychotherapeutics cope with our death fears not by denying death but by making us more aware of those fears and what they mean for our life, there is further affinity between the two. In psychological terms, both emphasize that what passes for normality (*samsara* in Buddhism) is a low-grade of psycho-pathology, unnoticed only because so common; that the supposedly autonomous ego-self is conditioned in ways we are normally not aware of (*karma, samskaras*); and that greater awareness of our mental processes can free us (*samadhi, prajna*).

The crucial link between the two traditions is the Buddhist doc-trine of *anatta*, "no-self." *Anatta* is essential to Buddhism, but to make sense of it we need to relate it to another concept: *dukkha*, usually translated as "suffering," better understood more broadly as frustration or unhappiness. The four ennobling truths into which Shakyamuni often summarized his teachings focus on this: life as *dukkha*, the cause of that *dukkha*, the end of *dukkha*, and the path to end *dukkha*. It is no exaggeration to say that this is the most important concept in Bud-dhism. On more than one occasion, the Buddha said that he taught only one thing: how to end *dukkha*.

Although psychotherapy today has more specific insight into the dynamics of our mental *dukkha* (repression, transference, etc.), I believe that Buddhism points more directly at the root of the problem: not dread of death, finally—that fear still keeps the feared thing at a distance by projecting it into the future —but the more immediate and terri-fying (because quite valid) suspicion each of us has that "*I*" *am not real right now.* No-self implies a subtle yet significant distinction between fear of death and fear of the void—that is, terror of our own ground-lessness, which we become aware of as a sense of lack and which motivates our compulsive but usually futile attempts to ground our-selves in one way or another, according to the opportunities for self-grounding that our particular situations seem to provide. In short, our lack represents the link between *dukkha* (our inability to be happy) and *anatta* (our lack of self).

Although Shakyamuni Buddha did not use psychoanalytic terms, our understanding of the Buddhist denial of self can benefit from the concept of repression and what Freud called the return of the repressed in symbolic form. If something (a mental wish, according to Freud) makes me uncomfortable and I do not want to cope with it consciously, I can choose to ignore or "forget" it. This allows me to concentrate on something else, yet what has been repressed tends to return to consciousness. What is not willingly admitted into awareness irrupts in obsessive ways—symptoms—that affect consciousness with precisely those qualities it strives to exclude. Existential psychologists such as Ernest Becker and Irvin Yalom argue that our primary repression is not sexual desires, as Freud believed, but the awareness that we are going to die. *Anatta* implies a slightly different perspective.

Buddhism analyzes the sense-of-self into sets of impersonal mental and physical processes, whose interaction creates the illusion of self-consciousness—i.e., that consciousness is the attribute of a self. The death-repression emphasized by existential psychology transforms the Oedipal complex into what Norman Brown calls an Oedipal *project*: the attempt to become father of oneself, that is, one's own origin. The child wants to conquer death by becoming the creator and sustainer of his/her own life. Buddhism shows us how to shift the emphasis: the Oedipal project is the attempt of the developing sense-of-self to attain autonomy, to become like Rene Descartes's supposedly self-sufficient consciousness. It is the quest to deny one's groundlessness by becoming one's own ground: the ground (socially conditioned yet nonetheless illusory) I "know" as being an independent self.

Then the Oedipal project derives from our uncomfortable, repressed awareness that self-consciousness is not "self-existing" (*svabhava*) but ungrounded, because a mental construct. Consciousness is like the surface of the sea, dependent on unfathomed depths that it cannot grasp because it is a manifestation of them. The problem arises when this conditioned consciousness wants to ground itself—i.e., to make itself *real*. Since the sense-of-self "inside" is an always unfinished, never secure construct, its efforts to real-ize itself are attempts to objectify itself in some fashion in the world. The ego-self is this never-ending project to realize oneself by objectifying oneself, something consciousness can no more do than a hand can grasp itself, or an eye see itself.

The consequence of this perpetual failure is that the sense-of-self is shadowed by a sense-of-lack, which it always tries to escape. The return of the repressed in the distorted form of a symptom shows us how to link this basic yet hopeless project with the symbolic ways we try to make ourselves real in the world. We experience this deep sense of lack as the feeling that "there is something wrong with me," but that feeling manifests, and we respond to it, in many different ways. In its "purer" forms lack appears as what might be called an ontological guilt or anxiety that gnaws on one's very core. For that reason ontological guilt tends to become guilt for something, because then we know how to atone for it; and anxiety is eager to objectify into fear of something, because we know how defend ourselves against particular feared things.

The problem with all objectifications, however, is that no object can ever satisfy if it is not really an object that we want. When we do not understand what is actually motivating us—because what we think we want is only a symptom of something else (according to Buddhism, our desire to become real, which is essentially a spiritual yearning)—we end up compulsive. According to Nietzsche, someone who follows the Biblical admonition literally and plucks out his own eye does not kill his sensuality, for "it lives on in an uncanny vampire form and torments him in repulsive disguises." Yet the opposite is also true: insofar as we think we have escaped such a spiritual drive we are deceiving ourselves, for that drive (to escape our lack and become real) still lives on in uncanny secular forms that obsess us because we do not understand what motivates them.

Then the neurotic's anguish and despair are not the result of symptoms but their source. Those symptoms are necessary to shield him or her from the tragedies that the rest of us are better at repressing: death, meaninglessness, groundlessness. "The irony of man's condition is that the deepest need is to be free of the anxiety of death and annihilation [i.e., lack]; but it is life itself which awakens it, and so we must shrink from being fully alive" (Becker 1973, 66). If the autonomy of self-consciousness is a delusion that can never quite shake off its shadow feeling that "something is wrong with me," it will need to rationalize that sense of inadequacy somehow.

This shifts our focus from the terror of future annihilation to the anguish of a groundlessness experienced here and now. On this account, even fear of death and desire for immortality symbolize something else: they become symptomatic of our vague intuition that the ego-self is not a hard core of consciousness but a mental construction, the axis of a web spun to hide the void. Those whose constructions are badly damaged, the insane, are uncomfortable to be with because they remind us of that fact.

In more Buddhist terms, the ego-self is delusive because, like everything else, it is an impermanent manifestation of interdependent phenomena, yet it feels alienated from that interconditionality. The basic difficulty is that insofar as I feel separate (i.e., an autonomous, self-existing consciousness) I also feel uncomfortable, because an illusory sense of separateness is inevitably insecure. It is this inescapable trace of nothingness in my "empty" (because not really self-existing) sense-of-self that is experienced as a sense-of-lack. In reaction, the sense-of-self becomes preoccupied with trying to make itself self-existing, in one way or another.

According to Otto Rank, contemporary man is neurotic because he suffers from a consciousness of sin just as much as premodern man did, but without believing in the religious conception of sin, which leaves us without a means to expiate our sense of guilt. Why do we need to feel guilty, and accept suffering, sickness, and death as condign punishment? What role does that guilt play in determining the meaning of our lives? "The ultimate problem is not guilt but the incapacity to live. The illusion of guilt is necessary for an animal that cannot enjoy life, in order to organize a life of nonenjoyment" (Brown 240). Even a feeling of wrongdoing gives us some sense of control over our own destinies, because an explanation has been provided for our sense of lack. We need to project our lack onto something, because only in that way can we get a handle on it.

In contrast to the Abrahamic religions, Buddhism does not reify the sense of lack into an original sin, although our problems with attachment and ignorance are historically conditioned. Shakyamuni Buddha declared that he was not interested in the metaphysical issue of origins and emphasized that he had one thing only to teach: how to end *dukkha*. This suggests that Buddhism is best understood as a way to resolve our sense of lack. Since there was no primeval offense and no divine expulsion from the Garden, our situation turns out to be paradoxical: our worst problem is the deeply repressed fear that our groundlessness/no-thing-ness is a problem. When I stop trying to fill up that hole at my core by vindicating or real-izing myself in some symbolic way, something happens to it—and therefore to me.

This is easy to misunderstand, for the letting go that is necessary is not something consciousness can simply do. The ego cannot absolve its own lack because the ego is the other side of that lack. When ontological guilt is experienced more "purely"—as the unobjectified feeling that "something is wrong with me"—there seems to be no way to cope with it, so normally we become conscious of it as the neurotic guilt of "not being good enough" in this or that particular way. One way to describe the Buddhist path is that the guilt expended in these situations is converted back into ontological guilt, and that guilt endured without evasion; the method for doing this is simply awareness, which meditation cultivates. Letting go of the mental devices that sustain my self-esteem, "I" become more vulnerable. Such guilt, experienced in or rather as the core of one's being, cannot be resolved by the ego-self; there is nothing one can do with it except be conscious of it and bear it and let it burn itself out, like a fire that exhausts its fuel, which in this case is the sense-of-self. If we cultivate the ability to dwell as it, then ontological guilt, finding nothing else to be guilty for, consumes the sense-of-self and thereby itself too.

From this Buddhist perspective, our most problematic duality is not life against death but self versus nonself, or being versus nonbeing. As in psychotherapy, the Buddhist response to such bipolar dualisms involves recognizing the side that has been denied. If death is what the sense-of-self fears, the solution is for the sense-of-self to die. If it is no-thing-ness (the repressed intuition that, rather than being autonomous and self-existent, the "I" is a construct) I am afraid of, the best way to resolve that fear is to become nothing. The thirteenth-century Japanese Zen master Dogen (1985, 70) sums up this process in a well-known passage from *Genjo-koan*:

> To study the buddha way is to study the self. To study the self is to forget the self. To forget the self is to be actualized by myriad things. When actualized by myriad things, your body and mind as well as the bodies and minds of others drop away. No trace of realization remains, and this no-trace continues endlessly.

"Forgetting" ourselves is how we lose our sense of separation and realize that we are not other than the world. Meditation is learning how to become nothing by learning to forget the sense-of-self, which happens when I become absorbed into my meditation exercise. If the sense-of-self is an effect of self-reflection—of consciousness attempting to grasp itself—such meditation practice makes sense as an exercise in *de-reflection*. Consciousness unlearns trying to grasp itself, real-ize itself, objectify itself. Liberating awareness occurs when the usually automatized reflexivity of consciousness ceases, which is experienced as a letting go and falling into the void. "Men are afraid to forget their minds, fearing to fall through the

Void with nothing to stay their fall. They do not know that the Void is not really void, but the realm of the real dharma" (Huang-po 41). Then, when I no longer strive to make myself real through things, I find myself "actualized" by them, says Dogen.

This process implies that what we fear as nothingness is not really nothingness, for that is the perspective of a sense-of-self anxious about losing its grip on itself. According to Buddhism, letting go of myself into that no-thing-ness leads to something else: when consciousness stops trying to catch its own tail, I become no-thing, and discover that I am everything—or, more precisely, that I can be anything. With that conflation, the no-thing at my core is transformed from a sense-of-lack into a serenity that is imperturbable because there is nothing to be perturbed.

This Buddhist account of the sense-of-self's sense of lack (developed at greater length in *Lack and Transcendence*) provides a psychological and existential explanation of the self-built mental disorder that Koestler noticed. If that gives us insight into the individual human condition, can it also shed light on the collective dynamics of societies and nations? If, as Nietzsche puts it somewhere, madness is rare in individuals but the rule in groups, peoples, and ages, does our history demonstrate a group dynamic of lack?

This issue is explored in the chapters that follow. To appreciate the argument, it is important to keep in mind that such an understanding of lack straddles our usual distinction between sacred and secular. The difference between them is reduced to where we look to resolve our sense of lack. If that lack is a constant, and if religion is understood as the way we try to resolve it, we can never escape a religious interpretation of the world. Our basic problem is spiritual inasmuch as the sense-of-self's lack of being compels it to seek being one way or another, consciously or unconsciously, whether in overtly religious ways or in "secular" ones. What today we understand as secular projects are sometimes just as symptomatic of this spiritual need. Rather than reductionistically viewing the sacred as a deluded projection of the secular, this book argues that many of our modern worldly values acquire their compulsiveness, and many modern institutions their authority, from this misdirected spiritual drive. Our lack is a constant, but how we understand it and how we try to overcome it have varied greatly throughout history. We need to look at the ways our personal senses of lack have plugged into the collective unconscious of our social behavior and institutions. We shall see that trying to resolve our sense-of-lack collectively has compounded the problem, and that such compounded lack objectifications have often assumed a life of their own.

The first chapter, The Lack of Freedom, looks at the Western ideal of freedom as it originated in classical Greece and Rome. This value has become so deeply involved in how we understand ourselves that it is hard for us to look *at* it, yet this ideal is not something "natural": it has its own history. Why did the idea of freedom arise when and where it did? This chapter argues that making freedom into our paramount value is more problematic than we have realized, for freedom conceived in secular, humanistic terms is fatally flawed. As the intellectual history of the classical period shows, it does not and cannot give us what we seek from it.

A lack perspective has two important implications for the way we view freedom. First, any culture that emphasizes the individuality of the self will inevitably come to place highest value on the freedom of that self. So it is not surprising that the Western history of freedom has been strongly associated with the development of the self, or, to put it another way, with subject-object dualism. Insofar as freedom is understood as freedom from outside control, we discriminate between internal (that which wants to be free) and external (what one is freed from). But that dualism is delusive, according to Buddhism, and one of the main sources of our *dukkha*.

Moreover, if the self-existence and autonomy of such a self is an illusion, then such a self will never be able to experience itself as enough of a self—that is, it can never feel free *enough*. It will try to resolve its lack by expanding the sphere of its freedom, which can never become large enough to be satisfactory. The history of the Stoic tradition culminates in the realization that such freedom cannot bring personal fulfillment or even peace of mind. The psychic introversion encouraged in Hellenistic philosophy broadened the sphere of one's subjectivity, but identifying that freedom with reason provided no way to cope with the increased sense of lack shadowing it. Freedom understood in such secular terms proved to be insufficient. This set the historical stage for return to a more explicitly religious perspective: the Augustinian discovery/construction of sin. Christianity offered a more attractive way to understand our lack.

Chapter 2, The Lack of Progress, traces both the dynamism of the West and the authority of its law back to the Papal Reformation, which occurred in Europe in the eleventh century. Although most of us know little about it, this was arguably the most important revolution the West ever experienced, and it was incontrovertibly a *spiritual* one, not so much because it transformed the Papacy, but because it involved a radically new understanding of our human condition and its salvation. It was based upon a novel theological doctrine about what sin is and how we can be redeemed—in other words, a new explanation for our human lack and how that is to be resolved. This led to a bifurcation of the world into the sacred and the secular spheres, whose disengagement led to "a release of energy and creativity analogous to a process of nuclear fission" (Berman 88). For better and worse, this was the crucial turning point that shifted us from focusing on an other-worldly solution to the problem of life, to constructing a this-worldly one.

The development of canon law led to a new view of sin, before understood simply as a condition of alienation from God. Sin came to be defined in legalistic terms, as specific acts and thoughts, for which painful penalties must be paid either in this life or in the next. This was an important shift from the earlier meaning of penance—acts of contrition symbolizing a turning away from sin back to God and neighbor—into a more objectified sense of sin as an entity that, as the Church soon discovered, could be commodified. In my Buddhist terms, this was a novel way to understand what our lack consists of and how it is to be resolved. The elaborate system of payments for spiritual debts implied a new type of grip on one's ultimate destiny. It also plugged nicely into the reform of this world: "progress" was born.

> The most important consequence of the Papal Revolution was that it introduced into Western history the experience of revolution itself. In contrast to the older view of secular history as a process of decay, there was introduced a dynamic quality, a sense of progress in time, a belief in the reformation of the world. No longer was it assumed that "temporal life" must inevitably deteriorate until the Last Judgment. On the contrary, it was now assumed—for the first time—that progress could be made in this world toward achieving some of the preconditions for salvation in the next. (Berman 118)

The third chapter, The Renaissance of Lack, addresses some of the changes that occurred around the time of the Renaissance. It argues that three particular types of delusive craving, which today we take for granted as natural, are in fact historically conditioned ways of trying to resolve our lack: the desire for fame, the love of romantic love, and the money complex. These three tendencies are not bound to any particular time or place, of course, yet in the West they became especially important as Christianity began to decline. As long as there was a truly catholic church providing a socially agreed method to cope with lack, such projects were not spiritually necessary and did not become obsessive. The stronger sense-of-self that began to develop in the Renaissance was shadowed by a stronger sense of lack, leading to greater individual need to real-ize this self and more radical attempts to do so.

The pursuit of fame and money are attempts to realize oneself through symbols; romantic love tries to fill in one's lack of being with the being of the beloved. All three are individualistic in that as they attempt a more personal solution to our lack, and all are secular insofar as they seek a salvation in the affairs of this world, but nonetheless religious in that they are still motivated by the spiritual desire to ground oneself and become real. Since they cannot fulfill that need, they threaten to spin out of control and become demonic.

In most Western societies belief in an afterlife has been largely replaced by a craving for fame, as an alternative way to become more real. Since the real world for us has become what's in the newspapers or on television, to be unknown is to be nothing. Because our sense-of-self is internalized through social conditioning, the natural tendency is to cope with our shadow sense of unreality by continually reassuring ourselves with the attention of other people, and the more attention the better. But if fame is my project to end my lack, disappointment is inevitable: no amount of fame can satisfy me when there is really something else I seek from it.

Another "personal religion" widely accepted today as a way to overcome our sense of lack, and also historically conditioned, is romantic love. When we fall in love (Madame de Stael called it "self-love *a deux*"), our formless sense of lack projects itself onto a particular lacked person, which provides us with a project to gain the lacked thing. Now I know what is wrong with me: I do not have *her* (or *him*). Originally the romantic myth had strong spiritual overtones, but for us it survives mostly in our preoccupation with sex. Why has sex become so obessive for so many today? If we do not dualize secular from sacred, we can see the same "spiritual" urge: we want sex to fulfill us and heal us— that is, we want it to resolve our lack, but that is something it cannot do except for the briefest of moments.

Money is perhaps our strangest social construction: a socially agreed symbol worthless in itself, yet one that has more value than anything else because it is how we define value. The psychological problem with this approach occurs when life becomes motivated by the desire for such pure value, owing to an ironic reversal between means and ends: everything else is devalued in order to maximize a "worthless" goal, because our lack has become fetishized into that symbol. Today the most popular explanation for our lack—our contemporary original sin—is that we don't have enough money. This leads to a need for constant growth: an ever higher "standard of living" and the gospel of sustained economic "development."

These constitute a defective myth because they can provide no real expiation of lack. Today our temple is the stock market, and our rite of worship is communing with the Dow Jones average. In return we receive the kiss of profits and the promise of more, yet there is no atonement in this. Of course, since we have lost belief in sin we no longer see anything to atone for, which means we end up unconsciously atoning in the only way we know, by working hard to acquire all those things that society tells us are important—and then we cannot understand why they do not make us happy, why they do not resolve our sense that something is lacking in our lives.

Chapter 4, The Lack of Modernity, supplements the above account of our individualistic idolatries with a lack history of our institutional idolatries: the nation-state, corporate capitalism, and mechanistic science, all of them born out of the religious chaos of the sixteenth century. From a lack perspective, there seems to have been something compulsive and delusive about the development of these institutions, because it was motivated by a profound social anxiety—a collective sense of lack—which became aggravated in that century and then channeled into these directions.

In the sixteenth century the organic paradigm of a hierarchical cosmos created by God collapsed, along with the worldview and institutions that maintained it. This crisis was initiated by the Protestant Reformation, which led to a new understanding of our lack and eventually to new secular ways of handling it. Luther and Calvin eliminated the intricate web of mediation between God and this world that had constituted, in effect, the sacral dimension of this world. On the one hand, God was booted upstairs, far above the sordid affairs of this world; and on the other hand the principle of a direct and personal relationship with God became sanctified. Religion became privatized.

Without a truly catholic church to take the role of God's Vicar, who would assume the mantle of His authority on earth? The void became filled by charismatic rulers of the developing nation-states with their chartered corporations, assisted by new technologies and philosophies. Together they responded to the anxiety and groundlessness of the age by embarking on a new project, which today remains our project: to compensate for our lack of spiritual grounding by collectively grounding ourselves. From a lack perspective, however, "God" is still present in the functioning of the nation-state, the market economy, and the Enlightenment scientific/technological project, because these collectivities continue to be motivated by what might be described as *institutional lack*. The history of the nation-states system demonstrates that they are unstable, externally competitive and internally self-aggrandizing. Economically, GNP is never big enough, corporations are never profitable enough, and consumers never consume enough. And the same is true for our scientific and technological establishments: the Faustian problem is not that we do not yet know enough, but that we never can, since our functionalist perspective subordinates their knowledge to our drive for ever greater control over the world.

Each is a victory of means over ends. The objectification of our lack into impersonal "secular" institutions means that basic questions about the meaning of our lives—the central spiritual issue for a being that needs to understand and resolve its own sense of lack—have become alienated into a "not yet enough" that can never be enough. For all three, power has become an end in itself, which is why there is something demonic about each of them. Power, although it may be a good servant, is a bad master because you can never have enough power if power itself is the goal. That points to the basic nihilism of modernity: the lack of an overtly spiritual grounding to our lives means that this "secular" preoccupation has become compulsive. Because this compulsion is not understood by us, these institutions have taken on lives of their own that subordinate us to them while avoiding subordination to anything else.

Chapter 5, The Lack of Civil Society, offers a lack perspective on the origins and development of civil society. Rather than being another result of the supposed secularization that began in the sixteenth century, Anglo-American civil society originated as a movement to reform society in order to make it more religious. This led to the execution of Charles I and Oliver Cromwell's Commonwealth—a radical transformation possible only because it was understood as helping to fulfill Biblical prophecy about the return of Christ.

The legacy of those millennial expectations, and the ways those hopes transformed when frustrated by the failure of the Commonwealth, were essential for the development of civil society in England

and the United States (where civil society first developed). Far from being a secular alternative to Christian conceptions of political life, the new society that began to develop in the seventeenth century would have been literally unthinkable without its Christian presuppositions. Thomas Hobbes's state of nature is a secularized version of Calvin's "natural man" without God. Socialist critiques of private property originated in allegorical interpretations of Adam's Fall and God's curse upon him. Locke's theory of individual rights is rooted in a Protestant understanding of man's relationship with God. And the unique civic society of the United States evolved in large part out of Puritan millennialist ambitions to create another Holy Commonwealth in a new, still pristine promised land.

The important point is not simply that Anglo-American civil society has theological origins; our society remains theological in the sense that its values and institutions cannot help being based upon some ultimate view about our human nature—in my terms, about the nature of our lack and how that is to be overcome. Seventeenth-century discussions of the Bible produced the basic alternatives we still debate today in more secularized terms: Is human nature evil, in need of restraint? Or does an oppressive society deform our natural goodness? If we want to escape the stultifying standoff between them, we need to return to the basic existential issues and rethink them afresh. In order to know what to do socially about our sense of lack, we need to come to some social understanding of what it is and what causes it.

Then do the spiritual origins of Anglo-American civil society survive today as roots still necessary for its nourishment? Perhaps we cannot understand the development of our civil society without seeing how its current crisis is related to the atrophy of those roots. If so, our secular cynicism may need to recover some of the Puritans' idealism about working together to reduce the objectifications of lack that now endanger our world.

Chapter 6, Waiting for Something That Never Happens, takes a closer look at what might be called the means/ends problem in modern life: the way that contemporary culture has become so preoccupied with means that it loses ends. More precisely, they have become inverted: our means, because they never culminate in an ends, in effect have come to constitute our ends. It begins by considering what Max Weber wrote about the instrumental rationality (*Zweckrationalitat*) of the modern world, and, in reaction to that, our flights into hypertrophied subjectivity—

more private, innerworldly responses to the world's bureaucratization, which do not escape the problem but aggravate it. Weber focused on three such spheres whose nonrationality seems to offer us a personal relief from the world's inexorable rationalization: an absolute ethics of "brotherliness," aestheticism, and eroticism. Rather than providing an innerworldly salvation, however, each aggravates the problem it flees, for the deceptive possibility of a private escape encourages us to yield to the degradation of the public realm, which in turn further encourages the escapist hypertrophy of subjectivist culture.

The other figure who thought deeply about means/ends teleology was Georg Simmel, whose *Philosophy of Money* reflects on the inevitability by which such a perfect means becomes *the* end: "Money's value as a *means* increases with its *value* as a means right up to the point at which it is valid as an absolute value and the consciousness of purpose in it comes to an end" (Simmel, 232). But this is only part of a more fundamental paradox that characterizes all developing cultures, according to Simmel. The cultural forms that life produces to express and realize itself become objectified into cages for the life-force that created them but needs to transcend them. Lengthening teleological chains lead us to ask about *the* end, the ultimate purpose of life, in that way producing our modernist awareness of a split between them.

A lack approach provides the crucial link between Weber's dualism (instrumental rationality versus hypertrophied subjectivity) and Simmel's ramifying teleological chains that never reach their end. If the modern, more subjectified ego-self is a delusion whose lack is never satisfied, it will understand its dissatisfaction as caused by having failed to attain its goals, which generates a need to develop more ambitious goals, at the end of still longer teleological chains. . . .

The final chapter, The Religion of the Market, gathers together many earlier threads in arguing that the predominant religion of the modern world, in fact the most successful religion of all time—making more converts more quickly than any other belief system or value system in history—is our present economic system. From a religious perspective, the global victory of market capitalism is not inevitable but only one historically conditioned way of organizing (or reorganizing) the material world; it also implies a worldview, with an ontology and ethics, in competition with other understandings of what the world is and how we should live in it. Previous chapters present lack interpretations of the origins of the money complex and corporate capitalism, but a critical stage in their development occurred late in the eighteenth century, when new technologies led to the "liberation" of a critical mass of land, labor, and capital. Without denying the many ways we have benefited from this, we should remember that at the time it was experienced by most people as an unprecedented catastrophe that destroyed their communities—a catastrophe that continues today in much of the "developing" world.

From a lack perspective, the problem with market capitalism is twofold: greed and delusion. Desire for profit fuels it, and an insatiable desire to consume ever more must be generated to create markets for what can be produced. From a religious perspective, this greed is based on a delusion: the belief that happiness is to be found in this way, that this will resolve our lack. For Buddhism, in contrast, such desires are not the solution but a main source of the *dukkha* frustration that infects our daily lives.

As this suggests, lack as a category of historical interpretation does not aspire to be value neutral in the sense of making dispassionate "objective" claims. Our past is much too important to us for that. The Pali Buddhist term *dukkha,* along with the English words *greed, ill will* and *delusion,* are value laden, for that is what enables them to point to the increasingly obvious situation that, as increasing social problems in the "developed" world suggest, consumerism is unable to bring about the social happiness it promises. If that is so—and it is becoming increasingly difficult to deny it—don't we need to consider other ways to address our sense of lack?

ONE

# THE LACK OF FREEDOM

You have only to consider yourself free to feel yourself bound;
you have only to consider yourself bound to feel free.

—Goethe

The growth of freedom has been the central theme of history, Lord
Acton believed, because it represents God's plan for humanity. One
does not need such a Whiggish view of history to notice that the
history of the West, at least, has indeed been a story of the development
of freedom, whether actualized or idealized. We trace the origins of
Western civilization back to the Greek "emancipation" of reason from
myth. Since the Renaissance, there has been a progressive emphasis, first
on religious freedom (the Reformation), then political freedom (the
English, American, French revolutions), followed by economic freedom
(the class struggle), colonial freedom (independence movements), racial
freedom (civil rights), psychological freedom (psychotherapy frees us
from neuroses), and most recently gender equality and sexual freedom
(feminism and gay rights emancipate women and sexual "deviance").
Today deconstruction and other postmodern intellectual developments
free us from authorial intention and the strictures of the text itself—
what might be called "textual liberation."

So it is no surprise that freedom today is the paramount value of
the Western world, and through the West's influence it has become that

of the rest of the world as well. "People may sin against freedom, but no one dares deny its virtue." Yet is this virtue losing some of its luster? Recently it has become more obvious that the critiques of democratic individualism espoused by some East Asian nations are usually little more than the apologetics of authoritarian regimes.[1] Nonetheless, the history of freedom contains enough contradictions to make us pause. As important as the Renaissance was for the development of personal freedom, we also see in it the roots of the problems that haunt us today, especially the extreme individualism that liberated greed as the engine of economic development and that continues to rationalize the erosion of community bonds. The French, Russian, and Chinese revolutions resulted in Napoleon, Stalin, and Mao, respectively, vindicating Burke's warnings about the sudden disintegration of even oppressive political authority. And today our technological freedom to transform the natural world is despoiling it so effectively that we are in danger of destroying ourselves as well.

If freedom is our supreme value, then, it is a problematic one. This chapter explores that problematic from a Buddhist lack perspective. It argues that making freedom into our *paramount* value is dangerous, for freedom conceived solely in secular, humanistic terms is fatally flawed. It cannot give us what we seek from it.

Part of our resistance to such a conclusion is caused by the difficulty in considering freedom objectively. That ideal is so much a part of us, so deeply involved in the way we understand ourselves, that it is hard to look *at* it. But this value has a history. Rather than being "natural," it is the result of a complicated genealogy that needs to be examined. Therefore a comparative approach can help to delineate our situation: Why did the ideal of freedom arise in the West, when and where it did? How does it contrast with the primary values of non-Western cultures?

Another difficulty is that the very concept of freedom is extremely elusive. It is almost impossible to define in a satisfactory fashion, because the abstract concept loses meaning outside particular contexts: freedom *from* . . . or freedom *to* . . . In *Freedom in the Making of Western Culture* (1991), Orlando Patterson distinguishes what he calls the chord of freedom into three notes: personal (being able to do as one pleases within the limits of others' desire to do the same), sovereignal (the power to act as one pleases, regardless of the wishes of others), and civic (the capacity of members of a community to participate in its life and governance). Such a tripartite definition already suggests the tensions that have dogged the history of freedom from the very beginning. If freedom is a chord it is evidently an unresolved one. It is unfortunate that throughout history fighting for freedom has been much easier to do than to live freely. Why does that continue to be so?

Most studies of freedom emphasize that the West has made the major contributions to the theory and practice of freedom. Patterson also attempts to explain why freedom did not evolve in the non-Western world. His short and sketchy treatment of this question discusses North and South American Indian tribes, African preliterate societies, a group of South Pacific tribes, ancient Mesopotamia, and dynastic Egypt. It does not consider India and China, philosophically the most sophisticated non-Western cultures and therefore the ones we would expect to offer the most interesting alternatives to the Western understanding of freedom. In India, for example, *mukti* has long been acknowledged by almost all schools of thought as the highest spiritual goal:

> [S]ince human existence was traditionally conceived as a cycle of birth and death interspersed with experience or suffering, the freedom of the self could be described as freedom from this cycle of *samsara*. Freedom or *mukti*, thus, means freedom from ignorance about the self, that is, *avidya*, freedom from the passions or *klesa*, freedom from suffering or *duhkha*, and finally freedom from death and time. The Buddhists, the Jainas, and the Yogins also conceive the ideal of freedom from all limitations of knowledge, while the Siddhas seek freedom from all natural limitations. (Pande 448)

Oblivious of this, Patterson follows the received wisdom in concluding that the West's value complex of freedom is "superior to any other single complex of values conceived by mankind" (402–403). We may raise some questions about this by bringing to bear the Buddhist critique of the ego-self: the supposedly self-existing subject that, because it understands itself as separate from the world, is often preoccupied with liberating itself from the bonds that tie it to the world. For Buddhism, the ego is not a self-existing consciousness but a mental construction, a fragile sense-of-self dreading its own no-thing-ness. Our problem arises because "my" conditioned consciousness wants to ground itself—i.e., to make itself *real*. Its perpetual failure to do so means that the sense-of-self has, as its inescapable shadow, a sense of lack, which it always tries to escape. What Freud called "the return of the repressed" in the distorted form of a symptom shows us how to link this basic project with the symbolic ways we try to make ourselves real in the world.

Such a lack interpretation of the Buddhist no-self doctrine has two important implications for the way we view freedom. First, any culture that emphasizes the individuality of the self will naturally come to place paramount value on the freedom of that self. Freedom is usually defined as *self*-determination, and etymology (*de* plus *terminus,* to limit, set boundaries) reveals the implication of establishing boundaries between the self and the not-self. So it is not surprising that from its very beginning the Western history of freedom has been strongly associated with the development of the self, or, to put it another way, with increasing subject-object dualism. Insofar as freedom is understood as freedom from external control, a discrimination is implied between internal (that which wants to be free) and external (what one is freed from). This is important because what Patterson calls the "stillbirth" of freedom outside the West is related to the fact that non–Western societies have had different conceptions of the self and its relationship with the other.

The second implication, and my main working hypothesis in this chapter, is that if the self-existence and autonomy of that sense-of-self is an illusion, as Buddhism claims, then such a self will never be able to experience itself as enough of a self—that is, it will never feel free enough. It will try to resolve its lack by expanding the sphere of its freedom, yet that can never become large enough to be comfortable. This dynamic helped to generate what we know as the history of the West: a never-ending quest for "genuine," i.e., complete, personal freedom. But can there be such a thing, if there is no "genuine" self to have it?

We shall see that this relationship between the self and its freedom explains much about the curious development of Western freedom and perhaps as much about our predicament today.

## THE INTERDEPENDENCE OF FREEDOM AND TYRANNY

To understand the West in context we must begin with what existed before the West—in this case, before the classical Greek period. Some recent historical studies have emphasized that the value placed on freedom was generated out of its opposite, the "social death" of slavery. Since slavery was so common, however, this idea by itself does not go very far to explain why social freedom developed only in the West.[2] The basic problem is that among nonslaves the presence of slaves reinforced their own sense of group solidarity and participation; and what the slave desired was never freedom in our evolved Western sense (which would have been fatal, since there was no place for a "free" person in such societies) but reduced marginality and partial resocialization into the master's community.

This already shows something important about the relationship between the individual self and its valuation of freedom: there is no social context for esteeming freedom until there is a social role for the individual to function as an individual. Dynastic Egypt provides a good example. As Max Weber noticed, the "prevailing rule would be 'no man without a master,' for the man without a protector was helpless. Hence the entire population of Egypt was organized in a hierarchy of clientages." For Weber this reveals "the essential characteristic of a liturgy-state: every individual is bound to the function assigned to him within the social system, and therefore every individual is in principle unfree" (in Patterson, 36, 37).

This principle applied to the pharaohs as well, for although they were gods even gods had their role to play in maintaining the cosmic order. That is why every attempt of the pharaohs to free themselves from the power of the priests was thwarted. When everyone is fixated within a divinely sanctioned hierarchy, there is no social space for personal freedom because the social structure has no place for self-directed individuals.

Just as important is the implication for what Patterson calls sovereignal freedom, the power to do utterly as one pleased with another person. In spite of the authoritarian nature of most human societies, such sovereignal freedom did not normally exist, because all social relationships existed within a network of countervailing powers (including divine powers that limited human *hubris*). This points to one of the tragic paradoxes that have dogged the history of the West: personal freedom and totalitarianism are not opposites but brothers, for the historical conditions that made democracy possible also made totalitarianism possible. The self-directed individual could evolve only by the destruction or weakening of the "hierarchy of clientages" or (in more tribal societies, including pre-Cleisthenes Athens) of kin-based lineages; yet the authority vacuum created can just as well be manipulated by those in a position to seize absolute political power no longer limited by countervailing social forces.

This point may be made from the other side: the breakdown of hierarchies and lineages allows for the development of more autonomous, self-directed individuals, but it also allows for the creation of the *masses*. That brings out another disturbing aspect of this paradox: the eagerness with which the plebs have repeatedly embraced their autocratic rulers. Dostoyevsky's Grand Inquisitor emphasizes that man has "no more pressing need than the one to find somebody to whom he can surrender, as quickly as possible, that gift of freedom which he, unfortunate creature, was born with." We are not born free—what freedom we have is the result of complex historical conditions—but Dostoyevsky's arrow is otherwise right on target: if (as the sense-of-self's sense-of-lack implies) freedom makes us anxious, the more free we are the more anxious we will be, and the greater our need to resolve that anxiety one way or another—usually by surrendering it to some father protector or other authority figure.

The psychoanalyst Otto Rank divided our anxiety into two complimentary fears. *Life fear* is the anxiety we feel when we stand out too much, thereby losing our connection with the whole; *death fear* is the anxiety of losing one's personhood and dissolving back into the whole. "Whereas the life fear is anxiety at going forward, becoming an individual, the death fear is anxiety at going backward, losing individuality. Between these two fear possibilities the individual is thrown back and forth all his life." This can just as well be expressed in terms of freedom: we feel the need to be free, but becoming more free makes us more anxious and therefore more inclined to sacrifice that freedom to someone who promises us security (including absolution for our sense of lack). In short, human beings have two great psychological needs, freedom and security, and unfortunately they conflict. This explains the temptations of totalitarianism:

> Totalitarianism is a cultural neurotic symptom of the need
> for community—a symptom in the respect that it is grasped
> as a means of allaying anxiety resulting from the feelings of
> powerlessness and helplessness of the isolated, alienated indi-
> viduals produced in a society in which complete individu-
> alism has been the dominant goal. Totalitarianism is the
> substitution of collectivism for community... (May 212)

Today the anonymity of mass men and women within impersonal societies no longer offers the securities of clientage hierarchies and lineages, leading to an accumulation of anxiety (lack) that can seek a collective outlet. The history of Greece and Rome reminds us that this problem is not uniquely modern.

Yet there is another "solution" to this dialectic, or an opposite temptation: The members of a society may decide instead that they are not yet free enough, that they must struggle further to become truly free. Unfortunately, this approach threatens to become a vicious circle because it denies us any solace in community bonds, inasmuch as we never can feel free enough. To express it in terms of sense of lack, today one of our main ways to objectify our lack is by feeling that we are not yet as free as we deserve to be. This is not to deny that there are always many human wrongs that need to be human righted, but this does give us some insight into, e.g., the attraction of victimhood. Victimhood is learning how to address the problem of one's life by discovering how one is being exploited or has been abused; then one's anger and self-pity become justified, socially acceptable, and sometimes lucrative. From a Buddhist point of view, however, this is dangerous, since rather than pointing the way to overcome one's sense of lack it reinforces one's delusive sense of self as that which has been abused.

For the masses totalitarianism is a temptation to surrender our freedom, yet the sense-of-self's sense of lack also enables us understand this authoritarianism from the autocratic side. Another way to try to resolve one's sense of lack is by extending control over others. If the self is groundless and therefore naturally anxious, it can try to defend itself and gain control by seeking to dominate what is outside it. "This absoluteness, the sense of being one (my identity is entirely independent and consistent) and alone ('There is nothing outside of me that I do not control') is the basis for domination—and the master-slave relationship" (Benjamin 33). If, again, no amount of control can allay the insecurity that haunts the self, this search for control also has a tendency to become demonic. Stalin never felt secure enough because it is not possible to feel secure enough.

The need to surrender our freedom by submitting to an authority figure therefore meshes all too comfortably with the anxiety that drives tyrants to keep trying to totalize their power. They evolved together at the expense of those countervailing social forces that traditionally limited the exercise of such concentrated power as much as the exercise of personal freedom. Ironically, then, the development of tyrants' sovereignal freedom is not only the negation of personal freedom, it is just as much an effect of personal freedom.

## THE RELIGION OF THE SELF

> The many basic terms [the Greeks] contributed to our lexicon—history, physics, geometry, geography, logic, theology, ethics, politics, aesthetics, etc.—testify to the literally extraordinary range of their thought.
>
> There remains a significant exception: the Greeks did not develop a higher religion. (H. Muller 158)

On the contrary: the Greeks developed the higher religion of the self—i.e., humanism—and the result of their experiment was the discovery that such a religion does not work. The Greco-Roman experiment with secular humanism failed, not for extraneous historical reasons (e.g., the Roman conquest of Greece, the barbarian conquest of Rome) but because it self-destructed. Its distinctive contribution to the development of freedom (and the individual self) survived only as sublated into the Augustinian synthesis of Neoplatonic thought with Christian theology, which devised another way to cope with the greater anxiety of greater inwardness: by postulating an original sin, caused by Adam's misuse of freedom. Our lack is the result of his original sin. Fortunately it can be resolved, but unfortunately only in the afterlife.

In "discovering" the eternal psyche that persists unchanged, early Greek thought also discovered the idea of eternal substance (Parmenides' Being, etc.). That which was believed to persist unchanged (the psyche) sought that which was believed to persist unchanged (Being). Beginning with Parmenides, only that which is permanent can be grasped by genuine knowledge, for comprehending transient things provides merely a semblance of knowledge. From a Buddhist point of view, however, the knowledge that the Greeks sought was from the beginning a delusion, in retrospect an intellectually glorious but nonetheless vain quest of a constructed individual to ground itself by discovering the eternal Ground of all things.

In setting up reason as the method whereby this psyche and this Being may be discovered, the Greek thinkers opened a door to what proved to be a blind alley. Despite its other fruits, rationality, the science of thinking, does not by itself provide a handle to grasp and resolve the sense-of-self's sense of lack. The new religions of the self that tried to do so, such as Epicureanism and Stoicism, eventually reached a dead end in the speculations of Epictetus and Marcus Aurelius. Yet Neoplatonic emphasis on subjective inwardness survived in the Augustinian emphasis on the self's essential sinfulness. Sin required constant watchfulness and introspection, thus deepening the self's introversion, and it provided that self with a way to understand and cope with the deeper sense of lack shadowing it. As we shall see in the next chapter, faith that this lack will be overcome (initially, in the return of Christ and the millennium that it would inaugurate) generated a future orientation that would continue long after that faith had yielded to more secular preoccupations.

We have seen that in traditional societies lack was usually dissolved by dissolving the individual into his or her society—that is, by integrating the person into the social structure, as in dynastic Egypt. In such cases the issue of freedom does not arise because the individual does not exist. Questions about the meaning of one's life also do not arise because human society is likewise integrated into the cosmos, often through the vital role of a priest-king (at the top of the social pyramid) in helping to maintain the cosmos. In such societies there is no clear distinction between sacred and secular, which tends to preempt social revolution: to challenge the orders of a god-king would also be to challenge the order of the universe.

Since this pattern was widespread, it is rather our distinction between sacred and secular that seems curious. What needs explaining is not the integration of secular with sacred but our split between them: i.e., the belief in a transcendence that is distinct from and superior to the natural world. Elsewhere (1996, 154ff) I have argued that the category of transcendence is important for explaining the differences between South Asia (India, which emphasized it) and East Asia (China and Japan, which did not). In order to see this difference, however, transcendence must be understood to have at least three related but different meanings: as another "higher" reality, such as God or Brahman; as a universal or absolute ethic, such as the Mosaic Decalogue (usually derived from a higher reality, such as Yahweh); and (remembering its etymology: *trans* plus *scendere*, to climb over, to rise above) as that perspective by which we "rise above" the given in order to observe it critically and gain the leverage to change it. Although these three types tend to reinforce one another, Indian transcendence traditionally emphasized the first, Hebrew transcendence the second, and Greek transcendence the third.

Why did explicitly transcendental perspectives arise in these places and not, for example, in Egypt or Mesopotamia or Japan?

> "Transcendence," whether it takes the form of divine revelation or of theoretical cosmology, implies a search for authority

outside the institutionalized offices and structures of the
seeker's society. Even its most concrete form, the law code,
implies a transfer of authority from the holders of office to
the written rule. Transcendental impulses therefore constitute, by definition, an implicit challenge to traditional authority and indicate some dissatisfaction with it . . . new
transcendental visions are . . . likely to be presented by persons in a precariously independent, interstitial—or at least
exposed and somewhat solitary—position in society . . .
(Humphreys 92, 112)

In India a two-stage process created these conditions. First, the Vedic
development of complicated rituals led to a need to differentiate priest
from king, and then a new social role appeared: the renouncer who,
being outside of traditional society, discovered or invented a "discipline
of salvation"—e.g., Shakyamuni, the founder of Buddhism, and Mahavira,
the founder of Jainism. In Israel the "interstitial" Hebrew prophets,
especially Amos, Isaiah, and Jeremiah, developed the ethical monothe-
ism established in the Mosaic covenant by fulminating against the impious
people and their rulers.

While it is futile to seek the necessary and sufficient historical
causes for Greek self-consciousness, retrospectively we can observe how
a number of factors reinforced one another to promote that particular
type of transcendence (the third of the types mentioned above). In
general, the Greek distinction between sacred and secular may be traced
back to the "emancipation" of reason from myth and the correlative
distinction between *nomos* (convention) and *phusis* (nature); significantly,
those are still the categories that frame our debates today. Humphreys
finds the necessary precondition for such a transcendental perspective
on society in the privileged and relatively independent position of
axial-age intellectuals, such as the sophists, whose special linguistic skills
provided "the ability to recreate social relationships and manipulate
them in thought" (Humphreys 111).

This ability was a result of complex cultural conditions that encouraged the development of humanism. When the Indo-Europeans
invaded Greece their Aryan sky gods, patrons of vitality and power,
encountered the local chthonian fertility deities and learned to coexist
with them in a live-and-let-live manner that did not foster the absolutism of the Abrahamic heritage. Homer recreated the gods in man's
own image; his detached, ironical attitude toward them meant his dei-

ties authorized no sacred book, proclaimed no dogma, and set up no powerful priesthood.

Greek merchant fleets beat the Phoenicians at their own game, sparking a great colonizing movement that dotted the Mediterranean and Baltic seas with Greek city-states. Thales, Pythagoras, Herodotus, Democritus, Plato, and other pioneer thinkers continued traveling to other cultural centers such as Egypt and Babylon (and India?) to acquire more learning. The exposure to such different influences and contradictory customs encouraged skepticism toward their own myths. Thales founded natural philosophy when he did not use gods to explain the world. Unlike Moses, Solon did not get his tables from them when he gave Athens new laws. In his funeral oration, a profoundly religious occasion, Pericles did not even mention the gods but celebrated the virtues of Athenian democracy. Greek drama reduced the gods' role by emphasizing human motivation and responsibility. Socrates used the gods to rationalize his mode of inquiry, yet his quest for wisdom did not otherwise depend upon them.

One does not escape the gods so easily, however. Psychologically they serve a crucial function. We ground ourselves in a mythological worldview because it organizes the cosmos for us: it explains who we are, why we are here, and what we should be doing with our lives. In the process, mythologies usually explain what our lack really is and how it can be resolved. Even if that vision becomes too fanciful or constrictive, its disappearance is likely to be worse, because that not only liberates the self, it also liberates its lack. And that points to the problem with the Greek alternative of humanism and rationalism: it did not work and could not work insofar as it did not show the sense-of-self how to resolve its sense of lack. Instead, the increased individuality of the Greeks aggravated their lack.

This helps us to understand what we now know about the "harmonious Greeks." Since Burckhardt and Nietzsche it has become apparent that the Greeks were not Apollonian but profoundly anxious and troubled, "an unusually energetic, restless, turbulent people, given to excess," who idealized harmony and balance because it was a virtue they rarely achieved. As Thucydides noticed, they "were born into the world to take no rest themselves, and to give none to others."[3]

Although this restlessness was made worse by burgeoning Greek skepticism, it was originally connected with their religion. Homeric mythology had offered no hopes of a heavenly afterlife. Death is not even the peace of sleep, for everyone ends up in Hades, whose shades are aware that they will never again participate in the joys of life. It was an inauspicious origin for Greek humanism, and it got worse, as there was "an undeniable growth of anxiety and dread in the evolution of Greek religion,"[4] which is what one would expect if stronger sense-of-self means stronger sense of lack.

> [T]he individualism of the Greeks was more likely to become reckless and lawless, or simply selfish, because it was neither sanctioned nor disciplined by an explicit democratic or religious principle. It was rooted in the Homeric tradition of personal fame and glory and was nourished by habitual competition, as much in art and athletics as in business, but everywhere off the battlefield with little team play. . . the individualism was tempered by little sense of strictly moral responsibility, or in particular of altruism . . . (Patterson 218)

Greek competitiveness exceeded even our own. Despite their lack of lawyers, the Athenians were perhaps the most litigious people who ever lived, once they discovered that in this way one could conquer one's opponents without resorting to violence. The recourse to law would seem to be an improvement, yet sometimes the difference is hard to see. In the fourth century B.C. only three Athenian generals were killed in battle, while at least six (perhaps eight) were sentenced to death in the Athenian courts for losing a battle. The cultural flowering that continues to awe us today is easier to appreciate in retrospect. Because it so fundamentally challenged the old ways of doing things, such an explosion of creativity was profoundly disturbing to most people at the time. Most progressive thinkers were tried for heresy: Anaxagoras, Diagoras, Socrates, probably Protagoras and Euripides; later Plato and Aristotle wisely absented themselves. No one suggested liberating the slaves or emancipating women. When Athens became democratic, it became not less but more imperialistic and genocidal, as the Peloponnesian War demonstrates, which is to say that collectively the Athenians' impulses toward greed and domination may actually have increased because they had evolved a new mode of self-governance.[5]

But are such criticisms anachronistic? We should not criticize the Athenians for not living up to democratic principles that they were just beginning to develop. It is not surprising that there was no check on mob rule, for the problem with mob rule needed to be experienced for checks to be perceived as necessary. The concept of human rights—the notion that the individual should have some protection against the state and the will of the majority—requires a more evolved sense of autonomous personhood and the sanctity of the self, along with the development of empathy and altruism in place of the "stranger anxiety" that predominated in classical Greece.

Nevertheless, the problems mentioned above are precisely the sort to be expected if the increase in self-consciousness were shadowed by an equivalent increase in anxiety, i.e., lack. When this lack—the feeling that "something is wrong with me"—is not explained by a sacred world view that resolves my doubts in a faith that grounds me in the cosmos, I shall try to ground myself in more individualistic, self-ish ways.

There was another alternative: to forget oneself, and thus the burden of one's lack, in the temporary ecstasy of Dionysian catharsis:

> Dionysus was in the archaic age as much a social necessity as Apollo; each ministered in his own way to the anxieties characteristic of guilt-culture. Apollo promised security: "Understand your station as man; do as the Father tells you; and you will be safe to-morrow." Dionysus offered freedom: "Forget the difference, and you will find the identity . . ." He was essentially a God of joy [who] enables you for a short time to *stop being yourself,* and thereby sets you free. . . . The individual, as the modern world knows him, began in that age to emerge for the first time from the old solidarity of the family, and found the unfamiliar burden of individual responsibility hard to bear. Dionysus could lift it from him. (Dodds 76)

How did the more thoughtful members of Athenian society react to these developments? Aeschylus was proud of having fought in the Persian War that saved Athens from foreign domination; a generation later, Euripides wrote his last unfinished play in exile bemoaning that "we are slaves to the masses" and affirming popular kingship as an alternative. Many other examples could be cited, but the most important for us, of course, were the responses of Plato and Aristotle. We do not know how much the former's political views were colored by his personal experience of Socrates' trial and execution, yet there is no doubt about his dislike of democracy, which he dismissed as "an agreeable, anarchic form of society, with plenty of variety, which treats all men as equal whether they are equal or not" (*Republic* 565d). The basic weaknesses of democracy are mob rule, demagoguery, and a tendency toward anarchy, since the mass of people grow impudent from "a reckless excess of liberty" (701b). The main concern of *The Republic* is the problems with city-state democracy; it addresses the root of the problem by analyzing the democratic personality, which lacks a coherent organizing principle and therefore follows the strongest pressures of the moment— a recipe for social as well as psychological strife (561c-d). Further experience only deepened Plato's distaste for personal freedom, as this extraordinary passage in *The Laws* (XII 942a-d) reveals:

> The organization of our forces is a thing calling in its nature for much advice and the framing of many rules, but the principle is this—that no man, and no woman, be ever suffered to live without an officer over them, and no soul of man to learn the trick of doing one single thing of its own sole motion, in play or in earnest, but, in peace as in war, ever to live with the commander in sight, to follow his leading, and take his motions from him to the least detail— to halt or advance, to drill, to bathe, to dine, to keep watch . . . in a word, to teach one's soul the habit of never so much as thinking to do one single act apart from one's fellow, of making life, to the very uttermost, an unbroken consort, society, and community of all with all. A wiser and better rule than this man neither had discovered, nor ever will . . .

This is not totalitarianism in the modern sense, more the jaundiced view of an old man who has observed the development and the failures of personal liberty, for without self-control freedom becomes libertinism. Aristotle was almost as critical of the democracies in which he lived, for "in these extreme democracies, each man lives as he likes—or, as Euripides says, 'For any end he chances to desire'" (*Politics* 1310a). He preferred a mixed constitution combining the best of oligarchy and democracy, with a more "bourgeois" bias than Plato's ideal state.

These elitist views were a response to changing social realities. If the fifth century was one of civic freedom, the fourth century (which began with Socrates' execution) increasingly became that of individual freedom and self-indulgence. The integrity of the *polis* declined in favor of concern for personal advancement, which came to preoccupy those

who controlled economic life and many of those who controlled political affairs. Demosthenes lamented that politics had become the path
to riches, for individuals no longer place the state before themselves but
view the state as a way to promote their own personal wealth. It would
become a familiar complaint.

The consequences of this for Greek thought were profound.
About the end of the fifth century—that is, at the same time as the
above development—philosophical discourse on freedom took a
radically new turn: A critical distinction was made between outer
and inner freedom. Socrates' emphasis on knowledge, by which man
can share in the universal and eternal, paved the way by urging men
to place their passions and impulses under the control of self-reflection.
In the context of the philosophical inquiry that was primary for
him and his successors—a search for the Truth about the human
soul and human society—democracy had failed; but instead of freedom being renounced it came to be redefined.

The *Republic* makes a momentous analogy between harmony
in the state and harmony in the soul. Internalizing the Greek sociological understanding of freedom and slavery as requiring one aother, Plato
came to conceive of reason as the master (hence the free party) with
desire and emotion as its slaves. The virtue of freedom was retained by
reconceptualizing it in terms of the self-mastery of self-consciousness.
In contrast to the incoherent life of the democrat, who lives "for any
end he chances to desire," the psychic tendencies of the spiritually
developed individual harmonize with one another because they are
governed by reason (*Republic* 431).[6] Rather than solving the growing
problem with civic freedom, however, this aggravated it. Like the
merchants and politicians who retreated into the more private world of
their own self-advancement, those who succeeded Plato retreated from
committment to the *polis* into the more private world of abstract thought,
which for them became the only method by which *true* freedom might
be gained.[7] "Post-Aristotelian ethical philosophy was marked by a clean
break between morality and society, by the location of virtue firmly
within the individual soul" (Finley 120).

Restated in terms of lack: the democratic experiment in self-
government had not worked to resolve the increased anxiety that the
increased individualism of the "democratic personality" generated, for
the self-governance of the *demos* clearly did not entail the self-governance
of the self. Just as the sophists had realized that the state is a construction that can be reconstructed, so those after Socrates realized that the

psyche is a construction that can be reconstructed, with reason as the master. And the aggravated sense of lack that shadowed increased individualism required such psychic reconstruction.

Needless to say, that reconstruction did not appeal to many. This meant that new gods besides reason would have to be found. In the early Hellenistic age the cult of *Tyche* "Luck" or "Fortune" became wisely diffused, being "'the last stage in the secularising of religion'; in default of any positive object, the sentiment of dependence attaches itself to the purely negative idea of the unexplained and unpredictable, which is *Tyche*" (Dodds 242). In the second century B.C. astrology suddenly became popular: "for a century or more the individual had been face to face with his own intellectual freedom, and now he turned tail and bolted from the horrid prospect—better the rigid determinism of the astrological Fate than that terrifying burden of daily responsibility" (Dodds 246). In the first century B.C. people became increasingly preoccupied with techniques for individual salvation:

> There was a growing demand for occultism, which is essentially an attempt to capture the Kingdom of Heaven by material means—it has been well described as 'the vulgar form of transcendentalism.' And philosophy followed a parallel path on a higher level. Most of the schools had long since ceased to value the truth for its own sake, but in the Imperial Age they abandon, with certain exceptions [notably Plotinus], any pretence of disinterested curiosity and present themselves frankly as dealers in salvation. (Dodds 248)

Dodds's conclusion is hard to dispute: "once before a civilized people rode to the jump—rode to it and refused it." The great experiment of Greek rationalism, as a humanistic alternative to religion and superstition, had failed.

In retrospect, the fateful Platonic move was equating freedom with reason and understanding psychic reconstruction in terms of the domination of reason. The immediate philosophical heirs to this were Cynicism, Epicureanism, and Stoicism, which developed into religions of the self, straddling between more conventional religions and philosophy as we know it today, which has become a search for propositional truth. In place of salvation through ecstatic mysteries they offered a salvation to be gained from rational self-cultivation, but they were just as much religions in that they were designed to cope with the personal lack caused, as they now understood it, by the self's desires and passions. Their ultimate aim was *autarkeia,* inner freedom from negative emotions and their entanglements. For the Stoics the soul of the sage was in a permanent *apatheia,* without excessive emotions, and for Epicureans the ideal psychic state was *ataraxia,* imperturbability of spirit. The aim of their theorizing was to contribute to the development of such states of tranquillity, which they equated with *autarkeia.* The metaphor of fortress became common; as the cynic Antisthenes put it, "wisdom is the safest wall, and a fortress must be constructed of our own impregnable reason." Yet the sense-of-self's sense of lack remained a fifth column that no fortress could defend against.

The irony of their goal is that as they worked to develop and preserve the self's freedom from emotional bonds to the external world, they also contributed to the further bifurcation of self from other, of subject from object, that aggravated the sense of lack. The three stoas of Stoicism reflect this increasing introversion: the first stoa emphasized harmony between self and cosmos, but the second stoa was more concerned about whether the psyche controls the body, and the third stoa became preoccupied with the personal freedom of the self-controlled individual, as described in the *Discourses* of Epictetus and the *Meditations* of Marcus Aurelius.

And just how lack-free was the self-controlled individual? Marcus Aurelius always held the deepest reverence for Epictetus, but when Epictetus, after one of his discourses on "the road which leads to freedom," was asked if he himself were truly free (*Discourses* 4.1.128–31), he had to admit that while he wanted and prayed to be so, he was still "not yet able to face my masters." Yet he could point to someone who is, or was: Diogenes the Cynic, who had died over four hundred years earlier! Evidently none of the Stoic masters since then had achieved it.

Patterson's discussion of Epictetus and Aurelius is insightful regarding their ultimate failure even by their own criteria. "The uniqueness of Marcus and Epictetus was in searching not so much for freedom as for the source of the yearning for, and meaning of, freedom. Shifting the terrain from the outer to the inner world was the beginning, not the end, of the struggle" (278). A Buddhist could not put it better. By both the philosophical and the social standards of his time, Marcus the Roman emperor should have been one of the freest men who ever lived; what his *Meditations* unwittingly reveal, then, is how little such freedom meant, both his sovereignal dominion and the reason-able freedom developed by his self-control. With him the Stoic tradition culminates in the realization that such freedoms do not by themselves bring personal fulfillment or peace of mind. In my Buddhist terms, they cannot resolve one's sense of lack.

The increased introversion entailed by psychic reconstruction enlarged the sphere of one's subjectivity, but identifying that freedom with reason provided no way to cope with the increased sense of lack shadowing it. Freedom understood in such secular terms proved to be unsatisfactory.

The stage was set for return to a more explicitly religious perspective: the Augustinian discovery/construction of sin. If even the internal freedom of dominant reason does not satisfy, but freedom still remains one's ultimate value, then there must be yet another, even more internalized kind of freedom. . . .

## THE ANCIENT SIN

Their Egyptian and Babylonian captivities taught the Hebrews the value of freedom, and even their allegiance to God was a voluntary contract (Abraham's covenant, Genesis 15:18). Nevertheless, the Hebrew prophets, and later Jesus, were not very concerned about individual freedom. Instead, they emphasized obedience to God. The moral earnestness of Amos, Isaiah, etc., generated an ethical interpretation of history that traced evil back to humanity and made it our business to overcome it. This introduced a concern for social justice rather than the valuation of personal freedom. Jesus taught submission to the will of God, a surrender that led not to freedom but to love. Neither he nor the earlier prophets had any time for the humanism and relativism that created the conditions for the Greek valorization of freedom.

Paul, however, employed the terminology of freedom to express the Christian message in a way that appealed to the many freedmen of the Roman empire. In Christ we are redeemed from the spiritual slavery of sin into spiritual freedom: "for freedom Christ has set us free; stand fast, therefore, and do not submit again to the yoke of slavery" (Galatians 5:1). When we try to unpack the metaphor, though, it becomes difficult to work out exactly what freedom can mean in the context of our submission to God.

To understand the failure of classical humanism is to appreciate the importance of Augustine, who salvaged the inwardness of its enhanced subjectivity and bequeathed it to the Western tradition that developed after him and out of him. He was able to recuperate and revitalize this interiority of self-presence because he added a new element, or perspective: the awareness of sin, and particularly the incorrigibility of original sin. "The Ancient Sin: nothing is more obviously part of our preaching of Christianity; yet nothing is more impenetrable to the understanding." Needless to say, this did not deter Augustine from explaining it.

Sin provided precisely what the classical Greco-Roman tradition lacked, a way to understand and cope with the sense of lack that shadows the groundless sense-of-self. Human beings have been dislocated by an ancient Fall. Now I know what is wrong with me: I have sinned. And now I know what must be done: atone for my sins (including that of our father, Adam) and strive to sin no more in the future. The classical emphasis on reason is replaced by the primacy of will, a faculty unknown to the Greeks; the problem of reason, which is error, is superceded by the problem of will, which is sin. The rigorous self-examination and never-ending watchfulness that required encouraged an ever-deepening inwardness exemplified in Augustine's own *Confessions*.

Yet there is an important difference between the Christian understanding of sin and my Buddhist understanding of lack, and their identification was a fateful confusion. Belief in sin does not in itself actually show the way to resolve lack; rather, one's anxiety is short-circuited by the belief that one's lack will (or can be) alleviated in the future. For the first Christians this would happen at the Second Coming, which was imminent but later became attenuated into a preoccupation with the future.

Augustine played a crucial role in this development. In his early years as a Manichaean and then a Neoplatonist he shared the classical belief in the possibility of self-perfection. With his conversion to Christianity he brought Neoplatonic free will with him: Man is the author of his own degradation. Yet postulating an original sin made this degradation more foundational and difficult to cope with, as he himself soon discovered. The extraordinary book ten of the *Confessions* "is not the affirmation of a cured man; it is the self-portrait of a convalescent." But the convalescent never fully recovered. What became distinctive in Augustine's religious attitude was "a sharp note of unrelieved anxiety about himself and a dependence upon his god" (Brown 177, 123). The later sermons and letters reflect his terrible realization:

> that he is doomed to remain incomplete in his present exist-
> ence, that what he wished for most ardently would never be

more than a hope, postponed to the final resolution of all tensions, far beyond this life. . . . All a man could do was to "yearn" for this absent perfection, to feel its loss intensely, to pine for it. (Brown 156)

For Augustine, then, true freedom could only culminate a long process of healing—a process so difficult that we cannot expect it to conclude during our lifetime. As Peter Brown adds, this marked "the end of a long-established classical ideal of perfection" (156). But if perfection is not attainable in this world, it must be postulated as attainable some-where else: There must be another world, after death, in which our lack can be resolved. The stage was set for the success of the late medieval church, which as God's agent on earth would gain a monopoly on the dispensation of lack.

This was a complex, many-sided legacy. Sin offered a way—indeed, led to the development of a spiritual technology—to cope with lack, but the increasing subjectivity it promoted also deepened the sense of lack that needed to be coped with, as the example of Augustine himself shows. According to how it was handled, sin could liberate you from consider-able anxiety or enmesh you more tightly in labyrinths of self-doubt and self-hatred. Understood metaphorically, the doctrine of original sin con-tained at its core an invaluable grain of liberating truth: Our sense of lack is the price of our individuality and freedom; my lack teaches me that I am not self-present but conditioned by something that it is my spiritual responsibility to discover. Understood more literally, however, original sin enslaves my incipient freedom to those religious institutions that claim to control its dispensation.

Yet the radical inward turn Augustine encouraged, by seeking God within, opened the door for what seems to have been the spiritual freedom of the great Christian mystics, such as St. Francis and Meister Eckhart, who discovered what according to Buddhism is the only true way to resolve our lack: liberation from self in nondual union with something greater than the self, a loss of self-preoccupation that can lead to identifying oneself with all creation—not only with the needy and sick, but with Brother Sun and Sister Moon.

Not surprisingly, it took centuries for such a complex intellectual inheritance to be adjudicated. One Augustinian tension, in particular, had great implications for the future of personal freedom. His influen-tial *City of God* went further than had any of the earlier Church Fathers in endorsing the powers of emperors. This divine sanction of secular authority was used to justify the subordination of church to state that was so characteristic of Christian Europe until the eleventh century. During this period kings were considered semireligious personages and had great influence on church affairs, while prominent churchmen played important roles in secular affairs as advisers, administrators, and rulers of ecclesiastical principalities. The danger with this, from the transcendental perspective discussed earlier, is that such a conflation of sacred and secular authority tends to reproduce the all-encompassing social hierarchy of clientages found in non-Western civilizations (e.g., dynastic Egypt), a conflation that discourages individual solutions to the problem of lack by discouraging individuals.

> The *respublica christiana* was necessarily organized as a hier-
> archical system in which the lower ends were subordinate to
> higher, and inferior powers to superior; authority in the
> entire structure descended from above . . . Self-determina-
> tion, in this view, could only appear . . . as a violation of the
> very structure of reality, and political duty appeared to con-
> sist only in patient submission and obedience. (Bouwsma 6)[8]

Yet the *City of God* also discouraged this conflation. Written to justify the fall of Rome, it did not identify the City of God with the City of Man. Instead of being the privileged vehicle of God's will, the Roman empire was only one in a series of historical societies. It was neither sacred nor necessary for human salvation. This set the stage for the protracted late medieval struggles between papacy and monarchs, each claiming the higher authority—i.e., greater sovereignal freedom. This in turn encouraged the development of doctrines that justified resistance to unjust rulers. It was "a short step from the question which sphere of power—the spiritual or the secular—should dominate to the deeper question of the nature of power itself and the sources of its authority. Once the Western mind latched on to this problem, it set in train a series of reflections that became, in effect, the modern intellectual history of freedom" (Patterson 384).

The historical factors that encouraged more radical and "self-sufficient" subjectivity were complex, yet among the most important was the development of the religious idea that salvation was not to be earned simply by engaging in religious rituals, for it required the effort of self-transformation. Because sin was now less in the act than in the intention, "the new view was an invitation to introspection, to exploration of the conscience. The apparatus of moral governance was shifted inward, to a private space that no longer had anything to do with the community" (Duby, 513). This signified the victory of Augustine's Neoplatonic inwardness, from being the spiritual exercise of philosophers to a requirement of all Christians. In 1215 the Fourth Lateran Council decided to make confession private, regular, and compulsory:

> The decision to make all Christians confess at least once a year was in part a repressive, inquisitorial measure; its purpose was to unearth insubordination and heresy lurking in individual consciences. But can there be a revolution more radical or an effect on attitudes more profound and prolonged that that which followed the change from a ceremony as public as penance had been (a spectacle of exclusion staged in the public square) to a simple private dialogue, as in the exempla, between sinner and priest, or between the soul and God (for oral confession was an inviolable secret, and worthless unless followed by a silent effort of self-correction)? (Duby, 531–32)

In this way the conditions for a transcendental perspective were preserved in medieval Europe and matured at the end of it. As we shall see in later chapters, the clash between sacred and secular authority again created space for the emergence of the individual by opening up the possibility of self-determination—and the valorization of personal freedom.

FREEDOM FROM FREEDOM

The above conditions encouraged a transcendence very different from that found in India or among the Hebrews, and help us to understand what has happened to transcendence in the development of the West. When we remember that the transcendental is, most fundamentally, that which provides a perspective on the world and leverage for changing it, we can see that transcendence has not disappeared from the modern West; rather, the transcendental dimension has become internalized into the supposedly autonomous, self-directed individual who began to develop again at the end of the Middle Ages.

The "rebirth" of Europe occurred when traditional Christian answers to questions of ultimate meaning and lack no longer satisfied the cultural elites who went on to find or make their own solutions to the problem of life. Later Luther encouraged this by sanctifying a more private relationship with God. Instead of believing in the corporate church as the means to resolve lack and gain salvation, now everyone must work it out for oneself. Personally having a direct line to transcendence provides the leverage to challenge all worldly authority, religious institutions as well as secular ones. Convinced he was following God's will, Luther refused to shut up: "Here I stand; I can do no other." This sanctioned the principle that one's personal understanding and moral principles can provide an appropriate perspective to confront social structures. Thus Luther was more than a prophet: after him everyone had to become his or her own prophet.

Eventually God could abdicate because by then his role had been largely assumed by the self-sufficient self-consciousness that Descartes described. The result was the Cartesian self: an increasingly anxious individual who relied on his or her own judgment, who measured the world according to his own standards, and who used her own resources to challenge the present situation, the social environment as much as the physical one. A condition of all these, of course, is personal freedom, which became and remains our paramount value.

What does all this mean for our lack now? For all the problems with sin, at least it taught a way to cope with the feeling that "something is wrong with me." Today, although our sense of self (and therefore our sense of lack) is stronger than ever, and our subjective alienation from the objectified world greater than ever, we no longer believe in sin. Therefore we lack an effective, socially agreed upon way to understand and deal with our lack, which means that it tends to manifest in individualistic ways that further weaken community bonds and relationships. One of these ways has already been noticed: If freedom is our ultimate value, then, when we feel that something is wrong with us, it must be that we are not yet free enough. This route is dangerous because it tends to become a vicious circle. It contains no resolution of lack, only its aggravation.

Today, however, we find ourselves in a radically different situation, which is beginning to transform our valuation of freedom. Like it or not, our paramount value must be reexamined from a new perspective. The ecological degradation of the earth, which threatens our own survival, supersedes other problems. This situation cannot be understood in terms of, or solved by, our need for greater freedom. On the contrary, freedom in this case is itself the problem, as the human species has attempted to enlarge the sphere of its own collective sovereignal freedom by commodifying the whole earth in its quest for ever-greater power. If totalitarianism is a form of government in which centralized authority exercises absolute control over all aspects of life, our humanistic domination of nature seems to describe a totalitarian relationship with the natural world and suggests what is wrong with it.

It is amazing that, although the ecological crisis is already seriously degrading the natural cycles upon which we all depend, life otherwise goes on almost normally. It is, quite literally, business as usual. No doubt our attention is circumscribed by consumerism and distracted by high-tech media addictions, but I think there is another problem as well: The environmental crisis is running up against the basic parameters of Western civilization, which has viewed progress in freedom as the solution to everything. As many have emphasized, what we need today is not a Declaration of Independence but a Declaration of Interdependence that tempers our understanding of freedom by emphasizing that "complete" freedom is a delusion too dangerous to tolerate anymore.

To conclude in a somewhat facetious way: what we need now is freedom from freedom, i.e., from our need for greater freedom, which is another way of saying that what we need today is responsibility. None of this denies the importance of freedom, any more than the Buddhist critique of self can be used to rationalize an Egyptian-like hierarchy of clientages. Yet it shows us that our understanding of freedom, like that of the self that values it, needs to be contextualized. The history of classical humanism and our present situation both show the problems that occur when the self and its freedom are understood solely in secular terms.

# Two

# THE LACK OF PROGRESS

Every time a society finds itself in crisis it instinctively turns its
eyes towards its origins and looks there for a sign.
—Octavio Paz

The more we learn about other civilizations, the more anomalous the
West seems. If we resist the presumption that Western culture is the
growing tip of social evolution, to be contrasted with the stagnation of
most non-Western ones, what becomes highlighted is its dynamism, for
better and worse. Rather than trying to account for the "undevelopment"
of non-Western societies—why they did not by themselves evolve further
along our path—it is the apparently self-generated and future-driven
"progress" of the West that needs to be explained. What caused it?

We cannot simply point to the Renaissance, for that rebirth is
itself the effect to be explained. What caused the Renaissance? Intellectuals at the time were inspired by the rediscovery of ancient texts, yet
in no sense was the Renaissance a return to the classical period: It was
a revolution that, like all revolutions, misunderstood itself to be restoring some pristine condition long lost in the past . . . as it created something quite new. In most ways the premodern West was not very
different from the other civilizations of its time, but we must find
something within the Middle Ages themselves to account for how the
modern West originated.

It turns out that answering this question will also shed light on another almost as important: the origins of Western law. The basic issue here is not only the development of legal codes but more the curious problem of the law's authority. Today we take for granted the peaceful transfer of power that occurs whenever the ruling party of a democratic nation is defeated at the polls, yet this contrasts starkly with what still occurs in many parts of the non-Western world, where the powers that be lack respect for such a political process and often subvert it. We say that in such countries the rule of law is weak, which prompts us to wonder: Where does the law get its authority? Why do we respect it, and yield to it? According to Harold Berman, "law—in all societies—derives its authority from something outside itself" (16). What is that something?

The answer to both questions turns out to be the same: The dynamism of the West and the authority of its law may both be traced back to the Papal reformation that occurred in Europe in the late eleventh century. This was not a reformation but a true revolution, in fact arguably the most important revolution the West ever experienced. Significantly, it was not primarily a secular revolution, as we might expect, but a spiritual one: not only in the sense that it transformed the Papacy, and from there the whole structure of medieval society, but even more because it involved a radically new understanding of our human condition and its salvation. It was based upon a new theological doctrine about what sin is and how we can be redeemed—in other words, a new explanation of our human lack and how that is to be resolved. Berman concludes his massive study of the legal revolution that accompanied this change by claiming, "Without the fear of Purgatory and the hope of the Last Judgment, the Western legal tradition could not have come into being" (558). Even that extraordinary claim is still too modest. This spiritual revolution led to a bifurcation of the world into the sacred and the secular spheres, whose disengagement led to "a release of energy and creativity analogous to a process of nuclear fission" (Berman 88).

The incredulity this invites is partly caused by our ignorance of historical fact, but more to a misleading periodization that for most of us still divides Western history into ancient, medieval, and modern (and now postmodern?) eras. This way of understanding our past originated in the Renaissance, whose intellectuals were eager to distinguish their times from the dark ages that preceded. Historians today distinguish the Low from the High Middle Ages (roughly, before and after c.1050), owing to the many extraordinary changes that began to occur late in the eleventh century: a self-generated economic expansion, with the formation of craft guilds and a merchant class; the growth of cities and universities; the development of vernacular languages and literatures, chivalry, and new styles of art and architecture.

To these must be added the significant changes within the church itself: first and foremost, the Papal reformation itself, and the complementary secular fissipation of the Holy Roman Empire into rudimentary nation-states; the end of lay investiture and married clergy; the final split between the Eastern and Western churches; growing emphasis on Confession, introspection, and the Eucharist, along with the formalization of the other sacraments; the cult of the Virgin Mary and her immaculate conception; the development of Purgatory; the Crusades (which encouraged, among many other things, the growth of anti-Semitism and led to the first massacres of European Jews); the Inquisition and other methods of persecuting heresy.

As Berman summarizes it, "in the West, modern times—not only modern institutions and modern legal systems but also the modern state, the modern church, modern philosophy, the modern university, modern literature, and much else that is modern—have their origin in the period 1050-1150 *and not before*" (4, his italics). This era opened the door for a new direction of human development, which has become our collective attempt to wrest control of our own fate on earth by aggressively restructuring human society and nature itself. The late eleventh century was the crucial turning point that, for better and worse, shifted us from focusing on an otherworldly solution to the problem of life to constructing a worldly one.

For Berman, the most consequential of these transformations was the development of law and its authority. Although this is something we now take for granted in democratic societies, it rests upon precarious historical roots, for law too depends on accepting a type of transcendence that challenges the authority of temporal powers, as the previous chapter has already noticed:

> "Transcendence," whether it takes the form of divine revelation or of theoretical cosmology, implies a search for authority outside the institutionalized offices and structures of the seeker's society. *Even its most concrete form, the law code, implies a transfer of authority from the holders of office to the written rule.* Transcendental impulses therefore constitute, by definition, an implicit challenge to traditional authority and indicate some dissatisfaction with it. . . .

> [N]ew transcendental visions are . . . likely to be presented
> by persons in a precariously independent, interstitial—or at
> least exposed and somewhat solitary—position in society;
> they are therefore particularly likely to occur in societies
> sufficiently differentiated to have specialized social roles with
> distinct bases of authority, but not complex enough to have
> integrated these roles into functionally differentiated struc-
> tures. (Humphreys 92, 112; my italics)

Humphreys is thinking of the Greek sophists and the Hebrew prophets, but as it turned out "precariously independent" applied as well to the Pope, whose situation in the early Middle Ages was quite interstitial: Although he was sometimes little more than the emperor's chaplain, his role was not fully integrated, for he had his own base of authority. Suddenly, within a generation, the Pope became the most powerful and important person in Europe, because he was able to articulate a new vision of God's transcendence and impose a new understanding of his own authority as God's vicar. It was a turning point in our understanding of human lack and how to address it.

How did this occur? Why did people accept it? This brings us back again to Harold Berman's extraordinary book *Law and Revolution,* which explains in detail the formation of the Western legal tradition, and which concludes by reflecting on the deterioration of that tradition today. At the same time that we need more from the law and its institutions—with the decline of religiously based morality, it has to substitute as a minimalist public morality—the law has lost its transcendental mandate, for we no longer accept it as reflecting anything more than social agreement, hence something to be manipulated and evaded when possible. For Berman, the basic problem is that the law has lost its spiritual foundations, something we are not even aware of, because today we understand the law only in terms of its rational codification. Therefore "the West no longer has confidence in the law as a way of protecting spiritual [and ethical] values against corrupting social, economic and political forces" (83). As we have become more contemptous and cynical about the law, itself becoming more subjective and expedient, there has been a "massive loss of confidence in the West itself, as a civilization, a community, and in the legal tradition which for nine centuries has helped sustain it" (40). In this way too we suffer from the loss of a transcendental dimension.

Is it a coincidence that this social crisis is occurring at the very same time as a life-threatening ecological crisis, both direct consequences of the dynamism of the West? Today that dynamism—our preoccupation with "progress"—has also become problematic: As technological and economic transformations have been accelerating into a state of permanent revolution, they seem less and less in our control, increasingly a future-obsessed growth-only-for-growth's sake. If both crises are the result of closely related developments that began at the same time, and have the same causes, it may be important to take a close look at their origins, which are our origins.

In the period between 1050 and 1150 our collective religious solution to lack first began to shift from an otherworldly to a this-worldly dimension, an approach that no longer looked up to the heavens but forward to what could appear on earth in the future. The shift was gradual, of course. In the beginning, the emphasis was on creating the spiritual and social conditions that could hasten the return of Christ and the new millennium he would inaugurate. Eventually we became more confident about our ability to reshape society and the material conditions of our existence. This implied new understandings of temporality, rationality, and technology itself—understandings now common sense and therefore oblivious of the spiritual motivations that formed them. Our new preoccupation with progress involved redefining time, in effect, as "a schema for the expiation of guilt" (Brown 277), which in my Buddhist terms becomes: Time originates from our sense of lack and our attempts to resolve that lack.

Today in a time of imminent ecological collapse it is more difficult to understand why future-oriented growth still obsesses us. The answer is that contemporary secular society, having lost faith in any spiritual solution, has become trapped in the future because that provides the only solution we can envision to our sense of lack. Nevertheless, the global threats of nuclear catastrophe, overpopulation, and social and environmental breakdown make it increasingly difficult for us at the beginning of the third millennium to believe in progress. The future is collapsing, which means our collective sense of lack is beginning to disinvest in the economic and technological projects whereby it hoped to become real. Before considering the possibility of new lack projects in the new millennium, however, we need a better understanding of the last one. How did we come to pursue secular solutions to what is essentially a spiritual problem? The answer is that those solutions were originally not secular at all.

## THE PAPAL REFORMATION

> The Papal Revolution was the most general and intensive
> social earthquake Europe has ever seen. (Berman 530)

In 1075 Gregory VII declared the political and legal supremacy of the
papacy over the whole church and indirectly over the whole of
Christendom. Independence of the clergy was unacceptable to Emperor Henry IV, who responded with military force. A civil war raged
intermittently through Europe until 1122, when the Concordat of
Worms agreed to distinguish the two spheres of power: There was a
difference between the allegiance owed to spiritual authorities and that
owed to temporal authorities. This was not the obvious solution it
appears in retrospect, for such a stalement was sought by neither party;
the religious and political unity of Christendom was generally believed
to be of the highest value. Such, arguably, was the origin of our distinction between sacred and secular.

A few years earlier, when the Normans of Sicily paid homage to
the Pope in 1060, their act of fealty changed the Holy See in Rome
from an adjunct of the imperial palace into an independent papal court.
This court invented central government when it granted the free right
of appeal to every Christian soul. Prior to this, no one could denounce
the corruption of a bishop or carry grievances outside that diocese.
Right of appeal led to the rapid systematization of canon law, with law
courts and a legal profession, legislation, and a legal literature, initiating
what soon became a "science of law."

In response, temporal rulers felt compelled to do the same, and
the nation-state was born.

Prior to this revolution, the emperor or king was considered the
head of the church and the Vicar of Christ. Charlemagne viewed the
Pope his chaplain, and admonished Hadrian: "Your part is to aid our
effort with your prayers" (Keen 91). Emperors usually crowned popes
and required an oath of fealty from them. Of the twenty-five popes
who held office in the hundred years prior to 1059 (when a church
synod first prohibited lay investiture of clergy), twenty-one were appointed by emperors and five dismissed by emperors (Berman 91).
Kings appointed the archbishops and bishops in their realms, including
even Anselm as Archbishop of Canterbury as late as 1093, for despite
his innovative theology Anselm was largely ignorant of the new development of canon law. The justification for this practice was that tem-

poral rulers were consecrated and therefore sacral rulers as well; after all, God gave them the power to rule.

This implied a legal order, but not a legal system. "Law was not consciously systematized. It had not yet been 'disembedded' from the whole social matrix of which it was a part" (Berman 50). Until the eleventh century the basic social unit remained the tribe, and within that the household, a community of trust based partly on kinship and partly on oaths of mutual protection and service. Violations by outsiders led to blood feuds that the king's law attempted to subvert, but it was not not easy to bring wrongdoers to trial or make witnesses testify or enforce a judgment. Later, fixed monetary sanctions payable by the wrongdoer's kin to the victim's kin worked to forestall vendettas. This solution did not need much of a state administrative system to regulate justice, which was fortunate since there was not much of a system.

The king ruled by holding court. His collections of law were less legislation than exhortations to keep the peace and desist from crime: "the king had to beg and pray . . . for he could not command and punish." Nor, for example, were the *dooms* of the Germanic folk assembly legislation in the modern sense; they were divinely inspired affirmations of ancient folk law, reflecting the will of the gods (after the introduction of Christianity, the will of God). "Men did not think of a ruler as the giver but rather the guardian of law." People expected a ruler to protect and be generous to them, not to administer efficiently; from the other side, he had the right to demand their loyal support (Berman, 53, 68, 62, 69). "What bound this society together was not a sense of obligation to a common weal, but the personal oaths of individual men to individual lords" (Keen 57).

In sum, early medieval law was not a body of rules imposed from above but a part of the collective consciousness: The bonds of kinship, lordship, and community *were* the law. That made it a mediating process for dealing with relationships, rather than a matter of rule making and enforcing. This bears comparison with the type of social control found in traditional Confucian and Buddhist societies, which emphasized not allocating rights and duties through a system of general norms, but maintaining right relationships among family and community members (Berman 77–78). The similar stress on restoring harmonious relationships supports the view that premodern Europe was not very different from much of the non-Western world at that time.

The folk law emphasis on honour and harmony was complemented by the Church's penitential law emphasis on repentance and forgiveness to preserve the spiritual welfare of the community. This involved no social program to reform society, for that was impossible. The hopelessness of life in the decaying "terrestrial city" was taken for granted. Christianity was an apocalyptic faith: one must patiently await the return of the Messiah, for that was how the world would be redeemed—in my Buddhist terms, the only way our personal and collective lack could be resolved. Events involving sin and justice were earthly manifestations of an ongoing cosmic struggle between God and Satan for our souls, which would eventually end when Christ reappeared to vanquish his nemesis once and for all. Sin was not objectified; it indicated a state of alienation between us and God, just as an earthly crime created a disharmony in the relationship between two kinship groups.

Although it never became officially adopted by the church, Anselm's theory of atonement offered a new perspective on how we are redeemed, which, in combination with the new authority of the Papacy, changed the course of history. By leading to a new understanding of how our human lack should be addressed, it opened up novel possibilities that would create the modern West.

## THE SPIRITUAL SOURCE OF LAW

More than anything else, it was the new vision of his own ultimate destiny that first led Western man to have faith in legal science. (Berman 164)

The Papal Reformation declared not only the independence of the church but its ultimate authority over temporal rulers. Lacking an army of its own, how could it hope to make these claims effective? In dealing with the new claimants its centralizing government encouraged, it discovered a new source of authority in its new means of control: the rule of law. The canon law that its scholars devised to replace natural law theory was the first modern legal system.

The church thereby set out to reform both itself and the world by law . . . but where did that new sense of law come from? Certainly there was a power struggle—Gregory VII was willful and proud—but the new role of law was based upon a revolutionary understanding of what redemption is: how Christ saves us, and what we must do to be saved.

Today we think of law as essentially a rationally ordered system, but canon law was primarily a response to new attitudes toward death, sin, punishment, and forgiveness, making its criteria as much spiritual and moral as rational. Berman concludes that "Western legal science is a secular theology, which often makes no sense because its theological presuppositions are no longer accepted" (165). But that does not mean we have escaped them.

Prior to this revolution, sin had been understood as a condition of alienation from God, which implied a diminution of one's being. The development of canon law led to a new understanding of sin, now defined in legalistic terms as specific wrongful acts, desires, or thoughts, for which painful penalties must be paid either in this life or in the next. This tended to reduce the importance of the Last Judgment and led to the "legalization," so to speak, of life after death in Purgatory, an intermediate realm where all one's remaining debts must be repaid. This was an important shift from the earlier meaning of penance—acts of contrition symbolizing a turning away from sin back to God and neighbor—into a more objectified sense of sin as an entity, which, as the church soon discovered, could be commodified. From my Buddhist perspective, this was a novel way to understand what our lack consists of and how it is to be resolved: The elaborate system of penances for debts enabled a new type of grip on one's ultimate destiny. "The route [to resolve lack] was charted by a system of punishments and rewards that extended from this world through the next, until the final goal was reached" (Berman 171).

The theological turning point was Anselm's theory of atonement in *Cur Deus Homo*, which outlined a theology of law. God is bound by his own justice, for mercy is the daughter of justice and does not work against her father. God cannot treat the disobedient will in the same way as the obedient one, for that would destroy justice and thus the order and beauty of the universe.

This goes against the earlier approach, which emphasized at least as much God's mercy and grace in saving us from the power of Satan. In the Eastern Church, sin continued to be understood mainly as the fallen state of one's soul, a disharmony in one's relationship with God rather than an act violating a divine legal code. For the Church that came to accept Anselm's perspective, redemption became essentially a legal transaction. Christ's sacrifice paid for our original sin, but we must suffer for all the sins we have committed since then. Justice required that all such violations be repaid with a penalty suitable to the violation (Berman 180–81). Inevitably, the nature and source of mercy also came to be understood in a new way: As God became more of a stern judge, Mary's role became more important as a compassionate intercessor.

By no coincidence this was also when the split between the Eastern and Western churches became final. The Eastern Church continues to follow the earlier view that emphasizes the resurrection of Christ: Christians die and rise again with Christ, who is the conqueror of death. In contrast, Western theology of the eleventh and twelfth centuries identified redemption with the crucifixion: Christ as the conqueror of sin. This changed the emphasis from God the Father to God the Son (hence the *filioque* clause in the Nicene Creed), the incarnation of God and the redeemer of this world. In place of a transcendental solution to our lack—awaiting an apocalyptic irruption of the sacred, with the return of Christ—the focus shifted to the process whereby the sacred becomes immanent in this world. "This released an enormous energy for the redemption of the world; yet it split the legal from the spiritual, the political from the ideological." The legalistic theological metaphors gave birth to a new conception of society, one that was able to transform itself over time by continuously infusing divine and natural law into legal institutions both ecclesiastical and secular. "The sacred was used as a standard by which to measure the secular order" (Berman 177–79, 197, 28).

This doctrine of atonement gave a new and universalizable significance to human justice by linking together the penalty imposed by a court for violating a law with "the nature and destiny of man, his search for salvation, his moral freedom, and his mission to create on earth a society that would reflect the divine will" (Berman 184). In my Buddhist terms, this understanding of our lack gave us a different handle on it, one that plugged nicely into the reform of this world. "Progress" was born.

> The most important consequence of the Papal Revolution was that it introduced into Western history the experience of revolution itself. In contrast to the older view of secular history as a process of decay, there was introduced a dynamic quality, a sense of progress in time, a belief in the reformation of the world. No longer was it assumed that "temporal life" must inevitably deteriorate until the Last Judgment. On the contrary, it was now assumed—for the first time—that progress could be made in this world toward achieving some of the preconditions for salvation in the next. (Berman 118).

Anselm himself was hardly a humanist, for his belief in the decline of this world, and the superiority of monastic life, was deeply conservative.

Like many other monastics since Augustine, he waited for a sufficient number of the saved to accumulate, which would bring about the Second Coming. Yet the future lay with minds of a different type, who would emphasize efficient administration as the way to duplicate on earth the pattern of things laid up in heaven (Southern 441, 345).

"God himself is law, and therefore law is dear to him," wrote the author of the first German law book in about 1220. Before 1075 no one in the West would have said it, but after 1122 it became a commonplace. "Law was seen as a way of fulfilling the mission of Western Christendom to begin to achieve the kingdom of God on earth" (Berman 521). The assumption underlying Anselm's argument, and canon law, was the belief that, as a God of justice, God operates a lawful universe, punishing and rewarding us proportionately although mercifully mitigated in special cases. Today state governors do the same when they mercifully (if rarely) commute a sentence, yet the political parallel goes much deeper. Just as sins became offenses against God, the supreme lawgiver and judge, so secular crimes were no longer against other people but against the king's law—against the state. "The Gregorian concept of the Church almost demanded the invention of the concept of the State" (Joseph Strayer, in Berman 404).

The notion that God operates a lawful universe would be just as important for the development of modern science and technology, for it encouraged the early scientists to search for natural physical laws. The necessary insight was provided by Galileo, who realized that "the Book of Nature is written in mathematical symbols" by "the great Geometer," so the key to its "hidden laws" is to be found by discovering the mathematical structure of the cosmos. That was part of a new understanding of the relationship between God and nature: God functions through his laws. This turned out to be a slippery slope; the more important those laws became, the less important became God, who began to disappear high up into the distant heavens.

The immediate earthly consequence of this new doctrine was to increase the authority of the Papacy immeasurably. As the Vicar of Christ, His temporal agent, the Pope became not only the ultimate spiritual authority but the arbiter of our salvation: the one who could resolve our lack.

In November 1095 Urban II addressed a great crowd in Clermont, calling on men all over Christendom to come to the rescue of their fellow Christians in the East. "Undertake this journey for the remission of your sins, assured of the imperishable glory of the kingdom of heaven." A great cry went up from the assembly: "It is God's will!"

Those who participated were promised remission of the temporal penalties for their sins; those who perished in battle were promised remission of all penalties for all sins, presumably going straight to heaven. In other words, dying on the Crusade was guaranteed to end your lack! Four years later the Crusaders entered Jerusalem, and the Roman Pontiff had succeeded as the leader of all Christendom in a great military endeavor to save the Holy Land. The organizational efforts that such a vast project required also marked a milestone in the development of the Papacy as a state.

The merit that Christ's sacrifice had gained was incalculable; as earthly dispenser of that merit, the power of the Papacy was theoretically immeasurable as well. Yet is spiritual power immune to the rule that power corrupts, and absolute power absolutely? The long-term consequences of such authority were predictable, owing less to the incompetence or corruption of certain individuals than to the humanity of the Pope and Curia, however much the Papacy might represent Christ on earth. Such a vast storehouse of spiritual treasure tempted the Pontiff to largesse, but that encouraged an inflation of the religious currency. Innocent's III's bull of 1209 gave an expedition against the Cathars of France the full legal and spiritual status of a Crusade: The same remission of sins was promised those who would serve for forty days in Languedoc. Later, Papal wars against the Hohenstaufen and the Aragonese also rated as Crusades. Large sums were raised by selling indulgences, originally as expedients to pay for the Crusades, but later relied upon as a regular source of income (Keen 141, 208, 279).

Dante's great poem records the moral consequences of the Church's temporal entanglements, by including Boniface VII, along with his predecessor and successor, in the simoniacs pit of hell. By Dante's time the Papacy had become so caught up in politics and ridden with vested interests that it was widely viewed as no longer able to promote either spiritual life or terrestrial peace. In lack terms, the authority of the Papacy as the arbiter of our lack had become dubitable.

According to Rosenstock-Huessy, "The great Revolutions break out whenever the power which has governed heaven and earth dries up at the fountain-head. The great Revolutions seem to destroy an existing order; but that is not true. They do not break out until the old state of affairs is already ended, until the old order of things has died and is no longer believed in by its own beneficiaries" (471). By the time of Luther, the gap between the Church and the life of the spirit had become viewed as irreparable, and the time was ripe for a new conception of our lack and what to do about it. Luther "delegalized" the church, burning its books of canon law and denying that it can have a legal character. His church was invisible, apolitical as well as alegal— which freed the state to develop a new theory of its own justice as morally neutral, only a means to manifest the policy of the sovereign. Luther may have denied the legality of the church but he believed strongly in the secular law of the ruler, assumed to be a Christian, of course. God was still a God of justice, but now that justice operated through a secular ruler. This was another slipppery slope. The new emphasis on the individual, on nature as property, and on economic relations as contract, led to the secularization of the state and the sanctification of property and contract (Berman 29–30, 197).

Much the same happened with rationality itself. Anselm did not exalt reason at the expense of faith: Reason was a supplement to faith, to help us understand better what we believe. Yet his belief that theology can be studied apart from revelation led to a conception of reason functioning by itself, as the sole guarantor of truth (Descartes, etc.). In a parallel fashion, modern law as a product of rationality has become disconnected from the ultimate values and purposes that motivated its development, thus alienating itself from its original spiritual foundations. Eventually not only religious belief but all deeply held convictions came to be understood as private affairs. "Thus not only legal thought but also the very structure of Western legal institutions have been removed from their spiritual foundations, and those foundations, in turn, are left devoid of the structure that once stood upon them" (Berman 198). The result is a legal system that focuses on precedent and procedure because in its "neutrality" it is unaware that it relies upon or embodies any values at all.

Today, of course, we no longer look at the law as a solution to lack. That is because we have in the meantime devised other ways to address our lack.

## A TIME FOR PROGRESS

> It is by the meaning that it intuitively attaches to time that one culture is differentiated from another. (Spengler, *The Decline of the West*)

In traditional societies, including the premodern West, time's structure is basically religious. Instead of being an undifferentiated Cartesian-like grid for mapping the affairs that happen in this world, a temporal schema provides the sacred pattern that gives meaning to the affairs of this world: "the supernatural and the passage of time as represented by the yearly cycle were so closely linked that they were virtually indistinguishable" (Thompson 2). According to this approach, our lack arises due to their disharmony, and the solution is not time as empty continuum but time as pattern to be renewed or reenacted. In contrast to our linear succession of cause-and-effect events, in this associative temporality history and cosmology are inseparable, for time and what happens in time are not to be distinguished. Rituals such as purification sacrifices are performed according to cyclic natural phenomena because they are needed at those times—which is to say, they do not occur in those periods but as a part *of* those periods (Aveni 65).

Mircea Eliade's scholarly legacy is controversial, yet he had an important insight into this distinction. For Eliade, archaic societies lived in a "paradise of archetypes" because their time structure was based upon periodic regeneration of the creation observed in nature (Aveni 65). This temporality presupposed that every re-creation repeats the initial act of genesis; by reenacting the creation myth, participants relived the creation of order out of chaos, of meaning out of meaninglessness. In this manner such events were never allowed to become "past" in the way that we understand the word, as historically superseded by the present. While we make history by choosing to separate ourselves from past events (a good working definition of "secular time"), more traditional societies deny that duality by reliving the past. For them history is not the burden it is for us, since the past is not a weight to be overcome nor is the future a set of novel possibilities that must be actualized.

It is dangerous to generalize about "archaic societies," but the classic Maya, one of the most time-obsessed cultures ever, provide a good example. They did not measure time by the sun; for them time *is* the sun's cycle (and they were on to something, for our time would certainly cease if the sun ceased). The sun was not a separate entity that followed a course through the heavens, nor did particular gods symbolize each day of their twenty-day cycle; rather, a day manifested its god. According to this schema, close attention to the demands of each day was necessary to preserve the parallel relationships between humans and the supernatural world. The past continued to repeat itself in the present because life's events were carefully timed and regulated: only by weaving the two together was the order of the cosmos maintained. In such a worldview the future is of little interest, for the important events will continue to recur as long as the same balance of cosmic forces is maintained (Aveni 190ff).

> These people did not react to the flow of natural events by struggling to harness and control them. Nor did they conceive of themselves as totally passive observers in the essentially neutral world of nature. Instead, they believed they were active participants and intermediaries in a great cosmic drama. By participating in the rituals, they helped the gods of nature to carry their burdens along their arduous course, for they believed firmly that the rituals served formally to close time's cycles. Without their life's work the universe could not function properly. (Aveni 252)

The Aztecs were even more devoted to the sun, for all their festivals were preoccupied with paying their "debt" to it by supplying the essential energy that would keep it on its course. Only by fueling the sun with enough of life's vital fluid—blood—could they maintain the balance of powers among the cosmic forces that would keep the world from being destroyed again. The primary responsibility of the state was ensuring that there were enough sacrifices. For the Aztecs, like the Maya, the nature of their time determined the nature of their lack and what they needed to do to overcome it.

From this perspective, perhaps the most interesting thing about modern temporality is how our unique understanding of a homogeneous space-time continuum ever evolved out of such spiritually charged schemas. By no coincidence, we again find the turning point in the twelfth century, for previously Europe had the same associative temporality that understands time as a meaning-providing pattern to be reenacted. "To understand our time is to chart the course of Western Judeo-Christendom" (Aveni 12). Our week has seven days because that repeats the pattern of creation at the beginning of Genesis; Jews worship and rest on the Sabbath because on that day the Lord rested (although early Christians changed that to the sun's day because on that day Christ rose from the dead to become the light of the world). The yearly cycle of church commemorations still reveals its associative origins. Our names for the seven days originate from the seven heavenly bodies known before the telescope, according to Aveni a scheme derived from ancient astrology.

None of these facts is very surprising in itself, but the important thing is to read the previous paragraph in the light of the earlier paragraphs about non-Western time. Contrary to the linear cause-and-effect continuum that we tend to project back upon our ancient world as well, our origins reveal the same associative temporality that does not distinguish between cosmos and history, between time and what happens in time, for there too, time is not a homogeneous continuum but a meaning-providing pattern to be reenacted. The pre-Christian world was not very concerned about determining the timing of one historical event by relating it to another; that presupposes our anachronistic belief in an objective and universal time-continuum in which everything can be precisely situated. So it is not surprising that the first clocks we know of, such as the Tower of the Winds in Athens, were not so much efforts to measure time as models of the cosmos constructed to represent and celebrate the beauty and simplicity of heavenly motion (Aveni 92).

Perhaps that helps us understand the extraordinary fascination of the first wave of cathedral clocks in the high Middle Ages: they symbolized the divine structure of time. The medieval Christian mind also did not yet conceive of history as our continuous chain of cause and effect. As Erich Auerbach puts it, "the here and now is no longer a mere link in an earthly chain of events, it is *simultaneously* something which has always been, and will be fulfilled in the future; and, strictly, in the eyes of God, it is something eternal, something omnitemporal, something already consummated in the realm of fragmentary earthly event" (Auerbach 64, his italics). Describing the monastic origins of our clock time, David Landes emphasises how the first clocks had the effect of creating

> "only one time, that of the group, that of the community. Time of rest, of prayer, of work, of meditation, of reading: signaled by the bell, measured and kept by the sacristan, excluding individual and autonomous time." Time, in other words, was of the essence because it belonged to the community and to God; and the bells saw to it that this precious, inextensible resource was not wasted. (68, quoting Albert d'Haenens)

Yet the notion that time is a resource is an anachronism that describes our attitude better than theirs, for it detracts from the essential point that time was God's and should be used to glorify Him (which is why usury was immoral: It profited from using something—time—that belonged only to God).

To sum up, medieval time largely retained the nonduality between cosmology and history—with one important difference. For traditional peoples such as the Maya and the Aztecs, the end of time, which might occur without their continual sacrifices to maintain the sun deity on his course, would be the greatest possible catastrophe. For Christians the second coming of Christ, which most still believed to be imminent, was a salvation devoutly to be wished for. That turned out to be a crucial difference.

Apocalyptic millenarianism can be characterized as belief that the tension between this world and the supernatural will be finally resolved in the (near) future when the transcendent manifests itself so completely that this world is purified and transformed. The crucial step toward modern time was the notion of a future golden age not outside human temporality but *within it,* and it seems to have been taken by Joachim of Fiore (1135–1202), the influential Calabrian abbot and hermit who had visions of complex patterns that drew together all the different threads of revelation and history. Berman, focusing on the influence of canon law, makes only one short reference to him, but Joachim visited three popes (who encouraged his radical exegesis) and spoke before the Curia; kings sought him out, including Richard I of England, Philip Augustus of France, even the emperor Henry VI; and Dante places him in the same circle of paradise as St. Bonaventura and St. Francis (West and Zimdars-Swartz 5).

Joachim retained the traditional belief that events on earth correspond to what is happening in another dimension, while envisioning a Christian utopia on earth *in the future,* a perfected society that would include the creation of new social structures. According to his exegesis the Old Testament corresponded to the Age of the Father, the New Testament to that of the Son, and the final Age of the Spirit, which would arrive by about 1260, would be a supremely happy era during which a renewed Church would regulate all aspects of life. "Without necessarily meaning to, he had made the crucial connection between apocalyptic change and political reconstruction. From the thirteenth century onwards, the two could never be entirely separated" (Thompson 128). The trajectory that would culminate in our cherished faith in progress was set, having grown out of

> the Christian belief that all things are made expressly for the end they fulfill. . . . Faith in the Second Coming pulls the true believer forward through the good life toward the ultimate judgment that gives reason to it all. In modern times,

this notion of advancement along a time line still prevails, except that technology has replaced religion as the force that propels events to succeed one another; nonetheless, the doctrine remains teleological. (Thompson 128)

Again we see that, far from being rational alternatives to religious apocalypticism, "many of the ideas we consider to be the very opposite of 'medieval,' such as faith in progress and the promise of utopia, have roots in the religious beliefs of the middle ages—and End-time beliefs at that" (Thompson 57).

If technology today has replaced religion for many of us, perhaps that is because our technology retains similar religious roots. David Noble's book *The Religion of Technology* makes a point parallel to the one that Berman makes about Western law: Our contemporary enchantment with modern technology—the very measure of our supposedly hard-headed rationalism—is in fact rooted in religious myth and the quest for spiritual salvation. "Although today's technologists, in their sober pursuit of utility, power and profit, seem to set society's standard for rationality, they are driven also by distant dreams, spiritual yearnings for supernatural redemption . . . their true inspiration lies . . . in an enduring, otherworldly quest for transcendence and salvation" (3). Again, we may have forgotten what originally motivated us, but that does not mean we have escaped it.

In the medieval period, "for reasons that remain obscure" (Noble 12), significant changes began to occur in the Christian attitude toward technology.[1] Medieval society believed that part of its fallenness was that it had lost knowledge of the ancient arts and sciences perfected by its predecessors. What was new was the belief that those mechanical arts could and should be resurrected—initially, not so much to improve society's worldly condition as to help create the temporal conditions that would hasten the return of Christ. "Over time, technology came to be identified more closely with both lost perfection and the possibility of renewed perfection, and the advance of the arts took on a new significance, not only as evidence of grace, but as a means of preparation for, and a sure sign of, imminent salvation." The influential Augustinian canon Hugh of St. Victor (1096–1141) emphasized that "the work of restoration included the repair of man's physical life," which had been damaged by sin and forfeited with the Fall (Noble 12, 19–20).

> An elite revitalization and reinterpretation of early Christian belief . . . situated the process of recovery in the context of human history and redefined it as an active and conscious pursuit rather than a merely passive and blind expectation. . . . The recovery of mankind's divine likeness, the transcendent trajectory of Christianity, thus now became at the same time an immanent historical project. . . . Technology now became at the same time eschatology. (Noble 22)

Noble describes Joachim's interpretation of *The Book of Revelations* as the "most influential prophetic system known to Europe until Marxism." It "ignited the greatest spiritual revolution of the Middle Ages" by revealing the millenarian meaning of history, God's plan for humanity. All wise men, wrote Roger Bacon, believe that the time of the Antichrist is nigh, and he urged his fellow churchmen to study Joachim's prophecies in order to be forewarned about the final events of history. According to both biblical and Joachimite prophecy, the gospel must be preached worldwide, as a necessary precondition for, as well as an unmistakable indication of, the approach of the millennium. This encouraged both exploration and the arts that promoted such exploration. Our prejudice in favor of economic explanations emphasizes the lust for gold, but if Christopher Columbus's unfinished *Book of Prophecy* can be trusted, he like many others viewed the colonization and conversion of the New World as necessary to fulfill Joachimite prophecy and help bring about the end of history. Understanding himself to be divinely inspired, he urged his Portugese patrons to use New World riches to finance a new Crusade to recover Jerusalem, another precondition for the new millennium (Noble 27–31, West and Zimdars-Swartz 108).

Later even Francis Bacon, the prophet of modern science, sought "a return to the state of Adam before the Fall, a state of pure and sinless contact with nature and knowledge of her powers . . . a progress back towards Adam" (Francis Yates, in Noble 50). Both Robert Boyle and Isaac Newton were fervent millenarians, and the latter spent much of his time on the interpretation of prophecy. For them, as for many other early scientists, the scientific quest was a devout effort to come closer to their Creator. "Armed with such foreknowledge, which included an anticipation of their own appointed role, the elect needed no longer to just passively await the millennium; they could now actively work to bring it about" (Noble 64, 24–25). We are still working to do that, but in the meantime we have forgotten exactly what it is we are supposed to be bringing about.

We have forgotten because our understanding of our lack has been displaced, and therefore our approach to resolving it. Instead of being the crux of creation and history, where the Christian story places it, our lack today has been marginalized and so its problematic shifted. We no longer appeal to the structure of the cosmos for our salvation, but try to work it out by ourselves. The new space-time of Descartes and Newton was homogenized, yet from this perspective it is somewhat misleading to call it secular. Rather, it provided us with a different kind of grid on which to work out our lack. In place of an intricate spiritual obstacle course to be challenged according to fixed rules, we began to live in a boundless universe where we had to set up the goals and decide which way to go. We decided to run into the future, and called the new game progress.

## WAITING FOR THE END

> And God shall wipe away all tears from their eyes; and there shall be no more death, neither sorrow, nor crying, neither shall there be any more pain: for the former things are passed away. And he that sat upon the throne said, Behold, I make all things new. (Revelations 21:4–5)

> Apocalypticism is "merely" the most explosive of forms that hope takes, and it resides at a very deep level of our cultural psyche. (Landes 1997, 24)

Norman Cohn's ground-breaking study *The Pursuit of the Millennium,* and the work of many other scholars since, have amply documented the role of apocalyptic millenarianism in the history of the West. It may seem very peculiar to us growth junkies today, but its influence has been immense—and from a lack perspective some such social tendency is not only natural but perhaps ineradicable. Cohn sums up his work by offering what is, in effect, a lack hypothesis about the cause of millenarian movements:

> It seems that there is in many, perhaps in all, human psyches a latent yearning for total salvation from suffering; that yearning appears to be greatly intensified by any frustration or

anxiety or humiliation that is unaccustomed and that cannot be tackled either by taking thought or by any institutionalized routine. Where a particular frustration or anxiety or humiliation of this nature is experienced at the same time and in the same area by a number of individuals, the result is a collective emotional agitation that is peculiar not only in its intensity, but also in the boundlessness of its aims. (in Strozier and Flynn, 40)[2]

Cohn shows how belief in the Last Days took on a revolutionary meaning and often led to explosive unrest in areas experiencing social and economic crisis, especially among those, such as newly urbanized casual workers, unsupported by traditional networks of social relationships. In my Buddhist terms, our lack is usually contained in and structured by such social relationships, which provide traditional ways to exorcise it; those unsupported by such a context are much more likely to seek a more apocalyptic resolution to their lack. The main argument of this chapter is that the West we know was created when our lack became channeled into creating the future, but the persistence of apocalyptic movements after the eleventh century, and the chiliastic influence of Joachim and others, shows that progress did not simply replace apocalypse as our social solution to lack. The idea of progress grew out of millenarianism, and retains the traces of its origins. The relationship between them remains uncomfortably close.

Early Christianity was apocalyptic, yet this soon received a nonchiliastic interpretation. For Origen the Kingdom of God was an event not in space or time but one that occurred in the souls of believers. When Christianity became the official religion of the Empire in the fourth century, millenarianism began to be strongly discouraged (Cohn 29). For Tichonius (d. ca. 400) the New Jerusalem was not an historical event but the present-day church; the *Book of Revelations* described in symbolic terms the diabolical attacks upon it. Augustine built on this allegorical approach by developing a great-week chronology that understood humanity to be already living in the new dispensation, although one that would decline until the Second Advent when history would end.

Joachim's addition to this vision was to restore primitive and still popular chiliastic beliefs in conceiving of a new world order that would prevail on earth for a thousand years before the Second Advent (West and Zimdars-Swartz 10–12). This was not easily reconciled with

Augustine's position, and some of Joachim's later disciples got into trouble with the Church authorities, but Joachim himself was never condemned. His approach resonated with the new collective consciousness of his time, and I conclude with some reflections on why that may have been so—on why people in the eleventh century may have been ready for the new understanding of our lack that the Papal Revolution initiated or enunciated.

As we ourselves experienced the advent of another millennium many of us wondered: What was the advent of the previous one like? The popular importance of apocalyptic expectations in medieval Chistianity suggests that many people must have expected the world to end in A.D. 1000. How did they cope with their disappointment?

Apparently with no difficulty at all, according to the received view, for there is little record of any such mass millennialism at that time, and many people then were not even familiar with our dating system. However, some contemporary historians, most notably Richard Landes, have challenged that conclusion, arguing that our historical sources were controlled by Augustinian monks who would naturally have downplayed the significance of such popular movements—especially apocalyptic ones that failed. According to Landes, lack of evidence in this case is not evidence of lack. Far from being insignificant, the mutation in apocalyptic expectations that this chapter describes was affected by what occurred (and did not occur) in A.D. 1000. How?

> The approach of the Apocalypse calls for all sinners to, in this final moment, "Repent, for the Kingdom of Heaven is at hand." If large numbers collectively feel this imminence, if a plague or an earthquake or a sign in the heavens shakes the confidence of even the most determined and powerful members of a society, if people gather in vast assemblies and engage in penitential activity, reaching unimaginable heights of confession and renunciation, then the fear can and will pass, not only because the end fails to come, but because the collective penance can produce a massive change of "atmosphere" in which people embrace their enemies in tears of mutual forgiveness. Thus the delay of the end might be viewed not merely as a reprieve, but as the salvation of God, bestowed on his chastened people; not the continuation of the world as we know it, but the inauguration of a new age in which the peace of men, the peace of iron, gives way to the Pax Dei.

> . . . Here one finds some of the most pregnant activity—the
> first and vigorous stirrings of a popular Christian culture of
> vast movements, of radical dissent and reform, of widespread
> pilgrimage, of collective actions. . . . It is in the transforma-
> tion of penitence to joy that new social bonds are made; that
> vendettas are abandoned, that feuding enemies embrace, that
> weapons are laid aside. (Landes, "While God Tarried" 6)

From many other examples we know that the extravagant hopes of
apocalyptic expectations do not usually disappear with failure. "Disappointment triggers not discouragement, but renewed efforts to reignite
the apocalyptic flames that had made the movement possible" (Landes,
"While God Tarried" 7).

Is this how it happened? Certainly the timing is curious. The
extraordinary developments of the High Middle Ages began more or
less in the middle of the eleventh century, which gave time for such a
change of consciousness to spread and develop. Of course, I cannot
pretend to adjudicate such a controversy. From my Buddhist perspective, however, it is interesting to interpret Landes's speculative scenario
in terms of the influence it might have on people's collective sense of
lack. Waiting for an End both welcomed and dreaded, one that would
destroy the world yet could bring about everything one hoped for,
would encourage those who were sincere to face their greatest fears
more consciously than ever before—that is, would prompt them to
confront their sense of lack more directly, cutting through the repres-
sions we usually hide behind. We know that to de-repress death denial
is not only to experience the terror of death more consciously, but
also—for those able to endure that—to become more *alive*. The same
should be true for our lack: to face one's sense of lack more consciously,
and to endure it, is to become more spiritually alive; and to experience
that with many others would create a special sense of community with
them. To face one's lack so immediately, to let go of everything in this
world and acknowledge one's nothingness before the mystery and majesty
of the cosmos, might be to be transformed and vivified—in Christian
terms, perhaps nothing less than to be filled with the Holy Spirit. Even
if this happened only for a minority, and incompletely, it could have
become a powerful influence on how people lived and how they wanted
to live—that is, on how they understood their lack.

Such an imminent experience of grace may have encouraged
them not to wait for a salvation to descend upon them from them, but

to work for their salvation here and now, by infusing what they had experienced of the sacred into the world and its institutions.

> Perhaps the single most enduring effect of this millennial generation was the development of a process of apocalyptic reform, in which movements like Pax Christi, which were launched at times of intense apocalyptic expectation, become, upon "reentry" into normal time, institutionalized as "reform" movements. Thus, the entire eleventh century is known as a time of fervent reform, beginning with the monastic orders (Cluny) and moving into the secular clergy with the reform of the canonical houses, finally becoming a full-fledged church reform in the second half of the century under the tutelage of the popes. . . . Reform is the post-apocalyptic form of the spiritual renewal that the advent of the millennium brought. (Landes, "The Apocalyptic Year 1000" 21)

Is that how the West was created, by a dramatic irruption of grace into the souls of believers, transformed by facing their lack more directly, and thereby inspired to transform the world around them?

And is it a coincidence that a new millennium begins just as we are losing faith in economic and technological progress as our collective way to resolve lack?

In one way, all religions worth the name are millennial: they critique the present condition and offer a vision of what could be. In that sense, religion remains inescapable. The issue for us becomes what new lack projects are possible.

# THREE

# THE RENAISSANCE OF LACK

If history is a nightmare from which we are trying to awaken, as James Joyce's Daedalus put it, what gives that nightmare its power over us? Perhaps it began as a daydream more attractive than the pain of being human—until the dream took on a life of its own and we became trapped in our own objectifications. Then the key to this puzzle is why we prefer daydreaming to waking up, and that brings us back to lack. If the autonomy of *self*-consciousness is a delusion that can never quite shake off its shadow feeling that "something is wrong with me," it will need to rationalize that sense of inadequacy somehow. Without a religious means of absolution, today we usually experience our lack as "I don't yet have enough of . . ." Most of us have lost faith in collective solutions, so we are more in the grip of individualistic ones, such as the craving for fame, the love of romantic love, and of course an obsession with money.

This chapter challenges the supposed secularity of modern individualism by arguing that these three may be understood as historically conditioned forms of delusive craving that gained their power over us because today they have become our main attempts to resolve such lack. These inclinations are not limited to any particular time or place, of course, but they began to gain special importance when Christianity began to decline in the late Middle Ages.

As long as there was a truly catholic church providing a socially agreed upon means to cope with lack, such projects did not seem spiritually necessary. Jacob Burckhardt, Johann Huizinga, and Philippe Aries all noticed a striking increase in preoccupation with death at the end of the medieval era. In psychotherapeutic terms, such an increase in death anxiety requires stronger psychic devices to cope with it. In lack terms, the greater sense-of-self that began to develop then must have been shadowed by a greater sense of lack, leading to greater individual need to realize this self and more radical attempts to do so. If we do not presuppose the usual distinction between secular and sacred, we can see the same drive operating in each case: the conscious or unconscious urge to resolve our sense of lack, by becoming *real*. To the extent that these three are motivated by such a spiritual need, they may be considered something like secular heresies. Since they cannot fulfill that need, they tend to spin out of control and become demonic.

The secular/sacred dualism seems important to us because we are wary of materialistic and psychologistic reductionism, yet there is another way to understand their nonduality. Rather than reducing the sacred to a function of the material, this chapter turns that idea on its head by suggesting that our modern worldly values (desire for fame, money, etc.) acquire their compulsiveness from a misdirected spiritual drive.

### THE FEVER OF RENOWN[1]

> Because the public image comes to stand as the only valid certification of being, the celebrity clings to his image as the rich man clings to his money—that is, as if to life itself. (Lapham 230)

"How can he be dead, who lives immortal in the hearts of men?" mused Longfellow, bestowing on Michelangelo our highest possible praise. "If his inmost heart could have been lain open," wrote Hawthorne of a character in *Fanshawe*, "there would have been discovered the dream of undying fame; which, dream as it is, is more powerful than a thousand realities." More powerful, because of such a dream is our reality woven, and the nature of this dream ensures that there is no lack of historical testimony to its power. Unfortunately, seeing through one aspect of this delusion does not immunize us against others. Horace warned that the race for public honors traps men, for the urge to glory and praise ruins both wellborn and lowly: "those who seek much, lack much." But this did not stop him from crowing at the end of his third ode: "I have wrought a monument more enduring than bronze, and loftier than the royal accumulation of the pyramids. Neither corrosive rain nor raging wind can destroy it, nor the innumerable sequence of years nor the flight of time. I shall not altogether die."Was Horace more vain than we are, or just more frank about his own motivations?

According to Alan Harrington, the urge for fame has only one purpose: "to achieve an imitation of divinity before witnesses." The gods are immortal, he says, but the rest of us will have to settle for a symbolic substitute, which requires witnesses. "Being recognized before many witnesses strengthens our claim to membership in the immortal company" (112). Yet Marcus Aurelius already saw the problem with witnesses (*Meditations* VIII 44): "Those that yearn for after-fame do not realize that their successors are sure to be very much the same as the contemporaries whom they find such a burden, and no less mortal. What is it anyway to you if there be this or that far-off echo in their voices, or if they have this or that opinion about you?" What is the advantage of having one's own name on the lips of future generations, when their overriding concern will be the same as ours: not to preserve anyone else's name, but to have their own name on the lips of *their* successors . . . How does that confer any reality on us? The second-century Buddhist philosopher Nagarjuna demonstrated the futility of such infinite regresses with his argument against dependent being: If there is no self-being there can be no dependent being either, inasmuch as dependent being acquires its being from the self-being of another.[2] Yet we strive to become real through (in) the eyes of others who strive to become real through the eyes of others who will strive . . .

Nonetheless, in Western secular societies such a craving for fame and the approval of posterity has largely replaced the afterlife as the way to fill up our lack. Physical death may come, but such symbolic life can continue forever. Reputation, primarily through public deeds, was also paramount for the Greeks and Romans: "a culture whose afterlife offered so little comfort to the soul was obsessed with preserving the fame of the dead on the lips of the living" (Murray 656). Like Derrida's elusive trace, however, genuine heroism is always receding if *true* greatness means achieving a sense of being without a sense of lack. A few generations ago, madhouses were said to be full of Napoleons, yet Napoleon was inspired by the example of Caesar, while Caesar lamented that he hadn't accomplished as much as Alexander, even as Alexander the Great modeled himself on Achilles . . . When lack is "the origin of the origin," such traces become unavoidable. "If he was real, I can become real by imitating him"—but not if his reality is a past that has never been present, in which case trying to recover the past in the future merely loses the present.

What little remains today of our discomfort with fame is a residue of the Judeo-Christian critique of Roman standards of public glory, for "in the wake of Jesus, public men of all sorts develop a kind of guilty conscience about their desire for achievement in front of an audience" (Braudy 56, 160). Christianity offered a different project to overcome lack. The success of this project accounts for the Middle Ages as we remember them; or, more precisely, that we remember so little about them. If history is a record of how humankind runs away from death, a society less preoccupied with death will make less history. Then it is no coincidence that at the end of the Middle Ages (when according to Burckhardt, Huizinga, and Aries man became more obsessed with death) man became more obsessed with symbolic immortality: "from the Renaissance until today men have been filled with a burning ambition for fame, while this striving that seems so natural today was unknown to medieval man." (Burckhardt 139). The crisis in Europe's collective religious project to cope with lack opened the door to a proliferation of more individualistic projects, both secular and sacred (e.g., personal mysticism). The Reformation worked to deinstitutionalize religion by shifting from a corporate orientation toward salvation (the Church as the body of Christ) to a more private relationship with God. If God is first and foremost the guarantor that our lack will be resolved, we can understand how God may be sought symbolically on earth—perhaps must be, if we no longer seek him in heaven.

In his comprehensive study *The Frenzy of Renown: Fame and Its History*, Leo Braudy traces the modern history of fame from late medieval glorification of the saint (e.g., St. Francis and Jeanne d'Arc) through the creative artist of the Renaissance (Michelangelo, Leonardo da Vinci) and the writer of the nineteenth century (Byron, Dickens, Victor Hugo) to today's performer (Madonna, Michael Jackson). It seems to be a gradual descent from sacred to secular: saints were believed to gain greater being from more direct contact with God; later Dante and John Milton strove to be worthy of fame; today we have celebrities whose only claim to fame is that they are famous. Fame has become self-justifying as an end to be sought for itself.

According to Braudy, the eighteenth century (also singled out by Aries for its death preoccupation) was a turning point in the development of our modern preoccupation with fame:

> [I]t is difficult not to characterize the latter part of the
> eighteenth century as a world in which the waning of belief
> in an afterlife has bred a twin obsession with posterity and
> death. . . . In a culture where talk of the afterlife was be-
> coming less and less important to theology, let alone the
> ordinary believer, the hope of fame on earth was part of the
> expectation that one might be fulfilled, that is, recognized in
> one's lifetime. Hope of heaven, hope of immediate fame, and
> hope of fame in posterity were becoming difficult to distin-
> guish. (Braudy 378)

This became tied up with earlier beliefs in progress (and, later, evolution): "The cult of progress, of growth, of achievement—the image of
new dawns, new tomorrows, and a new sense of time so prominent in
both the American and French revolutions—turned all eyes to the
future, where perfection and understanding would be achieved on earth"
(Braudy 429). The decline in a sacred afterlife was accompanied by a
rise in the importance of secular afterlife, for need to project a lack-free
time somewhere in the future remained. Diderot argued that in posterity fame will redeem one's work from the envy of the present, much
as the Christian afterlife redeems the reputation of the virtuous from
the persecutions of the wicked.

Gradually, however, this secularization of fame led to a decline of
belief even in a secular afterlife. William Hazlitt noticed that the young
value posthumous fame because they do not yet believe in their own
deaths, while the aged would rather have their celebrity on earth.
Nowadays it is becoming more difficult to believe in any future, so we
prefer our fame on the installment plan. This profanation of salvation
has eroded the distinction between good and bad fame. "How many
times do I have to kill before I get a name in the paper or some
national attention?" wrote a murderer to the Wichita police.[3] Only with
his sixth killing, he complained, had he begun to get the publicity he
deserved. When it is believed that recognition by others is what leads
to self-fulfillment, "fame promises acceptability, even if one commits the
most heinous crime, because thereby people will finally know who you
are, and you will be saved from the living death of being unknown"
(Braudy 562).

*The living death of being unknown.* When the real world becomes what's
in the newspapers or on television, to be unknown is to be nothing. Since
my sense-of-self is internalized through social conditioning—since others

teach me that I am real—the natural tendency is to cope with my shadow sense of unreality by continually reassuring myself with the attention of other people. However, if my sense of reality is dependent on others' perceptions of me, then, no matter how appreciative that attention may be, I am constrained by those perceptions. "The difficulty arises when to be free is defined by being known to be free, because then one might be more known than free." This applies to anything that constitutes one's claim to fame: you can't use fame without being used by it. Part of this problem is the fan, who seeks to bask in the glory—to share in the *being*—radiated by his or her heroes. "The audience . . . is less interested in what they [celebrities] think they 'really' are than what role they play in the audience's continuing drama of the meaning of human nature" (Braudy 589, 592, 590). That drama may be dangerous, as John Lennon and many others have discovered.

"[T]he essential lure of the famous is that they are somehow more real than we and that our insubstantial physical reality needs that immortal substance for support . . . because it is the best, perhaps the only, way *to be*." De Tocqueville, visiting America in the 1830s, noticed how democratic societies aggravate this tendency. Aristocracies fix one's social position so everyone knows who and where one is, while democracy engenders a need to stand out from the crowd. As de Tocqueville put it, democratic man usually has no lofty ambition; he just wants to be first at anything. (Braudy 6, 461–62). "And hence this tremendous struggle to singularize ourselves, to survive in some way in the memory of others and of posterity. It is this struggle, a thousand times more terrible than the struggle for life, that gives its tone, colour, and character to our society" (Unamuno 52).

The importance of fame as a secular salvation has become so pervasive today that we no longer notice it, any more than a fish sees the water it swims in. It has infiltrated all the corners of contemporary culture, even Christmas carols ("Rudolf the Red-Nosed Reindeer") and spaghetti sauce bottles (see the label on Newman's Own Spaghetti Sauce). The Guinness Book of World Records has become one of our most important cultural icons.

From a Buddhist perspective the struggle between fame and anonymity is another self-defeating version of dualistic thinking. We differentiate success from failure yet we cannot have one without the other because they are conceptually and psychologically interdependent: grasping one half also maintains the other. So our hope for success is equal to our fear of failure. And whether we win or lose the struggle for fame, we internalize the dialectic between fame and anonymity.

> Just as the titles of winners are worthless unless they are visible to others, there is a kind of antititle that attaches to invisibility. To the degree that we are invisible we have a past that has condemned us to oblivion. It is as though we have somehow been overlooked, even forgotten, by our chosen audience. If it is the winners who are presently visible, it is the losers who are invisibly past.
>
> As we enter into finite play—not playfully, but seriously—we come before an audience conscious that we bear the antititles of invisibility. We feel the need, therefore, to prove to them that we are not what we think they think we are . . .
>
> As with all finite play, an acute contradiction quickly develops at the heart of this attempt. As finite players we will not enter the game with sufficient desire to win unless we are ourselves convinced by the very audience we intend to convince. That is, *unless we believe we actually are the losers the audience sees us to be, we will not have the necessary desire to win.* The more negatively we assess ourselves, the more we strive to reverse the negative judgment of others. The outcome brings the contradiction to perfection: by proving to the audience they were wrong, we prove to ourselves the audience was right.
>
> The more we are recognized to be winners, the more we know ourselves to be losers. . . . No one is ever wealthy enough, honored enough, applauded enough. (Carse 72–73, his italics)

The more we are applauded, the more we feel our lack: If what I have sought for so long does not make me real, what can? "Many seek fame because they believe it confers a reality that they lack. Unfortunately, when they become famous themselves, they usually discover that their sense of unreality has only increased." Why? "The reception of the great work by the world can never satisfy the expectations its creator had for its own fame and his own" (Braudy 589). When fame symbolizes my need to end my lack and become real, such a disappointment is inevitable: No amount of fame can satisfy me if there is really something else I seek from it. From here there are two ways to go. One is concluding that I am not yet famous *enough*. Then each achievement has to top the last one, for if you're not going up you're headed down. The other danger with becoming famous is that one might accomplish one's project for overcoming lack without overcoming lack, with the effect of increasing one's anxiety about being unreal. From a Buddhist standpoint, however, this second problem is also a great opportunity since it opens up the possibility of confronting one's sense of lack more directly. The issue becomes how one deals with that heightened sense of pure lack.

## ALL YOU NEED IS LOVE

> Few people would fall in love had they never heard of love.
> (La Rochefoucauld)

A preliminary caution: the English word *love* means too much and therefore too little. This section addresses only that historically conditioned form of attraction between the sexes called romantic love ("self-love *a deux*" according to Madame de Stael). For some this type of love verges on the ridiculous, rather like someone dying of starvation because he could not find any Brussels sprouts. Then why does it so seldom seem ridiculous to us? Is it because romance has become one of the most widely accepted ways to overcome lack?

> Our eagerness for both novels and films with their identical type of plot; the idealized eroticism that pervades our culture and upbringing and provides the pictures that fill the background of our lives; our desire for "escape," which a mechanical boredom exacerbates—everything within and about us glorifies passion. Hence the prospect of a passionate experience has come to seem the promise that we are about to live more fully and more intensely. We look upon passion as a transfiguring force, something beyond pain and delight, an ardent beatitude. (de Rougemont 15–16)

A beatitude that transcends lack? Such beatitude may transfigure pain yet it remains dependent on it, since as we know there is nothing more fatal to passion than the completion that brings lovers down to earth. The course of true love must be hindered. Romance thrives on difficulties, misunderstandings, and forced separations, which postpone the complacency inherent in familiarity, when housekeeping emotions take over. Such a dismal encore to ecstasy being unendurable, suffering—the literal meaning of *passion*—comes to the rescue. The enmity between the families of Romeo and Juliet is necessary to challenge their attraction. Without it there would be no story to tell and (we have good reason to suspect) no such grand passion to begin with.

As Diotima taught Socrates in the *Symposium,* love thrives on lack, but the reverse is also true: our lack thrives on such love. We are not unaware that passion means suffering, yet we imagine that such passion is nonetheless exciting and vital in a way ordinary life is not. Therefore we revel in the pain, for all pain is endurable when we can see a reason for it and an end to it. Our formless sense of lack objectifies itself into an object lacked, which grants the possibility of a project to gain the lacked thing.

The Greeks and Romans were not unfamiliar with romantic love, yet for them it was the exception rather than the rule and they looked upon it more as an illness. Plutarch called such love a frenzy: "Some have believed it was a madness. . . . Those who are in love must be forgiven as though ill." Then how we have come to cherish this frenzy so highly? If salvation through romantic passion is an historically conditioned myth, where and why did it arise at the time it did?

Some of the answers are found in Denis de Rougemont's classic study *Love in the Western World.* It traces the myth back to the legend of Tristan and Iseult, a tale of unknown origins that became widespread in the twelfth century, about that time of the late Middle Ages singled out by Burckhardt and Aries as the turning point in our increasing awareness of death (and increasing awareness of lack). De Rougemont's analysis of the legend demonstrates:

> Tristan and Iseult do not love one another. They say they don't, and everything goes to prove it. *What they love is love and being in love.* . . . Their need of one another is in order to be aflame, and they do not need one another as they are. What they need is not one another's presence, but one another's absence (43, his italics).[4]

If absence gives us a project to overcome lack, presence must disappoint because it accomplishes one's goal without ending one's lack. Therefore each loves the other *"from the standpoint of self and not from the other's standpoint.* Their unhappiness thus originates in a false reciprocity, which disguises a twin narcissism." Narcissism, because the other is experienced not as he or she is, but as the opportunity to fill up one's own lack.[5]

Of course that is not the way Tristan and Iseult understand it. Like all great lovers, they imagine that they have been transported "into a kind of transcendental state outside ordinary human experience, into an ineffable absolute irreconcilable with the world, but that they feel to be *more real than the world.*" De Rougemont concludes that, unaware and in spite of themselves, the desire of Tristan and Iseult is for nothing but death. The approach of death acts as a goad to sensuality, aggravating their desire. *Love in the Western World* begins by quoting Bedier's version of the legend: "My lords, if you would hear a high tale of love and death . . ." We could listen to nothing more delightful, of course, for that is the fateful equation: "a myth is needed to express the dark and unmentionable fact that passion is linked with death, and involves the destruction of any one yielding himself up to it with all his strength" (55, 40–41, 15, 21–22). De Rougemont dismisses this as antilife but that misses the point: Death is linked with love because death, like love, symbolizes our fear of letting go of ourselves as well as our desire to let go of ourselves—which is the only way to overcome lack, according to Buddhism.

From a lack perspective, the most important aspect of de Rougemont's analysis is that he sees the "spiritual" character of romantic love: "the passionate love which the myth celebrates actually became in the twelfth century—the moment when first it began to be cultivated— a religion in the full sense of the word, and in particular a Christian heresy historically determined" (145). Again, it is unlikely to be a coincidence that the myth of salvation through romance arose just as the prevalent Christian myth began to decline, which cleared the way for more individualistic alternatives to develop, for more personal myths to overcome lack. De Rougemont relates the rise of the romantic heresy to the troubadours, who were probably under the influence of the Cathar heresy, itself likely to have been influenced by Manichaeism from Eastern Europe. He thereby marginalizes the infecting virus into an external "other" invading pure Christianity, which perhaps reveals as much about de Rougemont's anti-pagan bias as about the origin of the Cathars.

A famous twelfth-century judgment by a "court of love" in the house of the Countess of Champagne declared that love and marriage were incompatible, since the first is by choice and the second by duty.

But their judgment was also opposed to any physical "satisfaction" of love: "Of *donnoi* [courtly love] he knows truly nothing who wants fully to possess his lady. *Whatever turns into a reality is no longer love.*" Because whenever love is consummated we can no longer have the illusion that it is a way to become real? So the troubadours adored inaccessible ladies without hope of requital. The history of passionate love since then is the devolution of this courtly myth—still with strong spiritual over-tones—into more "profane" love, "the account of the more and more desperate attempts of Eros to take the place of mystical transcendence by means of emotional intensity. But magniloquent or plaintive, the tropes of its passionate discourse and the hues of its rhetoric can never attain to more than the glow of a resurgent twilight and the promise of a phantom bliss" (de Rougemont 35–36, 179).[6]

From spiritual transcendence through emotional intensity to . . . our present preoccupation with sexual satisfaction—why has sex become so important to us? If we do not dualize secular from sacred, we can see the same urge functioning in each: today we unconsciously seek a spiritual fulfillment from sex. *Spiritual* because we want sex to fulfill us and heal us—that is, to resolve our lack—yet that is to expect some-thing it cannot provide except for the briefest of moments. "It is once more the aspiration towards the life sublime," says Huizinga, "but this time viewed from the animal side. It is an ideal all the same, even though it be that of unchastity." And if we do not dualize the animal from the sublime, perhaps the main difference between troubadours and one-night stands is that the myth of sexual salvation is easier to see through. It is as easy as giving up smoking, which some people can do twenty times a day. Then the logical and demonic culmination of this myth is Don Juan, who turns out to be motivated by the same project as the troubadours. Not lust but the inadequacy of sex as a religion—its obvious inability to satisfy lack for very long—is what drives him from one woman to another.

De Rougemont contrasts passion-love with life. The first "is an impoverishment of one's being, an *askesis* without sequel, an inability to enjoy the present without imagining it as absent, a never-ending flight from possession" (300). Instead, he says, happiness depends on acceptance and is lost as soon as we try to gain it, since it pertains not to having but to being. "Every wish to experience happiness, to have it at one's beck and call—instead of *being* in a *state* of happiness, as though by grace—must instantly produce an intolerable sense of want" (294). Again, one can appreciate the wisdom in this without being satisfied with de Rougemont's solution, which is a simple return to more traditional Christian values, including a decision to keep troth. Religious faith and marital fidelity do not necessarily resolve the problem of lack, for that may simply replace one myth with another. Romantic passion is antilife, insists de Rougemont, yet he does not see what impels the widespread fascination with antilife: the lack dissatisfaction built into life as we ordinarily experience it, a frustration that must be addressed one way or another.

None of the above is a critique of love in its spiritual, emotional, or physical aspects; it is rather an attempt to explain the widespread inability to find happiness in such relationships. Of course, the Western tradition has other and older myths about love. One profound example is the story of Psyche and Cupid; another is found in the *Phaedrus* and the *Symposium*. In these dialogues Plato mentions a frenzied type of love that spreads from the body to infect the spirit with malignant humours, and contrasts that with a different kind of delirium conceived in one's soul by the inspiration of heaven (therefore to be called *enthusiasm,* "possessed by a god"). In the *Symposium* Diotima teaches Socrates that erotic passion at its best is transformed into a love delighting in beauty of every kind. The lover who has ascended high enough will therefore experience the perfect form of beauty, which is the reality and substance of everything we perceive as beautiful (211a–b).

This Platonic account of pure love and everlasting beauty does not survive Nietzsche's scathing attack on all such Real worlds, yet it touches on something that does: the ability of love to transform our way of experiencing everything. We smile on the man for whom the whole world has suddenly become inexpressibly beautiful, simply because his beloved reciprocates. But who, he or we, experiences the world more truly? Love shakes us out of the utilitarian, everything-for-the-sake-of-something-else way of seeing things and therefore it opens up the possibility of an even deeper transformation. Ernest Becker wonders if "the reason that love is one of the principle sources of anguish in the higher primates is because it stands at the threshold of a this-worldly liberation" (1964, 246).

A wonderful example of such liberation is Etty Hillesum's love for Julius Speier, as recorded in her wartime diaries. Soon after she met him in early 1941, the older Speier became the focus of her life and they became lovers, although he was more important as a "guru" figure for her. By the time that "dear spoilt man" died a year and a half later, however, her love had grown far beyond him, and during the Dutch

Holocaust she devoted herself wholeheartedly to helping all those who were suffering. Survivors from Auschwitz confirmed that she was "luminous" to the last, doing everything she could to comfort others. Such love has nothing to do with narcissism. Such inspiring examples imply that, instead of using the other to try to fill one's lack, one may participate in a deeper love that consumes self-love and self-preoccupation, and therefore their lack-shadow as well. Perhaps Etty realized, like Buddhist bodhisattvas, that when there is no self there is no other.

## THE MIDAS TOUCH

> If there is to be a psychoanalysis of money it must start from the hypothesis that the money complex has the essential structure of religion—or, if you will, the negation of religion, the demonic. The psychoanalytic theory of money must start by establishing the proposition that money is, in Shakespeare's words, the "visible god"; in Luther's words, "the God of this world" (Norman Brown 240–41).

> What I want to see above all is that this remains a country where someone can always get rich. (Ronald Reagan, quoted in Lapham 8)

One of Schopenhauer's aphorisms says that money is human happiness *in abstracto,* consequently he who is no longer capable of happiness *in concreto* sets his whole heart on money. The difficulty is not with money as a convenient medium of exchange but with the money complex that arises when money becomes desirable in itself. That desire is readily understandable when money truly improves the quality of one's life, yet what about those many situations when pursuing money impairs it? How does this happen? Given our sense of lack, how could this not happen?

Money is the "purest" symbol "because there is nothing in reality that corresponds to it" (Norman Brown 271). The coins and paper bills we pass around are in themselves worthless, just as Midas discovered about gold in itself. You can't eat or drink them, plant them or sleep under them. At the same time, money has more value than anything else because it *is* value. It can transform into everything because it is how we define value. The psychological problem occurs when we become preoccupied with the desire for such pure value. To the extent that life becomes focused around the desire for money, an ironic reversal takes place between means and ends: everything else is devalued in order to maximize a worthless-in-itself goal, because our desires have become fetishized into that symbol. "The crux of the matter is the general fact that money is everywhere conceived as purpose, and countless things that are really ends in themselves are thereby degraded to mere means. But since money itself is an omnipresent means, the various elements of our existence are thus placed in an all-embracing teleological nexus in which no element is either the first or the last" (Simmel 1907, 431).

When everything has its price and everyone his price, the numerical representation of the symbol system becomes more important—more *real*—than the things represented. We end up enjoying not a worthwhile job well done, or meeting a friend, or hearing a bird, but a bigger number on a bank statement. To find the method in this madness we must relate it to the sense-of-self's sense of lack, whose festering keeps us from being able to fully enjoy that birdsong (just *this!*), etc. Since we no longer believe in any original sin that could be expiated, what can it be that is wrong with us and how can we hope to get over it? Today the most popular explanation—our contemporary original sin—is that we don't have enough money.

The origin of money is puzzling: How did the transition from barter ever occur? How were human cravings fetishized into pieces of metal? The answer that Norman Brown provides is elegant because it reveals as much about the character of money now: money was and still is literally *sacred*. "It has long been known that the first markets were sacred markets, the first banks were temples, the first to issue money were priests or priest-kings" (Norman Brown 246). Simmel also noticed that Greek money was originally sacred, because it emanated from the priesthood (Simmel 1907, 187). The English word derives from the first Roman mint, in 269 B.C., in the temple of Juno Moneta, whose coins carried her effigy. The first coins were minted and distributed by temples because they were medallions inscribed with the god's image and embodying the god's protective power. Containing such *mana,* they were naturally in demand, not because you could buy things with them but vice versa: since they were popular you could exchange them for other things.

The consequence of this was that (as Becker puts it) "now the cosmic powers could be the property of everyman, without even the need to visit temples: you could now traffic in immortality in the marketplace." This eventually led to the emergence of a new kind of people who based the value of their lives—and their hope of ending their lack—on a new cosmology focused on coins. In this way a new meaning system evolved, which our present economic system continues to make more and more *the* meaning system. "Money becomes the distilled value of all existence . . . a single immortality symbol, a ready way of relating the increase of oneself to all the important objects and events of one's world" (1975, 76, 80–81). In Buddhist terms: Beyond its usefulness as a medium of exchange, money has become our most popular way of accumulating Being, to cope with our gnawing intuition that we do not really exist. Suspecting that the sense-of-self is groundless, we used to go to temples and churches to ground ourselves in God; now we work to secure ourselves financially.

Because the true meaning of this meaning system is unconscious, we end up, as usual, paying a heavy price for our ignorance. The value we place on money rebounds back against us: the more we value it, the more we find it used (and use it ourselves) to evaluate us. In *The Hour of Our Death* Aries turns our usual critique upside down. The modern world is not really materialistic, for "things have become means of production, or objects to be consumed or devoured. They no longer constitute a 'treasure.' . . . Scientists and philosophers may lay claim to an understanding of matter, but the ordinary man in his daily life no more believes in matter than he believes in God. The man of the Middle Ages believed in matter and in God, in life and in death, in the enjoyment of things and their renunciation" (136–37).

Then our problem is that we no longer believe in things but in symbols, hence our life has passed over into these symbols and their manipulation—only to find ourselves manipulated by the symbols we take so seriously, objectified in our objectifications. We are preoccupied not so much with what money can buy as with its power and status— not with the materiality of an expensive car, but with what owning a Lexus says about us. Modern man would not be able to endure real economic equality, says Becker, "because he has no faith in self-transcendent, otherworldly immortality symbols; visible physical worth is the only thing he has to give him eternal life." Or to give us real Being that can maybe fill up our sense of lack. In such fashion our spiritual hunger to become real, or at least to occupy a special place in the cosmos, has been reduced to having a bigger car than our neighbors. We can't get rid of the sacred, because we can't get rid of our ultimate concerns, except by repressing them, whereupon we become even more compulsively driven by them (Becker 85).

This lends psychological support to Weber's theory about the influence of the Protestant ethic on the rise of capitalism. You and I shall die, our children will die, but there is something else to invest in, which can take on a life of its own. "Death is overcome on condition that the real actuality of life pass into these immortal and dead things. Money is the man; the immortality of an estate or a corporation resides in the dead things which alone endure" (Brown 279). Instead of erecting time-defying monuments like the pyramids, now we find solace in the numbers sent to us by banks. "By continually taking and piling and accumulating interest and leaving to one's heirs, man contrives the illusion that he is in complete control of his destiny. After all, accumulated things are a visible testimonial to power, to the fact that one is not limited or dependent. Man imagines that the *causa sui* project is firmly in his hands, that he is the heroic doer and maker who takes what he creates, what is rightfully his" (Becker 89).

We tend to view the profit motive as natural and rational, but Brown's and Becker's summaries of the anthropological literature remind us that it is not traditional to most nonmodern societies and in fact has usually been viewed with some anxiety. For us the desire for profit defines economic activity, yet in premodern societies there was no clear division between the economic sphere and others. "Man's economy, as a rule, is submerged in his social relationships. He does not act so as to safeguard his individual interest in the possession of material goods; he acts so as to safeguard his social standing, his social claims, his social assets. He values material goods only in so far as they serve this end. . . . The economic system will be run on noneconomic motives" (Polanyi, in Norman Brown 262). Premodern peoples had no need for a financial solution to lack, for they had other ways to cope with it. R. H. Tawney brings this home to us by discovering the same truth in the history of the West:

> There is no place in medieval theory for economic activity which is not related to a moral end, and to found a science of society upon the assumption that the appetite for economic gain is a constant and measurable force, to be accepted like other natural forces, as an inevitable and self-evident datum, would have appeared to the medieval thinker as hardly less irrational and less immoral than to make the premise of social philosophy the unrestrained operation of such necessary human attributes as pugnacity and the sexual instinct (31).

We are not surprised to learn that the crucial transformation evidently began at the end of the Middle Ages. Once profit became the engine of the economic process, the tendency was for gradual reorganization of the entire social system and not just of the economic element, since, as Karl Polanyi implies, there is no natural distinction between them. "Capital had ceased to be a servant and had become a master. Assuming a separate and independent vitality it claimed the right of a predominant partner to dictate economic organization in accordance with its own exacting requirements" (Tawney 86). The economic globalization occurring now reminds us that this process of reorganization is still happening, indeed accelerating, as the individual money complex continues to supplant other personal meaning systems.

"Happiness is the deferred fulfillment of a prehistoric wish," said Freud. "That is why wealth brings so little happiness: money is not an infantile wish" (1964, 244). Then what kind of wish is money? "Money is condensed wealth; condensed wealth is condensed guilt" (Norman Brown 266). "Filthy Lucre," the most brilliant chapter of Brown's *Life Against Death,* develops this link between money and guilt. "Whatever the ultimate explanation of guilt may be, we put forward the hypothesis that the whole money complex is rooted in the psychology of guilt." The psychological advantage of archaic societies is that they knew what their problem was and therefore how to overcome it, according to Brown. Belief in sin allowed the possibility of expiation, which occurred in seasonal rituals and sacrifices. "The gods exist to receive gifts, that is to say sacrifices; the gods exist in order to structure the human need for self-sacrifice" (Norman Brown 265). For Christianity that sacrifice is incarnated in Christ, who "takes our sins upon him." Religion provides the opportunity to expiate our sense of lack by means of symbols—the Crucifix, the Eucharist, the Mass—whose validity is socially maintained. In such a context we do feel purified and closer to God after taking Holy Communion.

But what of the modern "neurotic type" who "feels a sinner without the religious belief in sin, for which he therefore needs a new rational explanation" (Rank 194)? How do you expiate your sense of lack when there is no religious explanation for it? As we have seen, the main secular alternative today is to experience our lack as "not yet enough." This converts cyclic time (maintained by seasonal rituals of atonement) into future-oriented and therefore linear time (in which atonement of lack is reached for but perpetually postponed, because never achieved). While the sense of lack remains a constant, our collective reaction to it has become the need for growth: an ever higher "standard of living" (but lack means the consumer never has enough) and the gospel of sustained economic "development" (because corporations and the GNP are never big enough). The heart or rather blood of both is the money complex. "A dollar is . . . a codified psychosis normal in one subspecies of this animal, an institutionalized dream that everyone is having at once" (LaBarre 173). Norman Brown is almost as damning:

> If the money complex is constructed out of an unconscious sense of guilt, it is a neurosis. . . . The dialectic of neurosis contains its own "attempts at explanation and cure," energized by the ceaseless upward pressure of the repressed unconscious and producing the return of the repressed to consciousness, although in an increasingly distorted form, as long as the basic repression (denial) is maintained and the neurosis endures. The modern economy is characterized by an aggravation of the neurosis, which is at the same time a fuller delineation of the nature of the neurosis, a fuller return of the repressed. In the archaic consciousness the sense of indebtedness exists together with the illusion that the debt is payable; the gods exist to make the debt payable. Hence the archaic economy is embedded in religion, limited by the religious framework, and mitigated by the consolations of religion—above all, removal of indebtedness and guilt. The modern consciousness represents an increased sense of guilt, more specifically a breakthrough from the unconscious of the truth that the burden of guilt is unpayable. (270–71)

The result of this is "an economy driven by a pure sense of guilt, unmitigated by any sense of redemption," which is "the more uncontrollably driven by the sense of guilt because the problem of guilt is repressed by denial into the unconscious" (Norman Brown 272). Nietzsche says somewhere that it is not only the reason of millennia but their insanity too that breaks out in us. Today our collective version of that insanity is the cult of perpetual economic growth, a faith that is difficult to see through because it has become, in effect, our religious myth. "We no longer give our surplus to God; the process of producing an ever-expanding surplus is in itself our God. . . . Schumpeter agrees: 'Capitalist rationality does not do away with sub- or super-rational impulses. It merely makes them get out

of hand by removing the restraint of sacred or semi-sacred tradition'"
(Norman Brown 261).

If so, we can see what the problem is: Money and economic
growth constitute a defective myth because they can provide no expiation of guilt—in my Buddhist terms, no resolution of lack. Our new
*sanctum sanctorum,* the true temple of modern man is the stock market,
and our rite of worship communing with the Dow Jones average. In
return we receive the kiss of profits and the promise of more to come,
yet there is no real atonement in this. Of course, insofar as we have lost
belief in sin we no longer see anything to atone for, which means we
end up unconsciously atoning in the only way we know, working hard
to acquire all those things that society tells us are important because
they will make us happy; and then not understanding why they do not
make us happy, why they do not resolve our sense that something is
lacking. The reason must be that we don't yet have *enough . . .* "But the
fact is that the human animal is distinctively characterized, as a species
and from the start, by the drive to produce a surplus . . . There is
something in the human psyche which commits man to nonenjoyment,
to work" (Norman Brown 256).

It is a cruel parody of Heidegger's resolute preoccupation with the
future. Where are we all going so quickly? "Having no real aim, acquisitiveness, as Aristotle correctly said, has no limit." Not going *to* anywhere
but running *from* something, which is why there can be no end to it as
long as that something is our own lack-shadow. "Economies, archaic and
civilized, are ultimately driven by that flight from death which turns life
into death-in-life" (Brown 258, 285). Or by that flight from emptiness
that makes life empty. If money, the purest symbol, symbolizes becoming
real, the fact that we never quite become real means we end up
with . . . pure deferral. Those chips we have accumulated can never be
cashed in, since doing so would dispel the illusion that money can resolve
lack, leaving us more empty and lack-ridden than before, because de-
prived of our fantasy for escaping lack. We unconsciously suspect and fear
this; the usual response is to flee faster into the future.

I think all this points to the fundamental defect of our economic
system, and any other system that requires continual growth if it is not
to collapse: What motivates it is not need but fear, for it feeds on and
feeds our sense of lack. In sum, our preoccupation with manipulating
the purest symbol, which we suppose to be the means of solving the
problem of life, turns out to be one of the most pernicious symptoms
of the problem.

Curiously, the best analogy for money may be *sunyata*, the "emptiness" that characterizes all phenomena according to Mahayana Buddhism. Nagarjuna warns that there is no such thing as *sunyata*. The term is a heuristic device to describe the interdependence of things, that nothing self-exists, but if we misunderstand this the cure is more dangerous than the disease. Also nothing in itself, also merely a symbol, money is indispensable because of its unique ability to convert anything into something else; but woe to those who grab this snake by the wrong end.

## FROM SACRED TO SECULAR

It is more than curious that the same karmic-like problem with objectification infects all these projects to resolve lack. One cannot use fame without being used by it. In *Being and Nothingness* Sartre argues that in order to win and keep the love of the other, I must present myself as a fascinating object. Pursuing the purest and most important symbol of all, we become preoccupied with what it symbolizes about us. And insofar as the sense-of-self uses these projects to fill up its sense of lack, each tends to become demonic, since none can grant the reality we seek. No one is ever rich or famous enough to fill up the sense of emptiness at one's core, and for us the myth of romance ends in Don Juan's joyless quest for sexual fulfillment.

Rather than being natural, as we tend to think, the contemporary importance of these three projects has been historically conditioned. Of course there have been people in most times and places who were greedy for money, fell in love with love, and sought glory. Yet the decline in collective faith at the end of the Middle Ages cleared the soil for these to take root and grow into "heresies" that have assumed a more central role in our psychic struggle against death anxiety and dread of groundlessness.

Another remarkable similarity among these three is that the modern history of each is a gradual devolution from (what might be called) sacred to secular. In the late Middle Ages saints were the most respected people. St. Francis did not seek fame; it was a by-product of what was believed to be his more immediate relationship with God. Dante and Milton strove to be worthy of fame but today fame is sought for its own sake and we celebrate celebrities. The troubadours adored noble ladies without hope of physical satisfaction or even the desire for it; later this became an emphasis on emotional intensity; today's version is sexual fulfillment. In exchanging the fruit of their labor for medallions with the god's image, early Greeks and Romans used the god to protect themselves by participating symbolically in the god's reality; later such cosmic powers were haggled over in the marketplace and now in the equities and foreign exchange markets.

These conclusions give us a new perspective on the Mahayana denial of any bifurcation between sacred and secular: "There is no specifiable difference whatever between *nirvana* and the everyday world; there is no specifiable difference whatever between the everyday world and *nirvana*" (*Mulamadhyamikakarika* 25:19). Without that dualism, how can Buddhism describe these three developments? The pattern translates into a devolution from nondual participation in something greater than the sense-of-self (and therefore greater than the sense of lack) to a more dualistic relation in which the reified sense-of-self uses objects in its Oedipal project to fill up its sense of lack. The historical tendency is toward greater objectification, which is also subjectification, since the sense-of-self is the first thing to be objectified. For Buddhism, however, "greater than sense-of-self" refers not to something transcending this world but to our interdependence. There is no need to appeal to another reality, just the need to come out from our own private and delusive hiding places—our sense-of-self—in order to realize *this* reality, in order to experience the full implications of our interdependence with everything else.

# FOUR

# THE LACK OF MODERNITY

When religion ceased to be a political force, politics became a substitute religion.

—Lewis Mumford

According to Buddhism the three roots of evil are *lobha* greed, *dosa* ill will, and *moha* delusion. Traditionally these are personal problems, but today they must also be understood more structurally, as institutionalized.

Our economic system promotes and requires greed in at least two ways: desire for profit is necessary to fuel the engine of economic growth, and consumers must be insatiable in order to maintain markets for what can be produced. Although justified as raising standards of living worldwide, economic globalization seems rather to be increasing inequality, unemployment, and environmental degradation. The United Nations Development Report for 1997 pointed out that 1.3 billion people now live on less than one dollar a day, and estimated that there are ninety-three countries having a per capita income below what they had a few decades ago.

Long after the end of the Cold War, the U.S. federal government continues to devote the largest percentage of its resources to maintaining an enormously expensive war machine. Most other countries continue to spend more on arms than social services. There is no sign that the military-industrial complex, or the lucrative international market in arms sales, will be diverted into plowshares anytime in the forseeable future.

The media that might inform us about these problems distract us with "infotainment" and sports spectacles in order to promote their real function, advertising. One would expect universities to be encouraging and developing the critical thinking necessary to reflect on these developments, but in the midst of the greatest economic expansion in history we are told that budget cutbacks are necessary because there is less money available for education. Increasingly, the need to become more market oriented is diverting academia into corporate research and advanced job training for those eager to join and benefit from a morally questionable world order.

In short, our global economy institutionalizes greed; the military-industrial complex at the heart of most developed nation-states institutionalizes aggression; our media and even our universities institutionalize ignorance of what is actually happening.

Unlike the original Buddhist roots of evil, these institutional roots of evil are rationalized as operating according to a logic (e.g., "laws of the market") that is inevitable because it is "natural." From my lack perspective, however, they are better understood as the results of particular historical forces that can and should be challenged. This chapter attempts to understand how those forces encouraged the development of such problematical institutions, which today control the earth and all its "resources" (including us). Nation-states have divided up the earth's surface and waters and airspace as well as its peoples; transnational corporations exploit the resources of these areas for their own purposes; these claims are policed by war machines that have the power to unleash irresistible violence against those who challenge this world order; and these three are serviced by scientific and technological establishments that exist primarily to meet their insatiable pursuit of ever greater power and wealth. . . . How did all this come to be?

This chapter argues that our collective sense of lack has been an important factor in developing these institutions. It offers another episode in the social history of lack, supplementing the previous chapter's account of our individualistic idolatries with a lack history of our institutional idolatries. "Men are literally hypnotized by life and by those who represent life to them," Ernest Becker has argued; replace "life" with "being" and we begin to realize how our sense of lack is also a source of social domination. All power is sacred power, Becker adds, "because it begins in the hunger for immortality, and it ends in the absolute subjection to people and things that represent immortality power" (1975, 49). Again, substituting "being" for "immortality" hints at the *spiritual* roots of our modern world. In particular, the supposed secularity of the nation-state, corporate capitalism, and mechanistic science may be problematized by summarizing what is known about their origins. We will see that there was something compulsive and delusive about their development because it was motivated by a profound social anxiety—a collective sense of lack—which became "liberated" in the sixteenth century and then channeled into these directions.

### THE ORGANIC PARADIGM

'Tis all in peeces, all cohaerence gone;
All just supply, and all Relation:
Prince, Subject, Father, Sonne, are things forgot,
For every man alone thinkes he hath got
To be a Phoenix, and that there can bee
None of that kinde, of which he is, but hee.

— John Donne, *An Anatomy of the World* (1611)

At the beginning of the Renaissance Europeans still understood the world and its creatures according to an organic paradigm: Everything, including human society, has its ordained place within a hierarchical cosmos created and maintained by God. Feudal society was unified, at least theoretically, in a Holy Roman Empire, which, as the joke has it, was not holy, not Roman, and not really an empire. But the messy reality matters less to us than the political ideal that provided a stability based on the authority of antiquity: a supposed continuation of the Roman empire, offering a groundedness in the past that was as much a feature of the organic paradigm as its opposite, groundlessness (and attempted self-grounding) is an essential feature of the modern world. Medieval groundedness was self-consciously religious in that civil authorities acknowledged the moral authority of the Church founded by Peter authorized by Christ.

A similar continuity existed for knowledge both sacred and secular: the spiritual and technological superiority of the ancients was taken for granted. Even in the sixteenth century doctors who trained at Padua, the foremost medical school in Europe, swore an oath to defend the authority of Aristotle. Later Francis Bacon still needed to rail against the myth that the ancients' arts and sciences existed in their purest form at the beginning of time. The medieval attitude has been the more common, however, not only in Europe but throughout world history, as in the four *kalpas* of Indian myth (which slowly deteriorate from an initial golden age) and the East Asian belief in *mappo* (the decline of the Buddhist dharma since Shakyamuni). If such myths are unbelievable today, our modern myth of progress would have been no more believable to medieval society; and so far as the medieval criterion of improvement was primarily a moral one, perhaps the evidence is no better for ours.

The church's understanding of sin and how to cope with it made the organic paradigm a self-contained system, which, despite wretched poverty and widespread suffering, "worked" in the sense that our human sense of lack was explicitly acknowledged and addressed: All of us inherit the original sin of Adam. Our lack was thus contained because its origins and solution were built into the structure of the Christian universe, which had an inescapable moral dimension. Chapter Two discusses how in the late eleventh century our sins became spiritual offenses against God the impartial Judge, for which we must bear punishment. Such an understanding of lack is quite different from a Buddhist one, but the important point is that each channels the effects of lack both individually and socially. To anticipate what follows: a mechanistic paradigm—the universe as a machine functioning according to objective and morally indifferent laws—implies very different ways of coping with our lack.

In the sixteenth and seventeenth centuries this medieval paradigm collapsed. From a lack perspective, it was like opening Pandora's box. An enormous amount of anxiety became liberated, because the worldview and institutions that had been managing it were overthrown. "In religion, politics, economics, and society, cherished authorities by the score were under attack, and centuries-old values no longer commanded unquestioned adherence. . . . The sense that all solid landmarks had disappeared pervades the writing of the age—either because men were toppling the landmarks or because they were seeking them in vain" (Rabb 37). The rug was pulled out from beneath religion (the Reformation), government (widespread insurrections and revolution), war (gunpowder made warfare more aggressive), the economy (the discovery of new lands and new forms of business organization), science (the collapse of Aristotelianism), and last but not least nature itself (an exceptional number of natural disasters, especially in the seventeenth century: bad weather, poor harvests, soil exhaustion, famines, and plagues, leading to riots, banditry, etc.). It is not surprising, then, that historians have consistently identified a widespread fear of chaos as the main feature of that era. It preoccupied the forms of discourse that have survived. "It is not difficult to believe that in that age of perplexing change many men and women, many of lowly position and simple understanding, but also not a few neither simple nor humble, were racked by anxiety for their future here and hereafter. It was a period of storm and stress seldom equalled and probably never surpassed" (Haller 27). The old order was dying, and no one knew what new order, if any, would replace it.

The main point of this chapter is that if we look at this collapse and the reconstruction that followed from a lack perspective, we can gain a new insight into what happened. The usual explanation is a triumphalist narrative about the decline of an otherworldly religious worldview, which had constrained social and economic development, replaced by the rise of a more dynamic secular society and free market economy. But if lack is fundamentally a spiritual problem, because susceptible only to a spiritual solution, the usual dualism between an earlier otherworldly society and a later this-worldly one does not fit anymore. If (to reformulate the Mahayana claim) the bounds of a secular society are not different from the bounds of a religious one, we should look for the conscious or unconscious *spiritual* motivations affecting the rise of modern institutions and perhaps still built into them. People in the sixteenth and seventeenth centuries needed to create new structures, intellectual and institutional, in order to cope with the disorder that threatened them on all sides—in my terms, with the lack-anxiety now liberated by the collapse of the organic understanding of sin and salvation. . . . What insight does this yield into the birth of our modern world?

## THE REFORMATION

A mighty fortress is our God,
A bulwark never failing . . .
—Lutheran hymn

The Protestant Reformation is a natural way to begin this story because the schism in Western Christendom between 1517 (when Luther posted his ninety-five theses) and 1564 (when Calvin died) was so instrumental in breaking down the organic paradigm. This is not the place to discuss the causes of that schism, but it is significant that the preceding centuries had witnessed an increasing preoccupation with death, suggesting that the Christian worldview—which offered a solution to death (and to lack)—was already losing its grip on people's

minds. During this period, writes Philippe Aries, the earlier acceptance
of death was replaced by more violent representations of it, including
a new fascination with bodily decomposition. He quotes Huizinga:
"No other epoch has laid so much stress as the expiring Middle Ages
on the thought of death" (Huizinga 134). The physical fact of death
replaced the images of final judgment; death was no longer a transition
to eternal life but an end in itself. "Those who were formerly Christians discovered their own mortality. They banished themselves from
heaven because they no longer had the strength to believe in it in a
coherent manner" (Alberto Tenenti, in Aries 128–29). This brought the
problem of our lack back into the center of human preoccupation.

As long as there was only one Church there was no church.
Religious institutions and ideals were not distinguished from secular
ones in the ways we now take for granted. Since the same worldview
was more or less maintained by everyone (except Jews and heretics,
which is why they were so threatening), salvation through the Church's
institutions and mediation "worked" because it was believed to work.
When that Church acrimoniously split and God helped neither side to
destroy the impiety of the other, the long-term effect of this contest
between lack solutions was to discredit that type of solution to lack
anxiety.

Martin Luther (1483–1546) had been a model Augustinian monk,
but his efforts within the Catholic framework of prayer, penance, charity, etc., brought no relief from his deep sense of sinfulness—i.e., did not
allay his sense of lack—and the extraordinary success of his alternative
suggests that many others felt the same way. His solution postulated a
wider gap between weak, corrupt humanity and the righteousness of
God. Left to itself, human nature is all falsehood and impurity, a condition hopeless without the intercession of God himself, the source of
all goodness and truth. Since humans by themselves can do virtually
nothing, the solution is through faith alone in his mercy. It is a free
acquittal of the guilty that has nothing to do with sacraments or any
other mediation by church or clergy; one can rely only on the Bible,
the sole infallible source of religious truth. This was an attempt to
return to the original Christianity of Biblical times as Luther understood it.

Two implications of this reformation turned out to be crucial.
Projecting all goodness onto a Deity who is elevated so far above our
world initiated a dangerous development that would empty this fallen
world of its spiritual and moral dimensions. The irrelevance for our

salvation of any institutional mediation or even personal good works closed the world off from being the place where religious activities could assuage our lack. Luther's emphasis on justification by faith alone offered a new interpretation of lack that precariously balanced pessimism about human nature with optimism about God, but in the process eliminated the intricate web of mediation that constituted, in effect, the sacral dimension of this world. "[T]o project the experience of the sacred onto an immaterial God is to shortchange sacredness as a dimension of material life and turn it into an object of worship that is beyond our world and thus alien to life. Sacrality hypostatized (or reified) can easily be sacrality lost" (Maguire 37). And so it would be.

The medieval continuity between the natural and the supernatural had meant that true reality manifested sacramentally in the spiritual potentialities of this temporal world, potentialities that could be developed. The new broom of the Reformers swept this away—not out the door but, as we shall see, under the carpet. What transformed the religiously saturated medieval world into the secular one we experience today was less the disappearance of God than the disappearance of this continuity between sacred and temporal.

Lack of mediation threw each Christian back upon his or her own lack. Luther could challenge the Church because he believed God wanted him to do so. This sanctified the principle of a direct and private relationship with God, which encouraged a proliferation of divisive interpretations of Scripture and, over time, an individualism that required working out one's own solution to one's own lack.

The doctrine of predestination taught by John Calvin (1509–1564) further developed both implications. Because of original sin humanity has lost its free will except to do evil. Without free will all our efforts to resolve our lack are useless. Only divine grace can restore the freedom to do good, but grace is bestowed only upon the elect, that small portion of the human race God has chosen for salvation. His salvation is a free act of his mercy, without any regard for human merit. Why does God condemn all others to eternal damnation? "For no other reason than that He wills to exclude them." Calvin himself admitted that this is a "horrible" doctrine, but God's omniscience and omnipotence allowed no other conclusion.

What effect did this have on the way Calvinists experienced their lack? All conventional religious activities were thrown out the window; there is absolutely nothing you can do that will qualify you for heaven, because it's all decided before you are born. Yet this powerlessness over our final destiny is not something we humans can live with. Predestination aggravates the anguish of our condition, our lack, unbearably. So a way out of this impasse must be discovered, and it was—or rather, several ways were constructed. If all religious expedients are discredited, secular ones need to be devised: expedients that (so far as motivated by the need to resolve our sense of lack) were infused with a spiritually driven dynamism, although (so far as that motivation is unconscious) a dynamism that tended to take on a life of its own.

## THE NATION-STATE

The Nation exists before all things and is the origin of all. Its will is always legal, it is the law unto itself.

—Emmanuel Joseph Sieyes, "What Is the Third Estate?" (1789)

"Nationalism" is the pathology of modern developmental history, as inescapable as "neurosis" in the individual, with much the same essential ambiguity attaching to it, a similar built-in capacity for descent into dementia . . .

—Tom Nairn (1977)

In the last few centuries the most successful god—that is, the god that people have been the most willing to die for—has been one's own nation. By far the most popular religion today is nationalism, argued Arnold Toynbee, the religion of the masses being the "worship of the deified community concealed under the fine name of patriotism" (98–99). Historians have noticed the curious fact that until the 1630s and 1640s the outcome of the religious struggles remained in doubt "and no government could ignore the force of the passions they aroused. Thereafter, however, religion ceased to be a violent issue" (Rabb 80). The sudden change makes sense when we realize that a new religion finally crystallized during that chaotic period. As this suggests, the nation-state has been one of the main beneficiaries of the Protestant Reformation. Its development was the political consequence of that schism, but it should be understood as a theological consequence as well. We cannot understand the state until we realize how it also serves a religious function for us.

The struggle between the church and its reformers increased the leverage of civil rulers and the balance of power between church (spiritual authority) and state (worldly authority) swung decisively to the latter. In the sixteenth century most kings were still basically feudal landlords. By 1650 they had become the supreme embodiments of a rapidly absolutizing state that in effect used them to centralize all civil authority and then discarded them.

The development of the nation-state was thus a two-stage process. Initially, the subordination of Christianity enabled some rulers to reappropriate the church's mantle of religious charisma. They became *absolute* (literally, "unconditioned") *rulers* because they filled the vacuum of spiritual authority by becoming "secular gods" accountable only to God—who was now conveniently far away, high up in his heaven. The long-term consequence was to centralize all political power in their persons. The eventual disappearance of such absolute rulers did not work to decentralize that absolute power; on the contrary, it in turn freed state institutions from any external authority. Since the state was now believed to represent and embody the people, the nation-state in effect became politically self-grounding and morally responsible to nothing outside itself.[1]

In lack terminology: since the Christian schism problematized that solution to our sense of lack and strengthened feudal overlords, an alternative was increased allegiance to those rulers, whose new aura of spiritual and moral authority radiated the promise of a more worldly solution to lack. Without an absolute sovereign the bureaucratic state could not have developed, for its institutions evolved as the way he or she exercised absolute power. But the sovereign's authority was a direct consequence of his new religious charisma—i.e., of the fact that his subjects came to view him as a person in whose majestic being they could collectively ground their own lack of being. "The kings and emperors who proclaimed themselves divine did not do so out of mere megalomania, but out of a need for a unification of experience, a simplification of it, and a rooting of it in a secure sense of power" (Becker 1975, 68). Here Becker refers to the early kings of Babylon and Egypt, but his point is just as valid for the sun kings that emerged in seventeenth-century Europe, whose majesty also offered the promise of a secure sense of power in a world falling apart.

The impersonal state evolved in order to mediate this relationship, with the gradual effect of distancing the sovereign so far from his subjects that his religious role (as a solution to lack) became differentiated from the state's bureaucratic role. With the eventual overthrow of such rulers, the lack that had empowered them continued to empower the nation-states that had coalesced around them. People's collective sense-of-self became increasingly constructed around, identified with, their nationality. In the process, however, the religious (i.e., lack) origins of the nation-state have been obscured and issues of moral responsibility impersonalized into the issue of what is best for the nation—e.g., *realpolitik*. The objectification of lack legitimized the new political institution only by becoming alienated from its original spiritual (and ethical) function. As usual with such objectifications, the state returned the favor by subjecting citizens to its own *raison d'etat*. Beware of the state, warned Nietzsche, for it will try to persuade you that it is the people. But it was the state that made the nation, and not vice-versa.[2]

Medieval feudalism tended to fragment because it was a loose structure of mutual obligations based on a hierarchical network of interpersonal relations. Contracts were symbiotic and this applied even to the monarch, who was by no means sovereign (although some polities were more theocratic than others, such as France). Kings usually understood themselves as sitting on top of a pyramid of personal loyalties, not as monarchs of the Roman or Byzantine sort. In the early middle ages the king was often regarded as an elected officer and his position was not necessarily hereditary; even later he was part of the community of the realm and responsible to its laws. Such a system diffused power and fostered what has been called a "massive sublife of numberless associations," which generated their own systems of rules and courts to adjudicate them. The society that resulted was criss-crossed with overlapping groups and conflicting loyalties and legal systems. One's *patria* was the town or region where one was born. Loyalty was personal, wars dynastic, and armies mostly mercenary.

Such personalized governance tended to reflect the idiosyncrasies of the local ruler. Since it operated through his household, it was portable and could be set up wherever the royal family established its residence. But such authority worked to undermine itself by shifting effective power downward to the lower links of lord-vassal relations. The long-term trend was fragmentation into increasingly autonomous systems that often quarreled with one another.

This tendency toward "feudal anarchy" was restrained by loyalty to the church, the only responsibility that transcended local group attachments. Because all authority ultimately derived from God, politics too was a branch of theology. Fallen humanity required repressive controls to help people live a Christian life; one must submit even to evil rulers who were scourges sent by God.

It is not surprising, then, that the final schism in the church's moral authority also created a political crisis that resulted in a century-long struggle for stability. The favorite conceit of seventeenth-century political thought was the chaos that threatened society if lack of imposed order allowed reversion to a state-of-nature. After an exhausting thirty years' war that reduced the population by a third and brought Europe to the edge of a anarchic abyss, the Treaty of Westphalia (1648) was widely celebrated as a once and for all settlement of all the outstanding problems by all the major powers. It enshrined noninterference in the domestic affairs of other states and (to counter the Papacy) recognized that only secular states could exercise political sovereignty. When Pope Innocent rejected the treaty as "null, void, invalid, iniquitous, unjust, damnable, reprobate, inane, empty of meaning and effect for all time," he could be and largely was ignored.

This signified the emergence of a new world order: a collection of individuating nation-states ruled by increasingly absolute sovereigns. Power came to rest solely with the monarch, but to exercise it

> he first had to increase his own prominence, had to magnify and project the majesty of his powers by greatly enlarging his court and intensifying his glamour. The absolute ruler's court was no longer the upper section of his household, a circle of relatives, close asociates, and favored dependents. It was an extensive, artifically constructed and regulated, highly distinctive world that appeared to outsiders (and to forcigners) to be a lofty plateau, an exalted stage at the center of which the ruler stood in a position of unchallengable superiority. (Poggi, 68)[3]

Such mystification worked to transfer spiritual authority from Pope to King. James I of England (1603–1625) emphasized that he was, in effect, the new stand-in for God. The monarchy is "the supremest thing on earth . . . accountable to none but God only." If to deny God was blasphemy, to dispute a king was sedition. "What God is to Nature, the King is to the State" (Toulmin 127).[4]

But how can one person wield such vast authority? New institutions were needed to make that authority effective. In England, for example, Tudor ministers had no army, no police, not even a corps of salaried civil servants to implement their policies. In most places the crown was dependent upon unpaid justices of the peace drawn from the ranks of the local nobility and gentry. This presupposed an accommodation with the interests of the landed classes. As the centralizing authority of the crown increased, however, one after another institution of the royal household "went out of court" to become a bureaucratic department of state, still subject to the will of the king but free from day-to-day interference. In the 1530s Thomas Cromwell, Henry VIII's chief minister and closest confidant, initiated the division of the royal household into the principle ministries of modern government. The King's council, originally an informal circle of advisers, evolved into the Privy Council, a more regularized committee of ministers who determined and implemented royal policy.

All this required a new conception of law, which by no coincidence paralleled the new understanding of natural law that the "natural philosophy" of Bacon and Descartes was helping to establish. The traditional understanding had based legal validity ultimately on the will of God, but his agency operated through the slow sedimentation of custom and negotiated accommodations among various semi-autonomous spheres (clerical law, guild regulations, etc.). The idea that the sovereign will of a ruler could replace common law with new statute law was revolutionary, borrowed as chapter Two shows from the Papal reformation. Because a ruler increasingly addressed himself to the whole population, in more uniform and abstract terms applicable everywhere and to everyone, there was a "leveling effect" that tended to eliminate the traditional plurality of overlapping authorities. In relation to the irresistible sovereignty of the king, everyone else was in principle equally subjugated—just as the absolute sovereignty of the Protestant Deity eliminated mediation and transcended everyone and everything equally.

Absolutism was not established without resistance. In the middle of the seventeenth century there were upheavals in many places, most dramatically in Cromwell's Commonwealth (1649–1659) and the French Frondes (1648–1652). In the long run, however, the revolutionaries were unable to maintain responsible national governments without sun-kings (or father-kings) to legitimize the fragile political entities that were still crystallizing. In other words, the best explanation of their failure may be a religious one: the problem of legitimacy and loyalty was how to transfer spiritual and moral authority from a fragmenting church to civil rulers, whose new charisma offered a more secular solution to one's felt lack of being. More pluralistic or impersonal alternatives lacked this charisma.

Absolute sovereignty nevertheless contained the seeds of its own destruction. As the king's power develops from a collection of various rights and prerogatives, it

> becomes instead more unitary and abstract, more *potential,* as it were. As such, it begins to detach itself conceptually from the physical person of the ruler; we might put it another way and say that it subsumes the ruler within itself, radiating *its own* energy through him. (Poggi 74)

Discussing the Prussian model, Poggi points out that:

> the state was made transcendent over the physical person of its head through the depersonalization and objectification of its power. Public law shaped the state as an artificial, organizational entity operating through individuals who in principle were interchangeable and who in their official activities were expected to employ their certified abilities in stewardship, loyalty to the state and commitment to its interests. (76)

As the king and his glamorous court ascended ever higher above the everyday workings of state power, they became less relevant and more dispensable to those workings: finally a mere theoretical foundation for absolute power that, once centralized into the state, no longer needed such a foundation.

The most important philosopher of the new nation-state was Thomas Hobbes (1588–1679), for whom politics is a secular affair detached from the usual theological argument for the divine right of kings. In place of divine right, he attempted to reconstruct society as a simple mechanical construct grounded on axioms about human nature. Following the metaphysical example of Descartes (whom he read and knew personally), he applied the new deductive method to human society.

Hobbes's social theory was a direct response to the social chaos he experienced first-hand. He prided himself as "the first of all that fled" the English civil war, and wrote his *Leviathan* (1651) during French exile. Hobbes concluded that the greatest evil is civil war and the greatest good civil peace. Man's distinctive quality is egoism, more precisely "a perpetual and restless desire for power after power, that ceaseth only in death." We may wonder whether this is truly "a general inclination of all mankind," but it has considerable validity as a description of how many people reacted to the political chaos of his times, when lack of social stability did not allow other inclinations to flower fully. The only antidote was "that great *Leviathan* . . . that mortal God, to which we owe under the immortal God our peace and defense," a sovereign who is able to establish order because it is to the advantage of all others to submit to his authority, as the wielder of supreme authority and who can guarantee his subjects' rights. A modern nation-state requires an irresistible force at the center that constrains the activities of all those under it. This solution provided

> order, peace and control through a set of accepted rules governing the operation of a machine. His sovereign, who was the external embodiment of contracted unity and dispenser of these rules, operated from outside the machine like a technician. The state, created *ex nihilo,* was an artificial ordering of individual parts, not bound together by cohesion, as an organic community, but united by fear. (Toulmin 211–12)

This Leviathan is "but an artificial man . . . in which the sovereignty is an artificial soul" providing not life but "artificial motion." One could not find a better image for the new bureaucratic machinery of the state. A society of individuals equally subjugated to an absolute ruler requires bureaucracy, which provides fairness and consistency because it is based on a set of rational rules applying to all. Its formality increases objectivity by reducing subjective decision making. In the Weberian ideal-type, bureaucratic role identification minimizes personal relations by maximizing functional relations. The more personal interaction is subordinated to functionally motivated interaction, the more efficient the bureaucracy and the more people become parts of a social machine—interchangeable parts, for such a bureaucracy "equalizes" people by abstracting the rights and obligations they have in common. From another perspective, it is the victory of means over ends, form over content. The impersonal efficiency of instrumental rationality overshadows the results of such procedures, perhaps most obviously in modern judicial systems.

"An artifical ordering of parts united by fear" gets at the heart of the issue: the contrast between the mutuality of an organic community and the fear that motivates Hobbes's contractual state. This ordering is externally imposed and supervised because in a social contract the self-interest of others is perceived as a constant threat to our own self-interest, for "except that they be restrained through fear of some coercive power, every man will dread and distrust each other." The absence of trust in the public realm precludes the possibility of mutuality; that is the reason for overarching law, which comes to be perceived as the only effective means to address conflict. The objectivity of bureaucratic procedure engenders trust in the institution, which takes the form of law and respect for law. But this develops at the cost of personal trust.

> As trust diminishes among individuals, bureaucracies, particularly legal bureaucracies, become more integral to the maintenance of social order and ultimately to the existence of society itself. In this context, law can be viewed as being inversely related to personal trust. With respect to trust, bureaucracy can be viewed as the antithesis of community. (Cordella 35)

The local breakdown of traditional communities creates "mobile and atomised populations whose claim to humanity rests more and more on the assertion of inidividual rights vis-à-vis an impersonal, distant and highly bureaucratised government apparatus." (Camilleri 24). This tends to become a vicious circle, benefiting only the self-aggrandizing state: the breakdown of personal trust and mutualist community makes citizens more dependent on the state to achieve safe and peaceful societies, and greater state sovereignty tends to replace the role of mutualist communities. That in turn generates the modern distinction between public and private (trust and mutuality become limited to the most intimate relationships) and thus promotes the very individualism that it postulates.

The Anabaptists (Mennonites, Amish, Hutterites, etc.) understood that such a state is inherently coercive and reacted against it. They rejected the Lutheran/Calvinist accommodation with the new nation-state (and the new capitalist mode of production) by refusing to engage in its civil affairs, because state authority was antithetical to their own mutualist vision of community. Today the Anabaptists are usually viewed as hopelessly old-fashioned, but perhaps they saw a basic problem that the rest of us are just beginning to understand.

No one would willingly invest his or her loyalty in such a bureaucracy, which is why a "mortal God" was needed. That deity became

dispensable once obedience to his institutions had been established at
the cost of localized authorities and mutualist loyalties. The sovereignty
of absolute rulers had been based upon their new role (taken over from
the church) as the temporal agents of almighty God's spiritual and
moral authority. Louis XIV believed that military victory or defeat was
God's reward or punishment, for a sovereign good or bad was an agent
of God. When that role became questionable sovereigns too became
disposable, leaving the nation-state as "no longer derived from the
divinely ordained harmony of the universal whole, . . . no longer explained as a partial whole which was derived from, and preserved by,
the existence of a greater: it was simply explained by itself" (Gierke 40).
Today the nation-state remains self-justifying and self-empowering,
devoted wholly to its own interests.

More precisely, a self-empowering *process*: for those interests
constantly need to be modified as demographic, military, economic,
and political environments change. The equilibrium of such an international system is thus precarious and requires constant readjust-
ment. This ongoing tension cannot be relieved by the operation of
binding international norms, for strictly speaking there are no such
norms except those that the greater powers temporarily agree upon
and can impose on lesser ones. *Self-justifying* means the disappearance of any overarching moral principles regulating states' conduct,
for what international law there is operates among states and not
above them. Hence:

> persistent tension between, on the one hand, the abso-
> luteness of the notions of sovereignty and *raison d'état*
> (which articulated and legitimated each systems' commit-
> ment to self-aggrandizement), and, on the other, the con-
> tinuous and inescapable presence of other states bounding
> that "will to sovereignty." Over and over again, each state
> came up against *limits* to its sovereignty in the form of
> competing states striving to satisfy their own self-defined
> interests. (Poggi 90).

Although much of the competition among developed nations has shifted
from military to economic, our situation otherwise remains much the
same. The present political polytheism is inherently unstable. The "sense
of insecurity, of which nationalism was supposed to be the cure, per-
sisted in the culture of the nation-state" (Nandy 265). At the time they

emerged nation-states were a plausible solution to the social chaos that enveloped the early seventeenth century, but the instability of such an international "community" led to incessant competition largely unbridled by any moral restraints, and eventually to two world wars. The political tragedies of the twentieth century make one wonder how much the cure was better than the disease.

With royal charisma replaced by impersonal state power, the religious grounding of civil authority finally disappeared—or did it? Do supposedly secular institutions merely obscure the religious basis of human allegiance even today? My point is that the nation-state has continued to derive its power over us from our sense of lack, which engenders a need to identify with and ground ourselves in something greater than ourselves. Each person, says Becker, "will knuckle under to some kind of authority, some source of sustaining and transcending power which gives him the mandate for his life"—for his very being. Our visits to the moon were commemorated not by leaving shrines or making offerings there, but by planting a cluster of national flags (Becker 1971, 151, 198). In a world no longer united by any ostensible religious belief, we have devised other sources of transcendent power to commit ourselves to. In his famous lecture on "Politics as a Vocation," Max Weber said that political entities have an ability shared only with religions—to impart meaning to death; the warrior's death in battle is a consecrated one. The basic problem, however, is that although nation-states have provided a weak substitution for community (citizenship) and an even weaker solution to the problem of life (patriotism), they are otherwise unable to fulfill the promise (to satisfy our lack) that nurtured them.

Perhaps this gives us some insight into the type of spiritual aberration that states are liable to, when they reject bureaucratic utilitarianism in favor of a quest for self-transcendence that involves surrendering to some higher supraindividual destiny. Since the instrumentalist and impersonal machinery of the state cannot give us what we unconsciously seek from it—a collective solution to our lack—one might learn from the Anabaptists; however, one might conclude instead that the nation needs to be transformed into a "purer" institution that can resolve our lack. If states retain the traces of their religious origins, as I am arguing, we can expect periods when its citizens are tempted to make it into a better religion. The results have been tragic, especially the fascisms and state socialisms of the twentieth century. Fascism, for example, was "an attempt to escape from the disciplines of 'stateness,' from not only the emphasis on depersonalization which follows from the state's bureaucratic and legal character but also the idea of state and society as distinct realms" (Dyson 59).[5]

As Friedrich Hölderlin put it, what has always made the state a hell on earth has been that man has tried to make it his heaven. This failure is not incidental but essential to its unconscious spiritual function for us. Insofar as we collectively try to become real through the nation-state, it can never become real enough to satisfy us, because it too is a human construct, "empty" and ungrounded despite the national origin myths spun to mystify it. In lack terms, our objectified and depersonalized lack anxiety internally feeds the unresolvable tension between state and civil society, and externally feeds the incessant competition among nations that constitutes the precarious "international order." In short, so far as the state has become a religious institution for us, it is doomed to be a poor one.

Yet what is the alternative? From its inception, there has been an ongoing argument about the proper activities of the state. The younger Johann Fichte, Alexander von Humboldt, and Immanuel Kant, for example, hesitated to acknowledge that the state has any common purpose except security. They saw it as a common framework within which subjects pursue their own ends. On the other side, Gottfried Leibniz, the later Fichte, and Johann Herder attributed a more substantive cultural mission to the state; for Hegel the people are that part of the state that does not know what it wants.

Historically, at least, the argument was settled by Karl Marx: the end of royal sovereignty led to states restructuring themselves to sustain capitalist domination.[6] Today this means states identify so much with the economy that they operate largely at the service of the industrial process. As Dan Hamburg concluded from his years in the U.S. Congress (D, Calif.): "The real government of our country is economic, dominated by large corporations that charter the state to do their bidding. Fostering a secure environment in which corporations and their investors can flourish is the paramount objective of both [political] parties" (25). Economic growth is unanimously endorsed by all political leaders as the standard to judge each state's performance, as self-justifying and validating whatever burdens it might cause the state to impose upon society (Poggi 133).

The result of this is very different from the pseudo-religious aspirations of fascism, but today we are realizing that such a state can be just as problematic.

CORPORATE CAPITALISM

> Gold constitutes treasure, and he who possesses it has all he
> needs in this world, as also the means of rescuing souls from
> Purgatory, and restoring them to the enjoyment of Paradise.
> (Christopher Columbus)

At the same time the nation-state was taking shape, other gods were also being born: other secular projects that, since they too seemed to offer a way to fill in our sense of lack, may also be understood as religious. As people began to have doubts about the afterlife, or at least confusion about the way to get there, economic success in this life became more important. But if the spiritual motivation behind this attraction was repressed and unconscious, one should also expect this economic drive to be distorted in some uncomfortable ways.

This brings us to what Max Weber wrote about Puritanism and the origins of capitalism; a lack reading supplements Weber's argument by adding another perspective on that development. If Weber is correct that capitalism originated in the "this-worldly" asceticism of Puritan ethics, lack implies that capitalism remains essentially religious in its psychological structure.

According to *The Protestant Ethic and the Spirit of Capitalism*, Calvinist belief in predestination encouraged what became an irresistible need to determine whether one was among the chosen. Such predestination devalued everything conventionally religious—ritual, confession, penance, acts of charity, etc.—in favor of economic success that came to be accepted as demonstrating God's favor. That had the effect of importing ascetic values from the monastery into worldly vocations, as one labored to prove oneself saved by reinvesting rather than consuming any surplus. This original motivation slowly evaporated but our preoccupation with capital and profit has not. On the contrary, it has become our main obsession. Since we no longer have any other goal, there being no other final salvation to believe in, in this way too the means has become our end. As Weber emphasized, the ascetic vocational ethos may have lost its original meaning yet that does not make it any the less powerful. Our type of salvation still requires a future orientation.

Lack fills in a psychological gap in this model. If my arbitrary Calvinist destiny is already decided and there is absolutely nothing I can do to qualify for heaven, why should I bother to exert myself in any way? The point is that we cannot live with this kind of aggravation to our anxiety; predestination exaggerates the anguish of our condition and destiny—our lack—unbearably. A way out *must* be discovered. There is no direct causal relation between material success and eternal salvation; wealth can only be a sign of God's approval. But psychologically there tends to be no significant difference: working hard for such a sign provides an opportunity to direct one's lack anxiety in a way that can hope to alleviate it—with the nice extra fillip that since you can never be sure of God's grace (your business might fail tomorrow) you can never relax enough to enjoy the fruits of your labors.

In a way analogous to the eventual overthrow of absolute sovereigns, the Calvinist God could also eventually disappear, but by then it did not matter because he too was not needed anymore. The psychological structures that had formed—use capital to get more capital; always jam tomorrow, never jam today—had taken on a life of their own and objectified into new economic institutions, which in turn have objectified us into their servants.

The main difference between medieval and modern economic thinking is that the former subordinates economic motivations to the moral authority of the Deity, while the latter accepts no such moral supervision. In secular terms, the first subsumes the economy to the society, the second subsumes society to economic expediency, which it liberates from social restraints (usually religious in form).

A good example of religious restraints against such a "liberation" was the medieval Church's condemnation of usury—what we now call interest, something necessary for money to function as capital. Usury was prohibited because a usurer profits from something (i.e., time) that belongs only to God; money is infertile, so it is against nature for money loaned to spawn more money. Jacques Le Goff's analysis of penance, purgatory, and usury in the late Middle Ages supplements Weber's argument by showing how the Church unwittingly undermined its own prohibition. Originally its doctrine of sin and penance focused on the act rather than the actor. Over time that doctrine became more internalized, as Confession changed from a collective and public event, reserved for the most serious sins, to a more private act that after 1215 was obligatory at least once a year. The confessor's priority changed from chastising a fault to cleansing the person.

This new preoccupation with daily intentions encouraged an introspection that would eventually transform ways of thinking and behaving. It also led to the development of a new intermediary realm,

Purgatory, for further contrition and cleansing the sinner. But the duration of this purgation could vary according to the prayers and concern of loved ones still on earth—which might show itself by buying masses and indulgences from the church to hasten their graduation to paradise.

Thus was built the system of "spiritual materialism" that Luther challenged. One unintended result was to legitimate usury. The accumulated wealth of a contrite usurer could be used, in effect, to buy his way out of Purgatory. "In a society where all conscience was a religious conscience, obstacles were, first of all—or finally—religious. The hope of escaping Hell, thanks to Purgatory, permitted the usurer to propel the economy and society of the thirteenth century ahead toward capitalism" (Le Goff 93). Since a usurer would need to save money to buy the services of the church, his psychological structure may not have been much different from the Puritan asceticism Weber described. In both cases, a new *religious* attitude inadvertently worked to make money the supreme value.

The development of modern economic theory, like modern political theory, is usually presented as a shift from a religious to a naturalistic explanation. The organic synthesis of medieval Europe fractured into different spheres—religious, political, economic, scientific—each assuming an independent vitality by acting according to the laws of its own nature. States operate according to their own *raison d'état,* and markets fluctuate according to a calculus of impersonal economic factors. From a lack perspective, however, this development is better understood as a shift from a conscious to an unconscious religious paradigm. If lack—our need to become *real*—is a constant spiritual drive, we can see religious motivations functioning both in the evolution of the nation-state and in the development of market capitalism. Once crystallized into institutions, those objectified motivations do not disappear along with the Calvinist Deity or the spectacular courts of sun kings. To be willing to die for one's country is to assign a spiritual role to the nation (cf. the eagerness of early Christian martyrs) that is impervious to any distinction we may make between church and state.

The same is true for market capitalism. Weber's sociology of religion distinguished more ritualistic and legalistic religions, which adapt to the world, from salvation religions more hostile to it, which seek to inject a new message or promise into everyday life. Their efforts to ensure the perpetuation of grace in the world ultimately require reordering the social system, including its economics. Weber noticed that adherents of this type of religion usually "do not enjoy inner repose because they are in the grip of inner tensions." This suggests that market capitalism began as, and still remains, a form of salvation religion: dissatisfied with the world as it is and compelled to inject a new promise into it, motivated (and justifying itself) by faith in the grace of profit and concerned to perpetuate that grace, with a missionary zeal to expand and reorder (rationalize) the economic system. Then our secular economic values are not only derived from religious ones (salvation from injecting a revolutionary new promise into daily life), they are much the same future-oriented values, although largely unconscious owing to the loss of reference to any otherworldly dimension.

The psychohistories (or religio-histories) that Weber and Le Goff outline might have been only footnotes to history had they not encouraged, and been encouraged by, some corresponding developments in economic organization. The first corporations with limited legal liability were established in the middle of the sixteenth century, perhaps the earliest in Florence in 1532. Both the place and date are revealing. Recent discoveries meant there were vast profits to be made in the East and in the New World; Vasco da Gama's trip to India in 1498 resulted in profits sixty times its costs. But such ventures were expensive and risky, given the debtors' prisons that awaited bankrupts and their families. The clever solution was limited liability: you could lose only what you invested. This required a special charter from one's ruler, which he was usually pleased to provide for a cut of the profits. The significant points here are, first, that from their beginnings corporations were involved in colonial exploitation, because that is what they were created to do; and second, that this has usually involved an incestuous relationship with the state, which used them to exploit distant resources that could not otherwise be "developed." Without the enormous resources that such corporations imported from the colonies—initially vast amounts of gold and silver (which resulted in severe and destabilizing inflation in the sixteenth century)—the bureaucratic nation-state could not have developed, for there was insufficient domestic capital available for such centralized control.

Prior to gunpowder warfare was primarily defensive: the issue was usually whether an army could wait out a siege. This changed forever in 1494, when Charles VIII of France used artillery to breach the walls of the Italian city-states. As the gunpowder revolution spread, "a feeling of insecurity swept all of Europe" (Herz 474). War became more aggressive, which led to the development of large standing armies and the expense of financing their military adventures, leading in turn to the development of the first banks. The result is that nation-states evolved early into what Lewis Mumford (1970) calls "war states": "all the great national states, and the empires formed around a national core, are at bottom war states; their politics are war politics; and the all-absorbing preoccupation of their governing classes lies in collective preparation for armed assault" (349). Paul Kennedy has more recently argued that war and its consequences provided more urgent and sustained pressures toward nation building than any philosophical considerations or social changes (90). Charles Tilly expresses the point most succinctly: "war made the state and the state made war" (42). But what motivated this aggression?

A Japanese colleague once commented to me that what he found most striking in the history of the West was its extraordinary aggressiveness. For approximately three-quarters of the sixteenth and seventeenth centuries Europe tore itself to pieces. From a comparative standpoint, it is curious that this did not result in forcible reunion. Every other "high culture" area had been dominated by an empire that believed itself to be supreme and essentially alone in its world; the states system that developed in Europe was therefore unique (Poggi 88). One factor was probably the religious disagreements that stiffened the backs of resisters, but another was the timely discovery of New Worlds, which increasingly diverted the attention of rulers to more profitable ventures overseas.

Nevertheless, I suspect that this aggression, whereby a tiny corner of the Eurasian landmass came to dominate the rest of the globe, is not something fully explained by religious civil war. Nor is it something we should take for granted, any more than we should accept the nation-state or the transnational corporation as something inevitable. Consider the timing: at virtually the same moment that the organic paradigm collapsed, liberating vast amounts of lack anxiety and preoccupying elites everywhere with the problem of subduing chaos, Western Europe began to conquer the rest of the world. Psychologically we know that one personal response to increased anxiety and fear can be aggression; does the historical development of Europe suggest that the same may be true collectively? One way to secure ourselves is to expand by dominating and incorporating the other. Thanks to new technological developments, the other was not only that nation-state coalescing next door; it was that newly discovered land across the sea, more vulnerable to conquest.

The New World also offered a new world for religious projection. As interminable internecine strife made Europe seem irredeemable,

America became much more than an abode of heathen to be converted and exploited. For some it was an empty land where religious and/or civil utopias could be achieved (as we shall see in the next chapter). For others its primitives exemplified a simple human happiness prior to the corruptions of civilization. For both, the New World became a place where our lack was or could be resolved.

The disintegration of the organic paradigm into different spheres, each operating according to its own objective laws, is usually taken to have liberated those spheres from any moral authority. If, however, the formation and function of these spheres reveal religious motivations, then a moral dimension is also inescapable insofar as religion always has ethical implications. Then, instead of accepting the moral neutrality that these "secular" spheres claim for themselves, we should look for the ways they deny or diffuse ethical responsibility.

A good example of such diffusion is provided by the limited-liability corporation and its twin the joint-stock market, the first chartered in England in 1553. Shares in a corporation could now be traded freely and even anonymously. Legally, the primary responsibility of a corporation is neither to its employees nor to its customers but to its stockholders, today mostly unknown, scattered here and there, usually with no interest in a corporation's business except its profitability. Medieval production had been mostly for local markets, which meant that responsibility for one's actions was also mostly local, to one's immediate community. Contrast that with what happened in Bhopal, India, in 1984, where a Union Carbide plant leaked toxic gases that killed up to 10,000 people and permanently injured another 50,000. The plant had been poorly supervised, and recommendations from earlier problems and accidents had not been implemented by top management. So who was responsible? The CEO and members of the board of Union Carbide, like the thousands of anonymous people who own it, live far away, and *legal* liability—usually only financial—is quite different from having to *live* with the consequences.

This difference has great consequences for the way that impersonal institutions like transnational corporations can conduct their business. It has been said that "a principle purpose of corporations is to shield the managers and directors who run them, and shareholders who profit, from responsibility for what the corporation actually does." Today the most powerful ones have learned to play off nations and communities against one another in order to obtain the most profitable operating conditions—the biggest tax breaks, the cheapest labor, the least environmental regulation, and so forth. Such corporations have become freer than nation-states, which remain responsible to their own borders and peoples. With no such fixed obligations, corporations can reinvent themselves at will, in a different location and even in a different business, if it is convenient for them to do so.

Of course, to be incorporated means that corporations gain a legal, not a physical, body. Like the bodies of humans and other animals, however, corporations are dissipative systems that absorb energy (e.g., raw materials) that is processed (e.g., manufacturing), and in order to thrive income must exceed expenditure. Unlike us, however, there is no intrinsic limit to their growth. The result is a fictitious but immortal person (because entitled to U.S. Bill of Rights protections)[7] with no emotional bonds to anyone or anything else, whose organizational structure diffuses all ethical (apart from legal) responsibility so thoroughly among anonymous stockholders that the possibility of genuine responsibility to anything else evaporates. Just like nation-states, transnational corporations have become self-justifying and self-empowering processes, with increasing access to all the world's resources but devoted solely to pursuing their own interests.

The problem, then, is not what corporations do wrong but what they do well—for themselves, that is. Thomas Hobbes called corporations "worms in the body politic," and in *The Wealth of Nations* Adam Smith's references to them are uniformly disparaging. Yet our depersonalized lack has made them into what they are. "The economy" is a collective objectification of our desire not so much for a "higher standard of living" as for an economic solution to our lack. Unfortunately for that ambition, there is no economic solution to our spiritual lack. Just as I can never be wealthy enough to feel real, so the economy can never be big enough, corporations can never be profitable enough, and consumers can never consume enough. All of this manifests a demonic preoccupation with growth as an end in itself. The tomorrow-that-never-actually-comes gives us hope of resolving the lack that gnaws on us today; the reality is that our future orientation has become a way of evading a present we are less and less able to cope with.

MECHANISTIC SCIENCE

My aim is to show that the celestial machine is to be likened not to a divine organism but to a clockwork. (Johannes Kepler)

Let's summarize the pattern so far. The collapse of the organic paradigm did not eliminate God; instead, it pushed him higher above human affairs, by severing the continuity between him and us, between the natural and supernatural. Yet denying the intermediaries that worked to sanctify this world merely created a need for more secular deities. Absolute rulers and the bureaucratic states that coalesced around them led to the formation of nations. In a parallel fashion, the asceticism of Puritan ethics filled the void by importing religious self-denial from the monastery. Thus both institutions, the nation-state and corporate capitalism, may be viewed as objectified forms of collective lack that have taken on a life of their own which nonetheless continues to draw its power from our identification with them. The lack of nation-states feeds upon our need to ground our hollow sense of self in something greater than ourselves; the lack of corporate capitalism feeds upon and legitimates the limitless desire for profit that was liberated by the loss of religious security. In both cases the institutionalization of this lack alienates it from our control (and our moral standards), so that today all of us, even CEOs and prime ministers, are subject to the impersonal dynamic of the market and the "national interest" of *raison d'état*.

If knowledge is power, as Francis Bacon famously put it, is a further parallel to be found in the new mechanistic science that provided technical support for the military and economic ambitions of the nascent states? What insight can a lack perspective grant into the origins and perspectives of modern science?

Copernicus's heliocentric hypothesis (1543) shook the firmament as much as gunpowder did. One could no longer trust even one's own senses, a problem aggravated by the invention of the telescope and microscope. Luther and Calvin thought they could refute Copernicus by citing the Old Testament, but their theologies unwittingly helped to banish its God from the new material universe.

Understood most broadly, science is a matter of learning how the world works, and in a religious society this is naturally a religious activity. When everyday life is permeated with the influence of a sacral dimension, scientific causality is also a sacred causality, and the impetus to understand that causality also spiritual. Today we take it for granted that scientific knowledge is something employed to manipulate the natural world, but our preoccupation with such power should not be anachronistically identified with the medieval attitude. As the old name for science suggests, the organic paradigm did not differentiate philosophy from "natural philosophy." The spiritual search for wisdom included an attempt to understand the workings of God in the natural world. How does nature manifest God's mind and will? How do its phenomena embody his "signature"? And, most important, what does this understanding of the world reveal about our role in it, i.e., about the meaning of our lives? Notice that this spiritual impetus does not separate facts from values: the quest to discover *what is* is not distinguished from our existential need to determine how we (part of *what is*) should live. In God's cosmic plan they are nondual.

Being so closely integrated, it is not surprising that the old theology and natural philosophy were overthrown together. The central concept that Protestant reformers and early scientists both challenged was hierarchy: the idea that the universe was composed of a graded chain of beings, extending from God in the highest heaven at the periphery of the cosmos, down through hierarchies of angelic beings inhabiting various celestial spheres, and then through the ranks to humans, animals, plants and minerals of the lowest terrestrial sphere at the center of the cosmic system. The Reformation worked to depopulate this hierarchy by denying any need for intermediaries between God and his world. Calvin, in particular, minimized the role of angels in governing the universe: "For the Holy Spirit designed to provide that no one should dream of primacy or domination in regard to the government of the Church" (*Institutes*, quoted in Mason 70). Since the Deity predetermined all events from the beginning, the workings of the Calvinist universe were orderly and in principle fully determinate.

This had important scientific implications. According to the theory of mechanics generally accepted in the late Middle Ages, a body in motion required the constant action of a mover, and the integration of Aristotelian natural philosophy with Christian theology had identified the movers of heavenly bodies with the angelic beings mentioned in the Bible. The physics of Galileo (1564–1642), Kepler (1571–1630), and Newton (1642–1727) can thus be understood as part of this larger process of moving away from the hierarchical conception of cosmic rule, with its multitude of spiritual powers, toward an absolutist theory of the governance of the universe, according to which physical events were subject to immutable laws—originally those decreed by the Creator, only later the impersonal laws of modern physics.

A similar development occurred in anatomy. Michael Servetus (1511–1553) first published his theory of the blood's "lesser circulation" (through the lungs) in a theological treatise, the *Restitutio Christianismi* (1553), for such a hypothesis was implied by his denial of the Trinity.

His medical training led Servetus to doubt that the human body was governed by a threefold hierarchy of natural, vital, and animal spirits, for "in all of these there is the energy of the one spirit and of the light of God." He concluded that there was only one type of blood.

These new theories suggested analogies with absolute rule that were not overlooked by the natural philosophers themselves. More than a century before Louis XIV (r. 1643–1715) was hailed as *le Roi soleil*, Copernicus in *De Revolutionibus* referred to the Sun enthroned as the ruler of the universe: "So the Sun sits as upon a royal throne, ruling his children, which circle around him." William Harvey (1578–1657) compared the heart to "the prince in a kingdom, in whose hands lie the chief and highest authority, rules over all; it is the original and foundation from which all power is derived, on which all power depends in the animal body." His book on blood circulation (1628) was dedicated to Charles I, "the sun of the world around him, the heart of the republic."

In addition to these specific implications, there was what has been described as a concordance between the early Protestant ethos and the scientific attitude:

> In their early days, both the Swiss and the German Reform-
> ers taught that man should reject the guidance and the
> authority of the priests of the Catholic faith and should seek
> for spiritual truth in his own religious experience: he should
> interpret the Scriptures for himself. Similarly the early mod-
> ern scientists turned away from the systems of the ancient
> philosophers and the medieval schoolmen to search for sci-
> entific truth in their own empirical and theoretical experi-
> ences: they interpreted Nature for themselves. (Mason 65–66)[8]

This led to a break with Aristotelianism and the Arabic theories that had been dominant. "The witches, the astrologers, the alchemists, the hermeticists, the cabalists, and even some of the neoplatonists, hungered to find the key that could unlock some all-encompassing secret. They would have access to the true structure of the universe if only they discovered the proper method" (Rabb 52–53). Galileo's insight turned out to be the revolutionary one: "the Book of Nature is written in mathematical symbols" by "the great Geometer," so the key to its hidden laws is to be found by discovering the mathematical laws of the cosmos.

Today we take this perspective so much for granted that it is difficult for us to realize how much it assumes a new and quite peculiar understanding of the relationship between God and nature. The Absolute Deity rules the universe not through a hierarchy of spiritual subordinates serving him but with a rational system of "hidden laws." As long as these laws constituted God's "signature" this was not quite a mechanistic view of the universe, but it was an intermediate step necessary for a fully mechanistic paradigm to develop. Again we encounter the consequences of depopulating the middle ground between God and us of all spiritual intermediaries. Where the medieval worldview saw the influence of God filtering through a hierarchy of agents, of varying degrees of blessedness and power according to their station and role in that hierarchy, the great Geometer was not to be identified with the fallen world he ruled impersonally from afar.

Since God was the ultimate source of all value, this was also the beginning of our bifurcation between fact and value. As the originator and guarantor of value gradually disappeared into the heavens, the world he left behind slowly but surely became de-valued.

This opened up exciting new possibilities: Those who comprehended his hidden laws could use them to manipulate nature for their own purposes. Originally this way of thinking was not very different from the magic employed by the Renaissance magus, who also tried to manipulate the world according to its secret laws. However,

> mechanizing the world picture removed the controls over environmental exploitation that were an inherent part of the organic view that nature was alive, sensitive, and responsive to human action. Mechanism took over from the magical tradition the concept of the manipulation of matter but divested it of life and vital action. The passivity of matter, externality of motion, and elimination of the female world soul altered the character of cosmology and its associated normative restraints. (Merchant 111)

Francis Bacon (1561–1626) kept the feminine imagery but turned it to rather different ends. He described nature as a "common harlot" who needed to be "tortured" in order to make her yield her secrets. Nature should be tortured to discover God's signature, and could be tortured because God was no longer "in" it. For this God needed to be far away, yet not *too* far away. Again, the political and economic parallels are instructive. Unless God were far away, there was no room and no need for absolute rulers; but if he were too far away they lost their divine right. Unless God were far away there was no space for the capitalist ethos to develop; but if he were too far away there was no incentive to import asceticism into the economic sphere. In each case God's new role was awkward and unstable, necessary for a while but soon to be supplanted.

The preoccupation of Bacon's era, subduing chaos, soon erased the traces of God's signature. Nature no longer signified something divine but appetites. "Matter is not devoid of an appetite and inclination to dissolve the world and fall back into the old Chaos," so bonds and handcuffs must be applied to its protean nature in order to restrain it. "The end of our foundation is the knowledge of causes and secret motions of things and of the enlarging of the bounds of human empire, to the effecting of all things possible" (Bacon, in Merchant 171, 186).[9]

Knowledge as power for the improvement of man's estate: a great, perhaps irresistible attraction for a culture of rampant lack in a world threatened by chaos. Without the religious security provided by a universal church, the only security to be found was one that humans made themselves.

The first writer to use the term "laws of Nature" consistently was René Descartes (1596–1650), whose *Discourse on Method* referred to "laws established in Nature by God." "God sets up mathematical laws in nature as a king sets up laws in his kingdom," he wrote to Marin Mersenne in 1630. Descartes became the foremost exponent of the new mechanical philosophy. In addition to founding analytic geometry, he was the first to outline a system of universal mechanics that would explain all changes in the motion of bodies as caused by the impacts between them. This was the scientific consequence of his radical dualism between the physical world, whose essence is extension, and the mental world whose essence is thinking. For Descartes too a deity was necessary to create and maintain the world, but God's role was shrinking fast. The English Puritans of the seventeenth century soon developed an idea abhorrent to Calvin but implicit in Calvin's writings: that the Deity was himself bound by his own ordinances.

The laws of Newton's mechanics (*Principia,* 1687) explained for the first time both terrestrial and heavenly motion, eliminating the need for anything more than a Creator. The Newtonian universe was now self-sustaining and completely mechanical, except for retaining God in the wholly passive role of a privileged observer. "The Deity endures for ever, and is everywhere present, and by existing always and everywhere, He constitutes duration and space . . . [He is] a being incorporeal, living, intelligent, omnipresent, who in infinite space as it were in his sensory, sees the things themselves intimately, and thoroughly perceives them, and comprehends them wholly by their immediate presence to himself."[10] Newton's postulation of an absolute space and time, and an ether pervading them, was thus connected with his understanding of such a single privileged observer in the universe.

On this account, the mechanistic worldview finally eliminated all traces of its spiritual origins only with Einstein's relativity theories. And with the refutation of ether the parallel with political and economic absolutism becomes complete. The Protestant "transcendentalization" of God gave the new Deity less and less to do, which reduced his day-to-day authority and led to his disappearance. But that disappearance had profound implications for the new intermediaries that had grown up to fill the vacuum between him and us. Once their sacral qualifications became dubious, absolute sovereigns were replaced by the bureaucratic states that had grown up to wield their authority. Puritan this-worldly asceticism for the sake of heaven yielded to the impersonal institutions of corporate capitalism and the more secular desire for profit. And the spiritual quest to discover the great Geometer's signature evolved into replicable experimentation to discover and exploit the impersonal laws of the physical sciences, including the indifferent natural selection motivating Darwinian evolution. Mechanism replaced organism in all three: in the functional bureaucratic rationality of Hobbes's "artificial man," in the supposedly objective laws regulating the operations of the market, and of course in the scientific laws determining the motion of physical objects and the development of living ones.

From a lack perspective, however, such scientific knowledge can never know enough, and our technological power can never be powerful enough, because they can never provide what we (motivated by that sense of lack) most want from them: an understanding of the world that also explains the meaning of our own lives by describing our role in the universe. Such value questions cannot be answered by an experimental discipline whose technique for pursuing knowledge involves determining the relationships among de-valued facts. Since facts cannot really be separated from values, scientists cannot avoid surreptitiously reimporting value implications (e.g., Daniel Dennett on Darwinism) by supposedly deriving them from the "objective facts." The basic problem with such attempts is not our inability to derive an "ought" from an "is," but the fundamental dualism between them that the scientific method takes for granted in the process of experimenting on the natural world.

Its mechanistic approach does not refute the sanctity of the world; it merely ignores such a perspective, since it has no way to deal with it.

As with the nation-state (which can never be secure enough) and the economy (which can never be big enough), the scientific/technological project represses this failure into its future orientation: We do not yet know enough. Important discoveries are made, but every important answer breeds several more questions, even as every technological application of those answers breeds more moral dilemmas that our science and technology cannot themselves resolve for us.

To sum up: insofar as modern science has become our collective effort to ground ourselves intellectually, by coming to an understanding of what the universe is and what our role in it is, it can never resolve our lack. Its experimental approach dualizes the one-who-wants-to-know from the objectified world that is known, because its functionalist perspective dervies from, and is at the service of, our drive for ever greater control over the natural world. Scientifically, we respond to this inadequacy by funding further research, that is, by deferring to the future. In the meantime we preoccupy ourselves with the power that our increasing knowledge defers on us. What should this power be used for? Our inability to answer this question makes the means, in effect, our ends.

THE COSMOPOLIS

The dream of *foundationalism*—i.e., the search for a permanent and unique set of authoritative principles for human knowledge—proves to be just a dream, which has its appeal in moments of intellectual crisis, but fades away when matters are viewed under a calmer and clearer light. (Toulmin 174)

Descartes is usually identified as the founder of modern philosophy, because Cartesian thought distinguishes itself from theology, or at least embarks on the path of that differentiation. Both in its methodology (self-grounding doubt) and in its conclusions (self-grounded subjectivity), Cartesianism broke with previous ways of thinking, which were mostly religiously oriented. Philosophy achieves its own ground, for the arguments are meant to be evaluated solely according to the merit of their own logic.

In *Cosmopolis: The Hidden Agenda of Modernity*, Stephen Toulmin offers a different understanding of these origins. Instead of accepting the usual self-description of modern philosophy, Toulmin places its foundationalist project in historical context. As we have seen, the problem for the seventeenth century was instability, and this instability had philosophical implications. The Christian schism and the fragmenting theologies originating from it were a serious challenge to the type of theologically oriented thinking that had prevailed up to then. The philosophical response to this intellectual disorder was foundationalism: a search for the permanent and authoritative principles of all human knowledge. These principles were to be discovered by human rationality alone, without dependence on divine revelation or any other authority. Such foundationalism became the preoccupation of philosophy until the middle of the twentieth century, and that approach is far from dead today.

Toulmin distinguishes the philosophical response to intellectual disorder into two historical phases: a more humanistic and literary period, exemplified by the influence of Michel Montaigne (1533–1592) up to about 1630, followed by a more rationalist and foundationalist period exemplified by Descartes. The eclipse of Montaigne's more broad-minded tolerance occurred because of a growing dissatisfaction with skepticism

> which led people, in turn, into an unwillingness to suspend the search for provable doctrines, an active distrust of disbelievers, and finally to *belief in belief itself.*
>
> If Europeans were to avoid falling into a skeptical morass, they had, it seemed, to find *something* to be "certain" about. The longer fighting continued, the less plausible it was that Protestants would admit the "certainty" of Catholic doctrines, let alone that devout Catholics would concede the "certainty" of Protestant heresies. The only other place to look for "certain foundations of belief" lay in the epistemological proofs that Montaigne had ruled out. On reflection, perhaps, human experience might turn out to embody clarities and certainties that Montaigne and the skeptics had overlooked. (Toulmin 55, his italics)

For Montaigne "there is nothing that throws us so much into dangers as an unthinkable eagerness to get clear of them" (*Essays* 124), but the widespread difficulty in coping with an excess of lack anxiety kept his skeptical tolerance from providing a viable alternative to *some* dogma to be believed in, either Christian or rational. In either case, nothing less than certainty would do. People will die for a dogma who will not stir for a conclusion, as Cardinal Newman put it, but in some cases the difference is hard to see. So Descartes founded modern philosophy and modern subjectivity by attempting to ground knowledge on the indubitability of his own doubt. This preoccupation with deductive logic based on axiomatic self-grounding was followed by Baruch Spinoza, who not only constructed his *Ethics* in deductive form but rewrote Descartes' *Meditations* into the same geometric format. Religious certainty had been wounded, but lack continued seeking to secure itself, and intellectually this meant a compulsive need for propositional certainty. If philosophical certainty is not to be found outside us, it must be located inside, in our mental processes. Cartesian dualism juxtaposed the mechanical causality of natural phenomena with the logical rationality of human thought and intentionality. The foundationalist trajectory of modern philosophy was set.

As Toulmin emphasizes, this self-grounding rationalist dream was always illusory:

> We no longer ground all our knowledge in universal, time-less systems today, only because the rationalist dream was always illusory. Descartes never faced classical skepticism *on its own ground;* instead, he pointed to subjects in which, within practical limits, formal logic can provide a kind of coherence to which Montaigne had done something less than full justice; but the implication that these examples were the model for all intellectual disciplines remains an unfulfilled dream. Nor does the fact that no such model is available today imply the "death" of Rationality; rather, it marks our awakening from a transient, ambiguous daydream. (174)

Again we can notice a parallel with the political, economic and scientific responses to a transcendentalized God. Descartes' break with the old paradigm was not very clean, for he soon found it necessary to reintroduce God to protect his cogitations from deceptions that might otherwise be introduced by an evil deceiver. Cartesian and other rationalist philosophy still required a deity to maintain the universe, but his tenure too proved to be limited. . . . And what secular god would take *his* place? We do not need to look very far. The eventual disappearance of the philosophers' God left his religious and moral functions to a

subjectivity increasingly alienated from a factual "objective" world des-
iccated of value and meaning. Philosophy today may have awakened
from the transient daydream of foundationalism, but the nihilistic implications of the Cartesian legacy continue to haunt our nightmares.

## THE IDOLATRY OF MODERNITY

> To what powers has a man given himself in order to solve
> the paradoxes of his life? On what kind of objective struc-
> ture has he strung out his meanings and fenced off his own
> free energies? . . . Each person *lives* his version of the real
> without knowing it, by giving his whole uncritical alle-
> giance to some kind of model of power. (Becker 1971, 186)

Our human lack was unable to cope with bifurcating the supernatural from the natural—with desacralizing the everyday world by
transcendentalizing God—so it filled the void by creating more worldly
deities, which have evolved into the "secular" institutions that now
control the earth and its creatures. Today each claims to operate according to its own objective and morally neutral laws, but those laws presuppose the mechanistic and atomistic paradigm of modernity. Rather
than escaping ethical issues, they deny or diffuse responsibility for their
consequences. "National interest" allows us to rationalize acts of state
that most of us would refuse to perform as individuals. The limited
liability of corporations and the anonymity of the stock market ensures
we remain largely ignorant of, and protected from, the social and ecological consequences of our pooled economic decisions. Scientific research and its technological application are perceived as neutral in
themselves, but nature divested of a spiritual dimension, and thus
of spiritual protection, can be freely dissected and divested of its
"resources."

We may summarize by contemplating what has happened to the
lack that was originally "built into" these now impersonal institutions.
If the human sense of lack is a constant, how does our collective lack
still manifest in them, now that absolute sovereigns, the Protestant ethic,
and God's signature have faded away?

The important point is that the deity has not really disappeared. From
a lack perspective, "God"—that is, the solution we cannot help seeking for
our lack—is still present in the functioning of the nation-state, the market
economy, and the Enlightenment scientific/technological project, because

these collectivities do not self-exist but are "empty" processes that depend on our energy input and continue to be motivated by what may be described as *institutional* lack. The history of the nation-states system demonstrates that they are externally unstable and internally self-aggrandizing. Economically, GNP is never big enough, corporations are never profitable enough, consumers never consume enough. And the same is true for our scientific and technological establishments: the Faustian problem is not that we do not yet know enough, but that we never can, so far as their functionalist perspective subordinates them to our drive for ever greater control over the world.

Each, then, may be considered a victory of means over ends. The objectification of our lack into impersonal "secular" institutions means that basic questions about the meaning of our lives—the central spiritual issue for a being that needs to understand and resolve its own sense of lack—have become alienated into a "not yet enough" that can never be enough. For all three, power has become an end in itself, which is why there is something demonic about them. Power, although sometimes a good servant, is a bad master, because you can never have enough power if power itself is the goal. That points to the basic nihilism of "secular" modernity: the lack of an overtly spiritual grounding to our lives means that this preoccupation has become religiously compulsive. Because this compulsion is not understood by us, these institutions have taken on lives of their own which subordinate us to them while accepting no subordination to anything else.

Secularity has been a basic concept for our understanding of modernity, but the distinction we usually make between a secular society and a religiously grounded one needs to be replaced by one between societies that are ostensibly spiritual and those that are unconsciously spiritual: spiritual, that is, in the basic existential sense of addressing our inescapable need to ground ourselves and feel *real*. Remember what Norman Brown said about the Oedipus complex, or rather Oedipus project: It is essentially the attempt to deny our conditioned origins and defend our fragile sense of independence by becoming self-sufficient. In my Buddhist terms, it is the ongoing (because never successful) attempt to overcome the sense of nonbeing or unreality that we become conscious of as a sense of lack. The problem with deifying the nation-state, corporate capitalism, and the Enlightenment scientific/technological project is, finally, that our lack cannot be resolved in those ways.

If the spiritual need to ground ourselves must be addressed, the issue becomes whether we will choose authentically spiritual versions of this quest, or whether we continue to pursue unconscious and therefore idolatrous ones. This chapter has offered a broader understanding of the three Buddhist roots of evil—greed, hatred, and delusion—which in turn suggests a broader understanding of idolatry. "Whatever idols man remains rooted to are idols designed precisely to hide the reality of the despair of his condition; all the frantic and obsessive activity of daily life, in whatever country, under whatever ideology, is a defense against full human self-consciousness" (Becker 1974, 194). Idolatry occurs whenever we try to "become real" by completely identifying with something *in* the world as the source of our power. Psychologically idolatry is akin to fetishism, and like fetishists, idolators gain their security at the price of living in a more constricted world, with narrowed perception and fewer possibilities. Insofar as our modern world is dominated by nationalism, corporate capitalism, scientism, and technopoly, today we all live in such a constricted world, with other possibilities foreclosed by our blinkered, socially permitted perceptions. This is the very "essence of idolatry—to let *what is* define *what could and ought to be*" (Lerner 25).

Yet what is the alternative? If idolatry is inauthentic religion, what does authentic religiosity look like? Again, I think Becker points the way: The problem of life is how to "grow out of" our idolatries by expanding our allegiances and preoccupations:

> Human beings believe either in God or in idols. There is no third course open. For God is the only object who is not a concrete object. . . . God is abstract necessity, the unconditioned, and this is liberating rather than opposing or confining, even though we submit our energies to it. Humanity achieves its highest freedom when energies are allied with the unconditioned cosmic process. Free human beings must turn to God as ultimate support for meaning because truly free people have nowhere else to turn. That is, to God as the highest ground for meanings, as the uncompromising critical perspective on earthly authority (Becker, in Liechty 59).

Buddhism uses a different vocabulary to make much the same point: all things, including ourselves and Buddhas, are "empty" (*sunya*), so we should not be attached to any of them. The touchstone of authentic spirituality is not whether one believes in God but whether one believes in and works to ground one's energies in what Becker calls the unconditioned cosmic process.

What does this imply for the modern institutions whose religious roots have been discussed in this chapter? I think it becomes obvious that we should not look to the nation-state nor to corporate capitalism nor to the scientific/technological establishments that service their ambitions for solutions to the problems they have created (e.g., the environmental crisis, addictive consumerism, increasing social injustice). This is not just because they have created the problems, but because to a large extent they *are* the problems. Instead of appealing to national governments for solutions, we need to work for more decentralized political institutions that will allow for increasing local self-governance and more direct participation. Instead of hoping that transnational corporations and market mechanisms can be used to solve the problems they themselves have created,[11] we need to rein them in by rewriting their corporate charters, the legal umbilical cords that could be used to subordinate them to greater social concerns. And since scientific inquiry is functionally unable to set self-limits on what it tries to discover and how those discoveries are to be used, scientific ambitions, like corporate ones, must be firmly subordinated to more democratically determined goals. Today the many ethical issues raised by genetic research, in particular, make this an urgent issue. It will not be easy to decide how this new knowledge should be developed and used, but it is becoming more evident that the worst solution may be leaving it to market forces and their political allies and technological servants.

This approach to history through a Buddhist understanding of our lack stands Marx on his head. Instead of reducing a superstructure of philosophical and religious ideology to some materialist infrastructure, I have argued that an unacknowledged repression of a spiritual character has played a significant role in the development of modernity. Yet Marx may have been right about something else. If the approach adumbrated here is valid, it is not enough for us just to understand it. The three roots of evil must be exposed and challenged, not only personally but structurally in the idolatrous institutions of modernity.

# FIVE

# THE LACK OF CIVIL SOCIETY

> Much like today, the emergence of the idea of civil society in the later seventeenth and eighteenth centuries was the result of a crisis in social order and a breakdown of existing paradigms of the idea of order.
>
> —Adam B. Seligman

Civil society has become an urgent topic, unfortunately. We do not usually notice things until they are broken, and the increasing attention of public leaders and scholars[1] is a sign that ours is in trouble. Everyone seems to agree that a strong civil society is essential for healthy democracy, which would be unremarkable except (as we shall see) there is no agreement on what civil society actually is. The unsurprising consequence is that there is also little agreement about what must be done to reinvigorate it.

The purpose of this chapter is to offer a new perspective on the origins and function of civil society, an approach that so far as I know has been overlooked in contemporary discussions. The modern development of civil society has been understood as a reaction to the rise of European nation-states in the seventeenth century, initially around absolute monarchs who weakened diffuse feudal centers of authority by consolidating power into their own hands:

> . . . [T]he transformation and subdivision of the idea of *societas civilis* was stimulated primarily by a specifically *political* development: the fear of state despotism and the hope (spawned by the defeat of the British in the American colonies, as well as by the earliest events of the French Revolution) of escaping its clutches. (Keane 1989, 65)

Civil society thus tends to be understood as another result of the secularization that began in the sixteenth century and culminated in the revolutions of the eighteenth century, by enthroning our cherished beliefs in the rights of man [*sic*] and the integrity of individuals. The previous chapter has questioned this supposed secularization by arguing that the rapid development of nation-states and corporate capitalism may also be understood in more *religious* terms, as a change of direction that did not so much supplant our spiritual concerns as pursue them in a this-worldly fashion. The Protestant Reformation did not just elevate God and free this world for more material pursuits: the decline of a Catholic church and its ecclesiastical paraphernalia (monasteries, sacraments, pilgrimages, etc.) meant that the duality in daily life between sacred and secular spheres was eliminated (or much reduced) without that resolving our lack. The diminution of church authority meant that new ways had to be found to address lack.

The spiritual concern and energy that had previously been devoted to supporting an ecclesiastical sphere found a new direction in the heightened individual responsibility of each person for his or her own spiritual life and destiny. This change also involved increased concern for the worldly conditions that affected such development, for others as well as oneself. One could no longer simply depend upon the established Church to take care of one's lack, especially when the *true* church was such a hotly contested issue.

Chapter Four looks at how this development contributed to the reorganization of political and economic institutions, which eventually took on a life of their own and now subordinate us to their own developmental imperatives. This chapter begins by looking at some countermovements that sought to reform society in a more ostensibly religious direction, so that it would better conform with God's spiritual plan. This movement eventually led, in particular, to the revolution in mid-seventeenth-century England that culminated in the execution of Charles I of England and the establishment of Oliver Cromwell's religiously based Commonwealth (1649–1660). That social ferment was as much religious as political, since it would be anachronistic to distinguish between them.[2] Such a radical political transformation became possible only because it was widely understood in millennial terms, as fulfilling Biblical prophecy about the return of Christ and the events necessary to help establish His kingdom on earth.

Such a religiopolitical revolution does not fit into the usual "secularizing" understanding of Western historical evolution, so its importance tends to be neglected in favor of the French Revolution, whose leaders exalted Reason—even to the point of deifying it! But the legacy of English millennial expectations, and the ways those hopes transformed when they were frustrated by the failure of the Commonwealth, have been vitally important for the development of Anglo-American civil society—and by no coincidence England and the United States are where the distinction between civil society and the state first developed (Keane 1989, 36). Hobbes's state of nature is a secularized version of Calvin's "natural man" without God. Socialist critiques of private property originated in allegorical interpretations of Adam's Fall and God's curse upon him. John Locke's theory of individual rights is rooted in a Protestant understanding of man's relationship with God. The unique civic society of the United States evolved in large part out of Puritan millennialist ambitions to create another Holy Commonwealth in a new and still pristine promised land.

In short, English and American civil society has spiritual origins. Furthermore, I shall argue that those origins survive today as roots still necessary for its nourishment. We cannot understand the development of our civil society without seeing how its current crisis is related to the atrophy of those roots. Does this imply that, in order for civil society to become revitalized, its spiritual dimension needs to be recuperated?

## THE ORIGINS OF CIVIL SOCIETY[3]

Much of our present confusion about the nature of civil society is due to the fact that its development in the West has been marked by at least three distinct bodies of thought, each of which offer quite different visions of what it is and should be.

The classical and medieval traditions generally did not distinguish civil society from politically organized commonwealths. Civilization was possible because people lived in law-governed states that had the power to protect them. Classical Greek philosophy emphasized that the public good was discoverable through public debate and organized by public action. Civic decay was a consequence of private calculation and the pursuit of individual interest. This left no room for an intermediate voluntary sphere between the citizen and the state. Civil society as we usually understand it today, a countervailing force to state coercion, did not exist, for the need of it was not yet recognized. In the first volume of *The Open Society and its Enemies,* Karl Popper attacks Plato for his "totalitarianism," yet such criticisms are anachronistic: Until the modern era the pressing social issue was not protecting subjects from their state, but protecting politically organized communities from the more immediate threat of barbarism. The problem was perceived as outside, not inside.

For Plato, political power exists to serve the welfare of the city and its citizens, and this requires firm restraints on the greed and ambition that constantly threaten that welfare. The glue that integrates civil society in his *Republic* is the power of reason, employed by philosopher-kings educated to discern the truth that alone can organize the world. Democracy, which had condemned his beloved Socrates, was itself condemned by its incompetence, mediocrity, and disorder. Political life must be grounded in moral wisdom and a life devoted to the good, which provided a counterweight to the disintegrative pull of personal interests.

Aristotle was more flexible in his conception of the ideal state, but like Plato he was suspicious of commerce. His teleological metaphysics made him conceive of politics as the moral consummation of all the other, more partial levels of human activity: politics should be morally redemptive. Like Hegel much later, both thinkers agreed that to be a member of a political society involved a life of collective involvement that should transcend private interests, for the state expresses the common moral life of the community. Today we have become more cynical about politics, yet our cynicism still reveals, in a disappointed and inverted fashion, those same moral concerns. If our lack is a constant irritant and challenge, the political sphere—the stage of collective social decision—cannot be ignored, for no human concern is immune to lack's projection and objectification.

We find a closer parallel to our times in the pervasive skepticism about politics during the declining fortunes of Hellenistic Greece. As the world outside deteriorated owing to greed and rivalry, the Cynics, Epicureans, and early Stoics redefined "the good life" in more private terms that offered some protection from a political sphere that less and less reflected Plato's and Aristotle's moral conception of the state. According to Epicurus, we must free ourselves from the prison of public affairs. Politics and civil society are no longer the source of ethical development, and the true self is not revealed in such public activities.

Cicero's Stoic conception of civil society rested on the universal human capacity for a rationality harmonious with the universe. As the Roman aristocracy degenerated into a group of competing and suspicious cliques, however, Rome became an expansionist war machine controlled by a small oligarchy. Curiously, this concentration of political power had some of the same effect as the rise of absolute rulers in Europe much later: it led to a legally acknowledged private realm that stood as a counterpart to the *polis*. The Roman *res publica* was understood to imply the existence of a *res privata*. Public law stopped at the doorstep: A private sphere was distinguished from the public citizen.

This distinction did not survive Rome's disintegration. What integration did survive was provided by the church, which was not sympathetic to the humanistic ambitions of the classical world. The optimistic ideal of self-sufficiency—that people could use their own powers of reason to cooperate and create a civilized society—was a pagan illusion and prideful error because it did not recognize our dependence on God as the only true source of justice and mercy. The doctrine of original sin led many church fathers to conclude that an oppressive state was one of the God-given consequences of our fallen nature, not only caused by sin but one of the remedies necessary to control our sinfulness. Humankind could not redeem itself, for we are too depraved to determine or follow moral values by ourselves.

The classical veneration of reason yielded to Augustine's unrelenting emphasis on faith and grace. He distinguished the City of Man from the City of God. The "goods" of the earthly city will always be elusive because of our unbalanced appetites, which drive us into a destructive scramble for power and wealth, leading to insecurity and mutual distrust, rebellion, civil war, and servitude. The institutions of the City of Man can have no sustained moral content, so a self-sufficient civil society as we conceive of it today is not possible. In its place is the church, God's institution, which works with the state to promote the salvation of fallen humanity by correcting error and punishing sin. In a degenerate world of sinful people, coercion is necessary.

The central aim of most medieval theory was to apply a single Christian ideal to the manifold conditions of life. Since the universe is hierarchical, earthly justice and harmony require human beings to understand and accept their role in God's creation. This left no place for any theory of civil society that could stand independent of theological presuppositions.

Thomas Aquinas broke with this by downplaying the Augustinian implications of Adam's fall. God's scheme of sin and salvation does not obliterate the value of human reason and human affairs. On the contrary, social and political life is fundamental to our condition, which revived the possibility that our own civil efforts could themselves serve moral purposes. Following the tentative steps of St. Anselm, Thomas Aquinas contributed to liberating reason from the requirements of faith, understanding it as the faculty that allows us a limited ability not only to understand but to participate in God's plan for our redemption.

Luther challenged the hierachy of the medieval Christian universe. The social division of labor does not imply a hierarchy of dignity or salvation. Differences of occupation among laymen, priests, princes, and bishops do not correspond to differences in their Christian status. We are equal before God, a doctrine that would later reincarnate in secular form as individual human rights for all. The true church is a "priesthood of all believers" in a community composed of autonomous consciences. Freeing the conscience, and unlinking our salvation from obedience to religious authority, created the conditions that would flower into modern individualism.

At the same time, Luther distinguished this inner life of the free Christian from an outer world of coercion and inequality. This separation between public and private spheres placed matters of conscience outside affairs of state, liberating not only conscience but secular powers from external restraint. "Luther's expulsion of politics from religion served to fortify it in the state" (Ehrenberg 70). He supported the harsh repression of peasant revolts in Germany. What he gave with one hand— spiritual equality and freedom of conscience—he took away with the other, subordinating us no longer to the church but to secular rulers and the new states that were forming around them. . . .

At this point in the story, histories of political theory and civil society usually jump to Thomas Hobbes and related attempts to theorize the basis of political authority in the idea of a *secular* social contract. Contracts imply obligations and therefore the complementary idea of an autonomous individual who is obligated to meet them; both concepts provide a more this-worldly basis for social order. Suddenly, we find ourselves in more familiar and comfortable ground for our political thinking, having escaped the otherworldly preoccupations that obfuscate so much of premodern social thought—or so we like to think. Yet this overlooks the crucial role of new *religious* ways of thinking in helping to create these novel "secular" understandings of politics and civil society. Rather than being a this-worldly alternative to Christian conceptions, the brave new sociopolitical world of the seventeenth century—which laid the foundations for our world—would have been literally unthinkable without those Christian presuppositions.

### THE REVOLUTIONARY BIBLE

> Sociological and psychological historians have not got very far in explaining why there was so much despair in the late sixteenth and early seventeenth centuries, leading some to suicide, some to atheism, some to conversion. . . . Where was certainty to be found? (Christopher Hill)[4]

Upon what certainty could a new society be founded in this "period of storm and stress seldom equalled and probably never surpassed" (Haller 27)? The notion of a social contract, which became popular among intellectuals in the late seventeenth century, meant nothing to the vast numbers of people preoccupied earlier with the no-holds-barred death grapple between Catholic and Reformed Europe (1618–48). This was probably the most vicious war in European history, because nothing less than our eternal destiny rested on the outcome. For Catholics, the challenge of the Reformers was a direct threat to their project to end lack: God's church, founded on Peter anointed by Christ. Protestants could no longer rely upon that Church to take care of their lack. "Protestantism retained medieval sin without the medieval insurance policy—confession and absolution. Men emancipated themselves from priests, but not from the terrors of sin, from the priest internalized—in their own consciences" (Hill 1975, 154–55). The authority of priests and their sacraments had been undermined. Where else could a religious people turn for grounding certainty?

To the Bible, newly translated and printed. "The Bible was central to all intellectual as well as moral life in the sixteenth and seventeenth centuries" (1994, 20).[5] Christopher Hill makes this claim for England, but much of his argument in *The English Bible* applies to the rest of Protestant Europe as well: for Christian societies in turmoil, lacking any other firm foundation, the Bible, now available cheaply in the vernacular, was widely studied because it was expected to provide solutions for urgent problems—social ones as well as religious, our distinction between them being anachronistic. For a civilization whose lack was now rampant, the Bible became essential as the only secure source of wisdom. It was almost universally acknowledged as the Word of God, hence of supreme and incomparable importance: not just a book, then, but *our sole remaining certain access to the Ground of being.* For a while, anyway.

> The Bible gave confidence and reassurance to men and women who badly needed it. Their times were out of joint; unprecedented things were happening to their world and their lives, apparently beyond human control. Some of the more daring of them came to conceive of solutions which were so novel that they could only be contemplated if they were envisaged as a return to purer Biblical days. (Hill 1994, 41)

Nothing that we would recognize as a civil society could have developed without a reading public, which presupposed the printing press and spread of literacy. Less noticed is that, for the majority of people in the sixteenth and seventeenth centuries, there was only one really important book: literally "the Book" (*biblos* is Greek for "book"). The Bible was the source of virtually all ideas, since it supplied the basic idiom in which men and women discussed all the questions of their day, issues that would have been dangerous to address in any other way. It was accepted as the ultimate authority on economics and politics as much as on religion and morality.

For John Milton (1608–1674) the Bible is "that book within whose sacred context all wisdom is enfolded" and his political tracts are as thoroughly Biblical as his religious poetry. This was so typical of the age that even Thomas Hobbes (1588–1679), prophet of the secular state, was not immune: 657 citations of Biblical texts have been counted in *Leviathan,* and a total of 1,327 in his six major political works. He denied being an atheist, claiming the authority of Scripture to support the logic of his *Leviathan* arguments, for "there ought be no power over the consciences of men but of the Word itself" (Hill 1994, 438, 20). Even those who wanted to challenge its influence needed to appropriate the Bible's authority in order to do so!

Its availability in English was a great encouragement to read, and it was how most children learned to read, for the Bible's many exciting narratives did not need to compete with the novel, which had not yet been invented. Immersed as we are today in print and electronic media, it is difficult for us to appreciate its unchallenged influence as the source of almost all the stories whereby men and women understood their own lives and times.

> In the censored society of sixteenth- and seventeenth-century England those who most wished to communicate, to discuss, were those who knew their Bible best. The Bible was what they wanted to discuss, for its guidance on the form of worship most pleasing to God in a society which had cast off one form and—some thought—not yet finally settled into a better one. Because church and state were one, religion became politics, with the Bible as textbook for both. (Hill 1994, 50–51).

In the fifteenth century merely owning an English Bible had been evidence of heresy, for its inconsistencies and ambiguities opened a Pandora's box. Even if "the rule and canon of faith is Scripture alone" (Milton), Scripture must be interpreted. Carrying the Protestant principle of the priesthood of all believers to its logical extreme, Milton declared that "Each man is his own arbitrator." In the long run, leaving decisions to individual consciences tended to undermine the authority of the text in favor of human reason and the spiritual "inner light" of believers. Once Bibles became widely available to the laity, so did theological controversy. "Error," wrote Joseph Hall during the reign of Charles I, "that could but creep then [before the Reformation] doth now fly" (Hill 1994, 374–75, 14). The most decisive period was the middle of the seventeenth century, when state censorship and the religious courts collapsed for two decades, leaving no restrictions on free discussion of the Bible, or of anything else for that matter. Radical new ideas spread quickly and widely, for printing presses were cheap and portable—an important factor if freedom of the press is restricted to those who own one.

With or without restrictions, the problem of error turned out to be insoluble, because the Bible was discovered to be "a huge bran-tub from which anything might be drawn. There are few ideas in whose support a Biblical text cannot be found. Much could be read into and between the lines." In the revolutionary climate of seventeenth-century England it was easy for both conservatives and radicals to quote scripture for their own purposes, due to the basic fact that "all heresy originates from the Bible, because the Bible itself is a compilation, a compromise; orthodoxy changes as it incorporates or over-reacts against a heresy—which itself originated from the Biblical text" (Hill 1994, 6).

> The Bible is one thing in a stable society, with an accepted machinery for controlling its interpretation. . . . But in the turmoil of the seventeenth century, the Bible became a sword to divide, or rather an armoury from which all parties selected weapons to meet their needs. . . . open to all, even the lower classes, to pillage and utilize. (Hill 1994, 5–6)

Those who knew their Bible well could find the answers they desired to most questions. One could find defenses of the status quo ("the powers that be are ordained of God," Romans 13:1), but one could also find severe criticisms of kings (Deuteronomy 17:14–20, I Samuel 8:6–19), defenses of the poor against the rich (Luke 6:20–21, 24; Matthew 19:21–22; Epistle of James 2:5), denunciations of oppression and celebrations of liberation (Exodus 2:7–9, Daniel 9–11). The New Testament, in particular, is full of libertarian ideas that could make a deep impression in a time of social oppression. Unfortunately, the Old Testament seems to take slavery for granted, and also the use of force against recalcitrant heathen; anti-Semitism could be justified by Thessalonians 2:14–16 as well as by the Jews' rejection of Christ; there were many passages to support the control of women by men, and the dominion of mankind over all other living things. Yet scripture did not give any clear direction about religious tolerance of nonconformists, although there is much intolerance in the Old Testament (Hill 1994, 66, 155–56, 179, 398–99, 409).

Unsurprisingly to us, then, but contrary to widespread expectations at the time, the Bible led those who studied it to no agreed political or social philosophy. Instead, it became used as a ragbag of quotations that could be mined to justify whatever one wanted to do. In the long term, this had the unexpected effect of encouraging men and women to think for themselves, by helping to rationalize the new possibilities they "found" within its pages. Trying to adjudicate those different ideas led to new confidence in their own reasoning powers. Paradoxically, this led to the eventual decline of Bibliolatry: "The world the Bible made dethroned the Bible" (Hill 1994, 441). But now we are getting ahead of our story.

The most popular books were Daniel and especially Revelation, which prophesied a time of great confusion—the present, obviously—

to be followed by a Christian utopia. Daniel had a vision of four monarchies: Babylon, Persia, Greece, and Rome. The first three had been overthrown, and the fourth—the Pope in Rome—would soon be, initiating a fifth and final monarchy, the Kingdom of God on earth. In *Revelation* John saw an angel descend from heaven and cast the dragon of this world into a bottomless pit, whereupon Christ would descend to reign over a new heaven and new earth for a thousand years, with his saints beside him. Countless sermons and pamphlets commented on these themes, and, as the Thirty Years War raged ever more chaotically on the continent, the conviction spread that England had been specially ordained by God to defend His cause against the Antichrist, in this final conflict between Light and Darkness.

The terrible times encouraged this apocalyptic thinking. During the seventeenth century land for the first time began to be widely used as a commodity that could be exploited for profit, and up to one-quarter of it was enclosed for private use. As the custom of community access was replaced by absolute rights of ownership, large numbers of people found themselves jobless and often homeless as well. Economically, the years between 1620 and 1650 were among the worst in English history; poor harvests meant that many did not have enough to eat. What would save them? "It is difficult to exaggerate the extent and strength of millenarian expectations among ordinary people in the 1640s and early 1650s" (Hill 1975, 96). In 1658, John Bunyan along with many others declared that "the judgment day is at hand."

Millennialism was not restricted to the lower classes. Tycho Brahe interpreted a new star he discovered in 1572 as a sign of the Second Coming; King James agreed with him. The greatest mathematicians of the time, including John Napier and Isaac Newton, were preoccupied with trying to extract a precise chronology from the Bible. A consensus emerged that the cycle of events that would lead to the end of the world was likely to begin in the 1650s or, at the latest, in the 1690s; some calculations suggested that 1656 or so would see the end of the Antichrist, who after 1640 was agreed to be the Pope (Hill 1994, 300). Milton confidently awaited "that day when thou the Eternall and shortly-expected King shall open the Clouds to judge the severall Kingdomes of the World [and] shall put an end to all Earthy *Tyrannies,* proclaiming thy universal and milde *Monarchy* through Heaven and Earth" (Haller 356).

In *The Eighteenth Brumaire of Louis Bonaparte* Karl Marx wrote that Oliver Cromwell (1599–1658) and the English people "borrowed speech, passions and illusions from the Old Testament" (Hill 1994, 40). According to Hill, the key to Cromwell's character as leader was his belief that his successes were achieved through God alone, for he was led by God. Despite his preeminent role Cromwell remained uninterested in political theory and organization, not only because he was pragmatic but because he was so religious: he preferred to leave such matters to God. All forms of government are "but a mortal thing," "dross and dung in comparison with Christ." We see this clearly in his role at the crucial turning point, when the execution of Charles I was proposed in Parliament:

> When it was first moved in the House of Commons to proceed capitally against the King, Cromwell stood up and told them "that if any man moved this upon design, he should think him the greatest traitor in the world; but since providence and necessity had cast them upon it, he should pray God to bless their counsels, though he were not provided on the sudden to give them counsel" (Hill 1972, 224–25, 135 and *passim*).[6]

Cromwell's belief that the millennium was imminent, and that God would solve the problems which the Rump parliament had found so intractable, contributed to the final tragedy (or farce) of the Barebones Parliament in 1653, whose inability to agree on a new form of government, in the absence of more direct divine intervention, eventually led to the restoration of Charles II after Cromwell's death.

Then was the English Revolution a consequence of religious belief or political aspiration? Again, it would be anachronistic to project our distinction between them. "The wrath of God from which some nonconformists decided to flee was demonstrated in the injustice of English society. The millennium, the reign of the saints and the promised land were the names they gave to their hopes for a better society, whether in New or old England" (Hill 1994, 439). Not just a better society: a more *spiritual* society, because it would (or could) bring about the end of lack. From a lack perspective, our distinction between religious and political aspiration is not obvious or inevitable, but a contingent result of our own social history, which very much includes the failure of the English Commonwealth. What most dreamt of at the time was not just the recovery of social stability—which offered little except to the elite—but a new social order that would bring an end to the inchoate sense of lack felt more immediately in those chaotic times.

My main point in this section is that our Anglo-American civil society originated out of this collective *religious* concern to reform the state and create a new society that (to use my term) would end our lack. Their millennial aspirations may have been naive, but we mock them at our cost, if (as I will argue later) the problem with our contemporary civil society is linked to the loss of such a religious dimension. In that case, our secular cynicism may need to recover some of their idealism about working together to reduce the objectifications of lack which now endanger our world. Among the Christians who attempted to use Biblical principles for truly radical social transformation, the most important were the Puritans.

According to William Haller's *The Rise of Puritanism,* English Puritanism was nothing new but a deep-seated tendency with medieval roots. What we now identify as historical Puritanism was a movement for religious reform that began early in the reign of Elizabeth I, owing to disappointment over what many saw as her reluctance to complete the reform of Christianity begun by her father, Henry VIII. Puritanism evidently spoke to some profound need in those unstable times. "In little more than a single lifetime it led to the founding of New England and the revolutionizing of English society" (Haller 5). Puritanism addressed the psychological problems of a dissatisfied minority by injecting new moral purpose into those who felt lost in moral confusion (213). It did this by offering a persuasive new understanding of what our lack is and how it is to be resolved.

Henry's reform had left England dangerously divided into a state church headed by the monarch, recusant Catholics who had to worship secretly, and Calvinist divines who criticized the official church as still too ceremonial and ecclesiastical. Nobody believed in toleration: There could only be one true church, and that church should be supported by the state, which was responsible for the Christian salvation of its subjects. Since her subjects could not agree on the true religion, however, Elizabeth's policy was to maintain a semblance of uniformity without wrecking her government. The Puritans were held in check but not crushed; in fact, they thrived. Their ambitions to reconstruct the official church rebuffed, they created instead a new type of spiritual literature that eventually went far beyond traditional religious bounds.

Puritan sermons and tracts tended to neglect theological abstractions in order to mirror the spiritual stress of the lonely conscience, "to convince the individual of sin in order to persuade him of grace, to make him feel worse in order to make him feel better, to inspire pity and fear in order to purge him of those passions" (Haller 6–9, 33). The most important metaphors were life as wayfaring (e.g., Bunyan's *Pilgrim's Progress*) and as warfaring, the struggle within each of us between good and evil.

Within each of us? Therein lay the problem. The Puritans were Calvinists, who believed in the predestined salvation of only a small number of souls, an elect chosen by God. Calvinist predestination presupposed universal human depravity: everyone deserves an eternity in hell. This turned out to have important social consequences, by implicitly challenging worldly hierarchy:

> The concept of universal depravity, by leveling all superiority not of the spirit, enormously enhanced the self-respect of the ordinary man. If none were righteous, then one man was as good as another. God chose whom he would and the distinctions of this world counted for nothing. The concept of free grace still further heightened his confidence. If the only real aristocracy was the aristocracy created by God, then nothing really counted but character and inner worth. (Haller 89)

Emphasizing an aristocracy of the spirit, over against the "carnal aristocracy" that ruled the world, assumed that salvation would be restricted to a limited number. Whatever we may think of this theologically,[7] it has its attractions, especially for those who believe they are among that elect. One of the main ways we have always tried to fill up our sense of lack is to become (or convince ourselves that we are) special, and therefore destined for a better fate than others. The Puritan version of this—to be one of the few regenerated by divine grace—was especially empowering. "Practical men in great numbers can be persuaded to commit themselves to a fight for a faith and a program when they can be induced to believe in the inevitability of a favorable outcome" (Haller 169). Hill makes the same point with explicit reference to Cromwell: "Men who have assurance that they are to inherit heaven, have a way of presently taking possession of the earth. . . . A man who really believed that God had included him among the handful who were saved from eternal damnation rather naturally felt under an obligation to make some voluntary return for this voluntary grace" (Hill 1972, 213, 216). If our sense of lack is not so easily overcome, however, the political (and, after the Restoration, commercial) energy of the

Puritans may also be explained by their need to continually reassure themselves that they were indeed one of those entitled to a special destiny. Psychologically, such certainty is not something gained once and for all, but a feeling of grace that needs to be renewed, hence requiring active moral perseverance. Puritan conversion was not the end of lack, rather the assurance that one's lack would be ended, although only in the hereafter.

In the middle of the seventeenth century English Calvinism collapsed, an unexpected reversal that Hill describes as one of the great turning points in intellectual history (Hill 1972, 206). One problem was the obvious failure of many of the "visible elect" to live up to expectations. It has always been difficult to argue that the elect are not saved by their deeds (implied by predestination) without also concluding that they cannot be damned for their deeds (implying antinomianism, which made it difficult to resist temptation). There was also the unseemly haste with which some leaders of the nonconformist movement returned to the established church after the Restoration.

The basic problem was more theological than carnal, however. The assumption that an omniscient and omnipotent God has from the beginning of history condemned the great mass of humankind to an eternity of torment became increasingly unacceptable. "Orthodox Calvinism leveled all men under the law, made all equal in their title to grace, and then denied to most all prospect of realizing their hopes. It made the individual experience of God in the soul all-important, enormously stimulating individual spiritual experience, and then denied any freedom to the individual will" (Haller 193). Instead of emphasizing the many who could not be saved, preachers focused on exposing everyone to God's covenant of grace; yet such efforts contradicted their theology, by acting as if every sinner could be converted into one of the saints. It was easy to draw the heretical inference that His grace was available to all who did not reject it, which also encouraged belief in the free will that made the moral efforts to deserve His grace. "The way was opened to a world in which the Protestant ethic, with its emphasis on effort and will-power, survived without the predestinarian theology which had originally accompanied it" (Hill 1988, 345).

> What the preachers as a whole believed was that heresy and schism should be firmly suppressed. But what they taught was that any man might be a saint and that the mark of a saint was that he obeyed his conscience at any cost. . . . The

> ultimate effect . . . was to encourage in their followers the habit of going each his own way toward heaven and the notion that it was every man's native right to save himself or not in his own way without interference from anybody. From the very beginning of the movement, therefore, heresy and schism dogged the steps of the Puritan reformers, and in the very day of victory, when prelacy lay overthrown, brought their schemes for the godly Utopia to confusion. (Haller 173–74).

Conscience, the voice of God in one's soul, became difficult to distinguish from reason, increasingly seen as necessary to understand the true meaning of God's voice in the soul as well as God's Word in the Bible. The influential *Satanae Strategemata* of Jacobus Acontius (English translation 1648) argued for two fundamental principles that appealed less to biblical authority than to reason and common observation of human behavior: unless we want to yield to Satan, nothing—learning, tradition, the church, nor any other authority—should be allowed to take precedence over conscience, the voice of God within us; and second, no man is immune from error. John Goodwin, who helped to rally the defense of London against advancing royalists during the civil war, came to the radical conclusion that redemption from sin was manifested not by infallible knowledge or absolute righteousness but by our ceaseless efforts to learn more truth and to live more like the son of God. This also had political implications. Like almost everyone else Goodwin conceded that kings were divinely appointed, but he argued that in order for justice to prevail the exercise of their authority must be based on discussion and agreement, and should be obeyed only in the light of individual judgment and conscience (Haller 196, 200).

Baptists were among the first to draw the obvious religious conclusions (retrospectively obvious to us, that is) and advance a claim for general toleration of nonconformity. They conceded the duty of obedience to civil laws, but since all of us are spiritually equal we must be left free to understand the truth for ourselves and to convert others as best we could (Haller 205). This way led to the future, although few could see it at the time, even though by the end of the century the religiosity of the English people had become so intense and so varied that no church could have enforced any uniformity.

One of the main reasons toleration became inevitable was the Bible itself. If its own attitude toward religious toleration was unclear—

well, that just highlighted the problem. Milton and most other radicals had believed that once an English Bible was widely available it would become the basis for reconstructing social norms and institutions. Yet intense and uncensored discussion in the 1640s and 1650s led to no agreement on what exactly the Bible meant, even among the godly (Hill 1994, 420–21).

The failure of confident predictions about the approaching millennium left even fervent believers skeptical and weary. Even to questions of church government—bishops or presbyters? state church or voluntary congregations? ordination or lay preaching? tithes or voluntary support?—the Bible produced no universally accepted solutions. Once it had been demonstrated that you could prove almost anything from it, the Bible lost its authority as the prime source of political ideas; and once churchly authority could not be enforced, each was free to believe what he wanted. Intellectual and congregational fragmentation was inevitable.

One response was to allegorize the Scriptures, and to stress the spirit within rather than the letter of the Bible—a spirit that became increasingly necessary to interpret God's ambiguous Word. Quakers and many others found an alternative authority in our "inner light." The Digger Gerrard Winstanley declared that important questions about our freedom were not to be answered by any Biblical text but by the light "which dwells in every man's heart and by which he was made. . . . We must throw off the tyranny of the Bible." The Ranter Jacob Bauthumley opined that Scripture was no better "than any other writings of good men" and added: "The Bible without is but a shadow of the Bible which is within." (Hill 1994, 224, 234).

The grace provided by that inner light was what enabled believers to understand the true meaning of the scriptures; but since even the godly continued to disagree, reason also needed to be employed to help adjudicate arguments and discriminate truth from falsity. Eventually that role became so important it overshadowed and then supplanted other aspects of the inner light. At first understood in a more spiritual way, as a function given to us by the grace of God, reason gradually became more calculative and instrumental, as we will see later.

The heretical attitudes of Winstanley and Bauthumley became more widespread after the failure of the Commonwealth, which also severely damaged the acceptance of the Bible as an infallible text that needed only to be applied. "In so far as the Biblical Revolution was defeated, the Bible shared this defeat" (Hill 1994, 40). But this did not mean a return to the orthodoxy that had existed before the vernacular Bible became available. Hill concludes his study by praising the many scholars and radicals "whose passionate desire to make sense of the Bible led them into the critical activity which ultimately dethroned it":

> To the extent that England ultimately became a democracy it owes much to the discussions initiated by these scholars— discussions whose ironical effect was in the long run to force men and women to rely on their own intelligence rather than on citations from a holy text. They cut off the branch on which they sat, letting in more light, to the great advantage of those who followed them. (Hill 1994, 441, 442)

This too had some unexpected political implications. The decline of Biblical authority undermined the Divine Right of Kings and the divine right of the clergy to collect tithes, "which did not mean that kings ceased to rule or tithes to be collected: it meant that different arguments had to be found to defend them. And in the long run these arguments were open to rational criticism" (Hill 1994, 431).

In the long run. After the Restoration in 1660 most nonconformists decided that Christ's kingdom was not of this world. The Quakers, for example, who in the 1650s had been notoriously belligerent in calling on Cromwell to fight against continental Catholics, became pacifist. Secular powers now must be obeyed except when their demands conflicted with God's, in which case resistance should be passive. Nonconformists accepted their exclusion from political life and turned their attention to commerce and quietist religion. *The Biblical solution to our lack—the infallible Word of God as our mode of access to His Being, and the attempt to help establish its Kingdom of Heaven on earth—had failed.* People began to look for answers elsewhere. Religious toleration became acceptable because for the first time religious commitment became a private matter. It became a private matter because it was no longer the ultimate issue.

The government of Charles II was preoccupied with avoiding the discontent that severe religious persecution had produced earlier. A compromise evolved because the two spheres split: people became free to worship as they wished, and an increasingly secular state became free to do whatever it wanted, without troublesome religious interference or troublesome responsibility for the salvation of its subjects' souls. An important freedom was gained, but at a cost: The loss of the state's moral responsibility has also been the loss of its moral accountability to anything "higher" than itself. Among individuals, tolerance became the norm, but at the price of our becoming "morally thin": As our chief social virtue today, such tolerance effectively "displaces morality" by "asking you to inhabit your own moral convictions loosely and be ready to withdraw from them whenever pursuing them would impinge on the activities and choices of others" (Fish 41). In other words, we now have the right to express our religious convictions as long as we do not act upon them in ways that affect other people, which leaves the sphere of social interaction religiously and morally neutral.

As this suggests, the failed religious revolution in seventeenth-century England left a mixed legacy. Stuart monarchy was restored, although in a weakened condition that survived only for a few decades before the "Glorious Revolution" of 1688–1689 imported a more Protestant lineage that accepted more limited powers. Parliament, now the deciding force, initiated the path toward an increasingly representative democracy. We tend to view the French Revolution as the prototype for radical social change, but the English were in the first in modern times to execute a ruling king, henceforth a possibility that other rulers and their subjects could not forget.

In another way too, the failure of the Commonwealth and the Barebones Parliament has been instructive. Since then we have learned again and again that societies cannot be made just simply by replacing one ruler with another—and this problem is more than the obvious realith that even well-intended people can disagree about what should replace a bad government. The English revolution was millennial because people expected it to bring about the end of lack, but our lack cannot be solved in such a way. What lesson can we draw from this? That our lack is not something that can be addressed collectively? Yes and no. From a Buddhist perspective, our lack is a spiritual (or existential) problem because resolving it requires personal effort to transform one's greed, ill will, and delusion into generosity, compassion, and wisdom. Such personal transformation cannot be legislated or conditioned into us from outside. This important realization is the foundation of our religious freedom and the separation of church from state.

But that is not all we can learn from England's Puritan revolution. Its enthusiasm fed on the Protestant Reformation but became something quite original: a concerted effort by people who tried to reform their own unjust government in order to make a better society.[8] We can focus on the utopian millennialism, or we can focus on their challenge to the entrenched greed, privilege, and violence of the state. If we focus on the latter, we see the origin of Anglo-American civil society in the religious concerns that brought people together to work for a vision greater than their own personal gain. Yes, they were deluded to expect a Kingdom of Heaven on earth, and in the end that naïvete was fatal to their hopes, as they expected too much from God's intervention and not enough from their own. As long as there is lack, human beings will never be able to create a utopia. Yet (to express it in lack terms) I think we today need to rediscover something that their spiritual preoccupations enabled them to see: that our lack is not only a personal problem (owing to one's lack of money, fame, etc., as we now commonly understand it), but something that often takes collective form in social and political institutions. When it does, those structures need to be challenged and transformed.

## THE BIBLICAL FOUNDATIONS OF POLITICAL THEORY

> The civil war of the seventeenth century . . . has never been concluded.
>
> —T. S. Eliot, *Milton*

The Bible did more than encourage millennialism. When the civil war began, the case against royal absolutism was most effectively presented by Henry Parker, in a very influential tract that "showed how impossible it was to keep spiritual warfare within spiritual bounds." Parker argued that whenever the existing laws of the state interfere with prosecuting the war against Satan, the Puritan spirit must acknowledge the higher law of conscience. That law now justified Parliament to act independently, and even to oppose the crown's commands. Parker supported this by basing a political theory of social contract upon the Puritan myth of the Fall of man and his eternal struggle with the Evil One. Before his Fall Adam had needed no governor but conscience, but afterward he became so depraved that it was necessary to agree on a temporal ruler. When, however, those rulers themselves became tyrannical, the law of nature (to protect oneself) began to operate again and found a remedy in Parliament, which expressed the people's will (Haller 365–68).

According to Christopher Hill, all serious English political theory dates from the middle of the seventeenth century (1994, 415), which is when critical and radical social attitudes first gained the freedom to develop alongside their more respectable conservative counterparts. Modern political philosophy is often understood to begin with Thomas Hobbes's social contract theory in the *Leviathan* (1651), which offered a closely argued secular alternative to divinely organized hierarchies, including the divine right of kings and popes. The influence of Henry Parker suggests that the line between sacred and secular approaches is less clear than we usually suppose, by offering what to us seems an odd mixture: a social contract deriving from Adam's Fall. Yet it was not so odd to Parker's contemporaries, for whom it served an important role in justifying resistance against the king. Nor should we dismiss it as merely a temporary or intermediate position in the development of a truly secular politics. In this section we will see that the political categories that continue to determine our thinking today are another legacy of the Bible and the spiritual preoccupations of those who turned to it for guidance. The political alternatives that still preoccupy us are grounded in contested notions of our human nature: notions derived from Biblical debates.

Luther had supported the repression of German peasant revolts because he feared what the peasants would get up to once they were free to do what they wanted. According to Henry Parker, "man being depraved by the Fall of Adam grew so untame and uncivil a creature that the law of God written in his breast was not sufficient to restrain him from mischief or to make him sociable." Many others traced our depraved nature back to the Fall. Sir Robert Filmer argued that "a natural freedom of mankind cannot be supposed without a denial of the creation of Adam." It was a strong argument for rule by the better sort, and that better sort agreed with Richard Crashaw that "the greater part [of people] generally is the worst part." Control by authorities was necessary, for as John Pym put it "if you take away the law, all things will fall into a confusion, every man will become a law to himself, which in the depraved condition of human nature must need produce many great enormities" (Hill, 1975, 157, 159). The radical antinomian William Walwyn was warned by seven nonconformist ministers that "surely a natural and complete freedom from all sorrows and troubles was fit for man only before he had sinned and not since. Let them look for their portion in this life that know no better, and their kingdom in this world that believe no other," for evidently those who *do* know better will wait with faith, patience, and self-denial for their reward in the world to come (Hill 1997, 331). Many agreed with Milton that the elect could be freed from all restraint, which needed to be applied only to the unregenerate, but it was a short step to Hobbes's view that the function of government is to restrain the depravity natural to us all.

For conservatives, who naturally included those with property to defend, the Fall could not be undone: Adam's sin had permanently affected human nature, for it had become an inherited characteristic transmitted by our sexual propagation. Evil is something that lurks in all our hearts, always ready to come out if we relax our grip. Calvin had encouraged the poor to endure their sufferings patiently, since their burden is imposed by God for their sins. The social consequence was to preserve property in the hands of those to whom God had given it. By what right can we sinners challenge His disposition?

On the other side were Ranters, Levellers, Familists, Diggers, and many other radical groups who emerged from the debates that occurred when censorship was relaxed. Among the most remarkable of them was a Digger whose forgotten (or censored) writings are once again available to us, thanks largely to the efforts of Christopher Hill: Gerrard Winstanley. Winstanley read the Bible rather differently from Sir Robert Filmer and Pym, and came to very different conclusions about our human nature, views that rejected inherited sin and the economic inequality that such sin was used to justify.

According to Robert Kenney, Winstanley's final pamphlet *Law of Freedom in a Platform* "was the first serious and sober attempt in the English language to restructure the whole of society along avowedly radical lines" (in Winstanley, 1). For Winstanley it was not the Fall that caused private property but private property that caused our Fall. Adam symbolizes the power of covetousness. Men began to fall when self-love arose. "When mankind began to quarrel about the earth, and some would have all and shut out others, forcing them to be servants; this was man's fall" (in Hill 1975, 163). This implied a more allegorical interpretation of God's inheritable curse on Adam when expelling him from the Garden:

> the power of enclosing land and owning property was brought into the creation by your ancestors by the sword; which first did murder their fellow creatures, men, and after plunder or steal away their land, and left this successively to you, their children. And therefore, though you did not kill or thieve, yet you hold that cursed thing in your hand by the power of the sword; and so you justify the wicked deeds of your fathers, and that sin of your fathers shall be visited upon the

head of you and your children to the third and fourth generation, and longer, too, till your bloody and thieving power
be rooted out of the land. (in Hill 1975, 132–33)

Again, this fable of lost grace made the Fall as much political as religious in its implications. Like many others before and since, Winstanley
appealed to the innocence of children, not yet corrupted by the world:
"Look upon a child that is new-born, or till he grows up to some few
years; he is innocent, harmless, humble, patient, gentle, easy to be en-
treated, not envious." The Fall happens when we surrender to covetousness in a competitive world. But this is not inevitable, or necessarily
permanent. Against it, Winstanley argued that the "poorest man hath as
true a title and just right to the land as the richest man" and "true
freedom lies in the free enjoyment of the earth." He had a vision in
which he was called upon to announce to the world that "the earth
should be made a common treasury of livelihood to whole mankind,
without respect of persons" (in Hill 1975, 391, 133, 112).

This metaphorical understanding of the Bible included a metaphorical understanding of Christ's return. In 1648 Winstanley declared
the salvation of all mankind, not by a physical descent of Christ from
the heavens but by His resurrection within each person: "Your Saviour
must be a power within you, to deliver you from that bondage within;
the outward Christ or the outward God are but men [i.e., not divine]
saviours." Those who work and eat together in a communal cultivation
of the commons do thereby join hands with Christ to lift up the
creation from bondage and restore all things from Adam's curse. True
freedom is found in a community of spirit that shares the earthly
treasury, "and this is Christ the true man-child spread abroad in the
creation, restoring all things unto himself." Since sin did not cause
property but vice versa, only abolishing private property can get rid of
the coercive state, which exists to protect property, and the coercive
church, which emphasizes our sinfulness to the same effect. In an
overpopulated land where enclosures were destroying the livelihood of
many, this was a hot topic. Winstanley believed that Christ rising in all
men and women would convince even the rich that cooperation and
mutual help are *natural* (notice that word again), and that everyone
would gain from establishing communal property (Hill 1975, 141, 392).

Winstanley eventually came to prefer the word *Reason* in place of
*God*, "because I have been held in darkness by that word, as I see many
people are." "In the beginning of time the great creator, Reason, made

the earth to be a common treasury, to preserve beasts, birds, fishes and man, the lord that was to govern this creation," but then "selfish imaginations . . . did set up one man to teach and rule over another" and thus "man was brought into bondage, and became a greater slave to such of his own kind than the beasts of the field were to him."

> There is no man or woman needs to go to Rome nor to hell below ground, as some talk, to find the Pope, Devil, Beast or power of darkness; neither to go up to heaven above the skies to find Christ the word of life. For both these powers are to be felt within a man, fighting against each other. (in Hill 1975, 141, 132, 143).

Winstanley used this new understanding to transform Joachim of Fiore's apocalyptic vision of the three ages (of the Father, Son, and Spirit, discussed in chapter Two) into a theology of reason that established democracy. God was equated with Reason, and Reason with the law of the universe. In the third age, which was now beginning, "the Lord himself, who is the Eternal Gospel, doth manifest himself to rule in the flesh of sons and daughters." Our hearts are returning to the Reason that pervades the cosmos, to "that spiritual power that guides all men's reasoning in right order to a right end." Every man subject to Reason's law becomes a son of God. He no longer "looks upon a God and a ruler without him, as the beast of the field does," for one's ruler is now found within. The Digger's aim was not just to remove "the Norman Yoke" and recover more ancient customs, but to restore this "pure law of righteousness before the Fall" (Hill 1975, 132, 148, 134).

From a Buddhist perspective, Winstanley's critique is perceptive in identifying the basic issue as our "selfish imaginations." The problem is not that we are *naturally* competitive, but that we are deceived by the way our minds usually work: "Imagination fears where no fear is: he rises up to destroy others, for fear lest others destroy him." Imagination "fills you with fears, doubts, troubles, evil surmisings and grudges, he it is that stirs up wars and divisions, he makes you lust after everything you see or hear of" (in Hill 1975, 389, 143).

The corrective to such imaginings is Reason, which for Winstanley is finally nothing other than Love, Christ resurrected in us His sons and daughters. Today, however, our conception of reason is much closer to that of Hobbes: the faculty of calculation, "nothing but reckoning (that is adding and subtracting)" (in Hill 1975, 393).

As this suggests, the contrast between Winstanley and Hobbes is instructive. For Hobbes, a truly civil society could not exist without a coercive state, since such a state is the only remedy to our perpetual desire for ever greater power. Because of our insecurity, we can never have enough: attaining something is only a spur to seeking something else. We are motivated by

> a general inclination of all mankind, a perpetual and restless desire of power after power, that ceaseth only in death. And the cause of this, is not always that a man hopes for a more intensive delight, than he has already attained to, or that he cannot be content with a moderate power: but because he cannot assure the power and means to live well, which he hath present, without the acquisition of more.[9]

This need to accumulate ever more power is our *natural* condition, intrinsic to the state of nature before a political solution. "In Hobbes's theory, nature replaces sin and depravity as the cause of humankind's ruin and the turn toward the state" (Ehrenberg 71).

A civil society becomes possible only with the establishment of a Leviathan or "mortal God" whose absolute sovereignty subsumes all other sources of power. Hobbes's deductive rationalism enabled him to construct a theory of the state that rested on a theory of human psychology that ignored revelation, the divine right of kings, and all other traditional arguments. Neither rights nor ethics exists before the state exists to enforce the sovereign's will. The atomized individuals that comprise such a civil society are linked together only by agreements that they enter into as rational and self-interested beings. These individuals are "owners" of themselves rather than members of larger communities. The "common good" can mean nothing except the sum of individual interests. Constituted only by state coercion and protection, society is an artificial network existing only to protect property and maintain an orderly economy. Contrary to Winstanley's spiritual vision of Reason as that which overcomes our covetous imaginations, reason for Hobbes is not a capacity that harmonizes or integrates our interests: it divides us because it is yoked to our competitive pursuit of our own individual concerns (Ehrenberg 70–73, 77–79).

Although Winstanley's vision is more attractive to Buddhists, this approach marked Hobbes as the man of the future, to be reincarnated in the philosophy of David Hume, in the economics of Adam Smith, and in their successors down to the cheerleaders of neoliberal globalization today.

Does this mean that Winstanley's religious understanding of property and society has been replaced by more secular contract approaches that better acknowledge our individual motivations? The contrast between the two is not so simple. Hobbes did not construct his understanding of human nature from scratch, in an intellectual vacuum. His philosophy is a secularized version of the Christian (especially the Protestant) understanding of our nature after the Fall. Hobbes's man in nature is Calvin's unregenerate natural man without God: a lonely individual dominated by evil, selfish passions. "Protestantism relied on the sense of guilt, of sin, to internalize an ethic of effort, thrift, industry. Hobbes hoped to achieve the same ends by an appeal to rational science, calculation of profit and loss, expediency, utility: not fear of hell but fear of social disorder" (Hill 1994, 388). According to this tradition, our lack is ineradicable because it is built into us. Whether it is caused by Adam's inherited sin or genetic evolutionary factors that sociobiology discovers, all we can do is strive to control it.

On the other side, the spiritual perspective expressed by Winstanley (and others in his day) has also reincarnated in more secular forms: most of all in socialism and the social-democratic political traditions. These see our lack as a function of economic exploitation and other social oppression. According to Jean-Jacques Rousseau, man is naturally good but is made wicked by his institutions. For Marx and Friedrich Engels, man is born free but everywhere finds himself in chains.

There are many other versions of this claim, down to the "bleeding heart liberal" stereotype that all bad behavior is caused by poor socialization. As Lewis Mumford put it, such "progressives" believe that human nature is deflected from its natural goodness by external circumstances beyond its control: "Having no sense of sin, they discounted inherent obstacles to moral development and therefore could not grasp the need for a 'form-giving discipline of the personality' " (in Lasch 1991). In Winstanley's day the better sort were afraid of the antinomianism this seems to encourage ("I myself am without sin, so I can do whatever I will"). Today a consumerist version of antinomianism ("since nothing is wrong with me, I should consume anything I can afford") has become not only socially acceptable but necessary to keep the economy growing (and growth is necessary to keep it from collapsing).

From a lack point of view, however, antinomianism of either sort is wrong, not so much for moral reasons but because it is a delusion to think that "I have no lack, so I can do whatever I want." If social oppression were the only source of our lack, removing that external oppression should remove our lack; it doesn't. Moreover, an unacknowledged lack is more dangerous than a conscious sense of lack, because it is more likely to be projected in a fashion resistant to our understanding. Although lack does become collectively objectified into oppressive institutions, those institutions are not themselves the source of our lack. That is why violent political revolutions always seem to fail, despite intentions that are often good. For Buddhism, our sense of lack ultimately derives from our lack of self-being and our inability to cope with that. There is good reason to fear the antinomianism of one's neighbor, even if we are not afraid of our own: Removing the chains that restrict our liberty can allow our lack to express itself in some of the very ugly ways we read about daily in the newspapers.

If most of this sounds familiar, that's because it is. This debate about the source of our lack, which originated in seventeenth-century controversies about the Fall and how Adam's curse may be rectified, continues in contemporary arguments between conservatives and liberals, the right and the left of an increasingly sterile political spectrum. Can remembering its source and recognizing this as a *spiritual* issue help us to escape the impasse between them? The problem is not merely a political one about the proper relationship between individuals and the state. Inescapably, the issue is as much religious as political, for political perspectives wittingly or unwittingly presuppose an answer to the fundamental question: What is our lack, and how is it to be overcome? Without an answer to that question, we cannot really know how society should be organized. We can ignore that basic issue only by falling back into automatized and polarized understandings whose origins remain unknown to us.

From a Buddhist perspective, Winstanley's understanding is more perceptive than many of the more secular critics who have succeeded him. Our Fall is both objective and subjective. Unequal and oppressive social relations are maintained by coercion. But that coercion could not be effective without the cooperation of our own "selfish imaginations." The lack that makes us unhappy is found both inside and outside.

Then any solution must address both, something that a socially engaged Buddhism is well equipped to do. Buddhism begins as a personal path that works to transform our own greed, ill will, and delusion into generosity, loving-kindness, and wisdom. But to overcome one's own *dukkha* is to become more aware of the *dukkha* maintained by unjust and unnecessary social arrangements. To overcome that institutionalized *dukkha,* we need to work collectively. So we need to avoid two extremes. One is a Buddhism that remains preoccupied only with one's own awakening and personal liberation. The other is a socially preoccupied Buddhism that loses its roots in personal transformation, because it identifies too much with a "progressive" understanding of our lack as caused mainly by social oppression. The challenge today is integrating these two concerns.

## COMMERCIALIZING SOCIETY

Although Hobbes's pessimistic view of human nature still prevails in many conservative circles, his conclusions about the need for absolute state power held little attraction for the English gentry struggling against would-be absolute rulers. They found a more congenial perspective in John Locke's *Second Treatise of Government* (1690), which argued that the chief end of human association is to defend private property. Contrary to Hobbes, our rights to freedom, property, labor, and exchange are not a function of the social contract; they already existed in the state of nature, which means an absolutist state is not necessary to establish them. Then why do we agree to give up some of our freedom by entering into a social contract? Because in the state of nature "the enjoyment of it is very uncertain, and constantly exposed to the invasion of others."

As with Hobbes, however, any notion of a common good is emptied by Locke's concern to protect personal interest, especially property. The state exists to guarantee the maximum possible liberty to individuals—that is, to self-interested proprietors (Locke himself was a land speculator); "individual interest was always clear and compelling in Locke's thinking, while common matters were derivative, thin, and inconsequential at best" (Ehrenberg 87).

If *that* looks familiar, it is because this approach was also attractive to gentry in the American colonies struggling to gain independence and establish a republic. Their constitutional decision to separate church from state does not mean that Locke's perspective on government was secular. Despite his debt to the natural-law tradition, Locke's understanding of individual rights remained grounded in a religious vision, in "a specific Christian, if not Calvinist, reading of man's relation with

God . . . itself rooted in a theological matrix—rooted, in fact, in the medieval Christian tradition of right reason and Christian Revelation" (Seligman 22). God survives on every other page of the *Second Treatise* because Locke's theory depends on Him for transcendental validation. There is no worldly authority that is intrinsically legitimate, for all authority is ultimately derived from God:

> The state of nature has a law of nature to govern it, which obliges every one and reason, which is that law, teaches all mankind who will but consult it, that being all equal and independent, no one ought to harm another in his life, health, liberty or possessions. For men being all the work-manship of one omnipotent and infinitely wise Maker—all servants of one sovereign master, sent into the world by His order, and about His business—they are His property, whose workmanship they are, made to last during His, not one another's pleasure, and being furnished with like faculties, sharing all in one community of nature, there cannot be supposed any such subordination among us, that may autho-rize us to destroy one another, as if we were made for one another's uses, as the inferior ranks of creatures are for ours. (Locke, Book II, 6)

Our independence and equality derive from our situation of being not only God's workmanship but continuing to be His property: an association that serves to *sanctify property*. Our existence remains rooted in a theological understanding of the cosmos that is necessary to justify our calling and our reason. "What is Calvinist in this reading is precisely the validation of this-worldly affairs and of the reason that governs them, in transcendent terms" (Seligman 24). Our supposedly secular affairs are validated by their role within a religious soteriology. God places us on this earth and guarantees that by obediently following our calling and employing our reason, our lack will be resolved.

Again, this transcendental precondition of civil society was not merely a short-lived relic of some premodern political understanding. Internalized, it became essential to the vision of civil society that de-veloped in America, for "if the Calvinist community of saints was no longer a viable social model by the end of the seventeenth century, a community of individualized moral agents pursuing the social good in conformity to the 'will of God' definitely was, at least in John Locke's vision of civil society." In the next section we shall see "just how central this internalization of the salvational doctrine of ascetic Protestantism was to the origin and development of the civil society tradition in the United States" (Seligman 25).

Hobbes's *Leviathan* had attempted to combine two inconsistent social tendencies: community bonds (to be fused in the absolute power of a sovereign) and increasing individualism, which makes each person an "owner" of himself or herself in an atomized society. The emphasis on ownership relations became central in Locke, and set the trajectory for modern social relations—a trajectory whose agenda still drives us today, in the commodification that economic globalization continues to extend to all corners of the earth and all aspects of human life. But Locke's transcendent method for grounding civil society became intellectually questionable as Deism distanced God ever further from human affairs. The commercial relationships that Locke emphasized needed to be justified in a more this-worldly fashion that disengaged our moral concerns from theology. If the validation could no longer be found outside, it would have to be found somewhere inside us, in an inner-worldliness that may or may not actually serve the unifying role we seek from it.

More than ever before, this emphasized the distinction between one's public role and private life. When the source of morality and human bonds lay beyond this world, in some transcendent vision of the social order, their distinction was largely irrelevant for living a good life. When the moral basis of society must be located in this world, however, the distinction between public and private, between the individual and society, becomes the fundamental tension that must somehow be resolved in order to have a truly civil society (Seligman 30). *This is still our problem with civil society, because the tension between individual freedom and the common good has never been resolved.* Market relations emphasize self-interested freedom often at the price of any common good; largely in reaction to that, fascist and state socialist regimes emphasized what they defined as the common good, at the price of individual liberty to define and pursue one's own good. The political history of the twentieth century is a story of the failure of such attempts, but we have so far been unable to discover any other social glue to replace the unifying moral bond that God provided.

One notable attempt was made by the eighteenth-century Scottish Enlightenment, which tried to revive the classical notion of human interaction as itself an ethical sphere of development. Emphasizing property relations, as Locke had done, made market exchange a neutral arena of conduct, but in fact markets are inescapably moral in their effects on participants. Humans do not become fully human in isolation; our capacities, including our ethical qualities and intellectual abilities, develop only in our social relationships.

The strongest case for this was made by Adam Ferguson in *An Essay on the History of Civil Society* (1767), which discovers the roots of human sociability (and thus civil society) in our general capacity to see the world through someone else's eyes and put ourselves in another's place. Property and self-interest are an unsatisfactory explanation for social bonds, for people are often motivated by generosity, altruism, and group solidarity. Above all else, we are moral creatures: individual competition and instrumental reason cannot by themselves provide us with a truly civilized life. Innate sociability is what enables us to live with others. We naturally want to help them and they naturally want to help us, which leads to mutual benefit. Although selfishness often divides us, there is nonetheless a stronger "habit of the soul by which we consider ourselves as but a part of some beloved community, and as but individual members of some society, whose general welfare is to us the supreme object of zeal, and the great rule of our conduct" (Ferguson 51).

Ferguson was skeptical of social-contract theories and refused to speculate on a prepolitical state of nature. It makes no sense to draw social conclusions from a time when humans were without social bonds, for without those we are not human. We are born into civil society and cannot conceive of ourselves without it.

This approach is consistent with contemporary social psychology, which since George Herbert Mead has emphasized how our sense of self is formed in relationship with others. It is also is attractive to Buddhism, since the Buddhist refutation of all self-existing individuality emphasizes our interdependence or "interpermeation."[10] As expressed in the Hua-yen metaphor of Indra's net, everything (including each of us) lacks self-existence because each "empty" node of Indra's infinite web reflects all the other nodes. I have no life apart from those other nodes, being both their cause and their effect.

So there may be much in Ferguson and the Scottish school that can be recovered. In its day, however, this sort of philosophical anthropology, unsupported by any transcendent grounding, turned out to be a fragile synthesis that could not resist the rapid growth of a new economy based on individual self-interest, accompanied by the spread of a more calculative and instrumental understanding of our rationality. Despite his firm belief that "bands of affection" were the only basis for a durable civil society, Ferguson realized that such moral ties would not be able to withstand the pressure of markets and their commodification of human relations.

An instrumental understanding of rationality had become irresistible after David Hume's *Treatise of Human Nature* (1739–1740), which sharply distinguishes fact from values, what *is* from what *ought to be*. This amounted to an attack on the moral sentiments and innate human benevolence that Ferguson would later use to found his concept of civil society. Hume posited a strict boundary between what reason could ascertain and what motivated human action, which was our personal "sentiments and affections." Although they could work together they could never join together: reasoning has no role in evaluating our motivations, for those are determined by our passions, which themselves have no knowledge of any universal truth about what "should be."

> Morals excite passions, and produce or prevent actions. Reason
> of itself is utterly impotent in this particular. The rules of morality,
> therefore, are not conclusions of our Reason. (Hume 185)

This approach denied the possibility of a common good. Anything we consider as moral has no foundation in reason, so a common good cannot exist except as the sum of individual goods based on our own individual preferences. The only role for reason is an instrumental one, to help us identify our interests and show us the best way to satisfy them. Transcendent morality and universal benevolence are replaced by habit and empirical experience as the criterion of truth. This philosophically grounds the speculations of Hobbes and Locke: Civil society is nothing more than a conventional arrangement for pursuing our personal goals (Seligman 37–39).

The power of reasoning that Thomas Aquinas had tentatively liberated from theological demands (because confident that it would support such beliefs), and Reason "the great creator" for Winstanley, become unrecognizable in Hume's narrowed calculative understanding, which today has become our collective understanding of reason: It is something we use to get what we want. The global success of capitalist economic relations would hardly have been possible without this reductive understanding of our mental faculties and their proper function. By devoting ourselves to making and consuming money, then, we are simply doing what it is our nature to do, for that is what our reasoning abilities are for. There is no place here for a different role—Socratic dialogue, for example, or a late Heideggerian meditative understanding of thinking. We think that our hardheaded this-worldliness has escaped the futile speculations of metaphysics, but in this way too we unconsciously live according to a diminished philosophical understanding of ourselves, which we now view as natural. This instrumentalization extends the modern tendency to commercialize everything: Restricting our thinking abilities to this way of using them subordinates the "used" (calculative reasoning) to the "user" (motivating desires). With Hobbes and Locke we became "owners" of ourselves; with Hume we complete the process by splitting reasoning from valuing, thus commodifying part of our own minds.[11]

The fruit of Hume's philosophy and Locke's politics was Adam Smith's economics. In *The Wealth of Nations* (1776) we find for the first time our modern conception of civil society as a sphere of self-interested and self-regulating economic activity, apart from the state but sympathetically supported by it. Rational self-interest replaces any shared vision of a cosmic order. Smith's world is a fully commodified one. Civil society is constituted by three components of production—land, labor, and capital—that yield three types of reward: rent, wages, and profits. Contrary to Ferguson, people assist each other only on the basis of mutual self-interest, but it turns out that that is enough. Smith's notion of an "invisible hand" provided "a powerful economic and moral argument for the untrammeled pursuit of individual self-interest and announced the appearance of civil society organized around 'economic man'. . . . The drive for wealth and economic advantage was now the force behind all human activity in civil society" (Ehrenberg 102).

> [Every individual] intends only his own gain, and he is in this, as in many other cases, led by an invisible hand to promote an end which was no part of his intention. Nor is it always the worse for the society that it was no part of it. By pursuing his own interest he frequently promotes that of the society more effectually than when he really intends to promote it. (*Wealth of Nations* 292)[12]

Today this is our great myth, providing the foundation for our notion of civil society by explaining how we live today: why we cooperate and why we do not. Yet Smith's understanding of it was more nuanced than that of many modern "Smithians." He never used the term laissez-faire and he expected government expenses to increase as civilization advanced (J. Muller 2 and *passim*). He believed that only the influence of society transforms us into moral beings, yet he had no illusions that self-interest works to the benefit of everyone, or even the majority: "Wherever there is great property, there is great inequality. For one very rich man, there must be at least five hundred poor, and the affluence of the few supposes the indigence of the many" (*Wealth of Nations,* 407). The role of a "sympathetic" state includes protecting power and extreme inequality.

In his lesser-known *Theory of Moral Sentiments* (1759) Smith notices how market exchange tends to corrode the very shared community values it needs to restrain its excesses: honesty, thrift, self-discipline, etc. He argues that the moral basis of our existence is the need that each has for recognition and consideration on the part of others. To be noticed with sympathy and approbation is the driving force behind "all the toil and bustle of the world . . . the end [goal] of avarice and ambition, of the pursuit of wealth" (50). This roots economic activity in something noneconomic. As with Ferguson, the marketplace—the realm of civil society for Smith—is not simply a neutral place where already morally constituted individuals meet to exchange; it is itself an "ethical arena" in which we become who we are through the perceptions that others have of us (Seligman 27).

This serves to remind us of something that modern economists (but not advertisers!) tend to forget: Most market exchange is for satisfying psychological "needs," not physical ones. Smith's point about our preoccupation with individual recognition and approval can also be understood in lack terms: the need of our "empty" ego-selves to feel *more real.* As we grow up, our sense of self develops by internalizing the attention of others, for they name us and treat us as if we are real. Since that sense of self remains an ungrounded psychological construct, however, we can never get enough attention to feel *really* real. The more individualized a person becomes, the more one must cope by using one's "inner" psychological resources, and the more "empty" one therefore feels. There are different ways to try to fill up this emptiness, but by no coincidence most of them involve the attention and approval of others.

Smith also has a somewhat Buddhist understanding of the way our dissatisfaction with the present motivates the "desire of bettering our condition." He sees this dissatisfaction as natural to human beings, a permanent feature of our lives experienced even in the womb. It is crucial for economic development and, insofar as it motivates the growth of our character, for moral development as well. This is why the competitive drive for wealth and economic success becomes the force behind all human activity in civil society. As with Hume, reason plays no role in regulating this self-aggrandizement or in balancing the relationship between private desire and public welfare—even though, as Smith acknowledges, *there is something delusive about our economic goals.* In the "languor of disease and the weariness of old age," the moral insignificance of worldly goods appears in its true light, for neither our possessions nor even the beauty and utility admired in "any production of art" prove capable of bringing true happiness in such adversity. However, we seldom look upon the matter in this "abstract and philosophical light" and "it is well that nature imposes upon us in this manner": "It is this deception which rouses and keeps in continual motion the industry of mankind" (*Theory of Moral Sentiments*[13]).

So the worldly fruit of our economic pursuits brings us no lasting happiness. Rather than seeking happiness in another way, however, this child of the Enlightenment encourages the deception, which is necessary to motivate our social and personal development. In other words, for Adam Smith the economic and civilizing glue of society is ultimately based upon a collective lie, or something we all agree to repress: that our self-interested economic activity can never give us what we seek from it.

If we reflect on why Smith—and we—accept this deception, the answer would seem to be: now that God is dead, or too far away to be relevant anymore, all we can do is distract ourselves from our mortality, and make the best of a bad thing by pursuing our own economic advantage. Our lack cannot be solved, so let's divert ourselves while we can.

Here the contrast with Buddhism is sharp, for the Buddhist path involves acknowledging our mortality and using that as our teacher. According to the foundational myth, Shakyamuni's spiritual quest was motivated by his shocked encounter with an ill man, an old man, and then a corpse. "Does this happen to everyone? To *me* too?" he asked his attendant—precisely the realization of our mortality that nature and Smith conspire for us to forget. But Sakyamuni's quest allows our thinking a spiritual role that Hume's and Smith's instrumental reason has no place for.

THE AMERICAN RELIGION

Why didn't socialism ever catch on in the United States? Because America had its own civil religion, to use Robert Bellah's term. Its ideology precluded the development of a socialist movement by offering a more individualist explanation of what is wrong with us and how to solve it.

By Hegel's time it had become evident that self-regulating markets increased not only wealth but poverty and inequality. His realization that the new economy could not solve this problem inspired his turn toward the state. "In the end, civil society is an alienated, unfree, and unjust sphere, for a power alien to the individual and over which he has no control determines whether his needs will be fulfilled. . . . The anarchy of a sphere of self-serving proprietors cannot produce integration, rationality, universality, and freedom" (Ehrenberg 126–28). The only thing that can reconcile the antagonisms created by the new civil society is the State, the locus of our highest collective ends and the final realization of Spirit in history.

Marx rejected this metaphysical fantasy, for the simple reason that by *his* time it was becoming obvious that the state was being shaped by civil society rather than vice versa. He looked forward to a future society where noncommodified human relationships would recover the communal bonds of a precapitalist past. Yet his alternative vision of civil society is best understood as a capitalist heresy because it shares the same economic presuppositions about what constitutes the social glue. Marx's materialist theory of history left no transformative role either for ideology (religion is an opiate) or for civil society itself. They are only effects of the technological developments and economic forces that drive our social evolution.

The communal and group-based feudal cultures of Europe resisted the full development of a civil society based upon autonomous individual agents. That resistance became socialism and syndicalism, which rejected the new class system. But appeals to the universal solidarity of an international working class were not persuasive in the United States, which had no feudal past with which to resist an identity founded on self-interested individualism. As Walter Dean Burnham put it, "no feudalism, no socialism" (in Seligman 104). In their place, "Americanism" provided "a highly attenuated, conceptualized, platonic impersonal attraction to a handful of notions—democracy, liberty, opportunity, to all of which the American adheres rationalistically, much like a socialist adheres to his socialism" (Sampson 426). According to Seligman, the components of this core ideology can be traced back to our sectarian Protestant origins—in particular, to the religious vision of the New England Puritans.

The key to understanding this is the question: What created the individual? What empowered us to break away from communal norms and become self-interested, able to decide for ourselves what to value and how to seek it? Again, the answer is found in a *religious* development: in the way that the source of moral (and hence social) order was relocated, from a transcendent God to one's own "inner light." This was not a rejection of the transcendent, for to become empowered as individuals, people must first be invested with transcendental qualities. As Seligman puts it, "our notion of the ethically autonomous individual— upon which the idea of civil society rested—is predicated on the introjection within the individual of a particular dimension of grace which had previously been defined in otherworldly terms" (67). Luther could stand up to the Church because he introjected God: He was doing what God wanted him to do. This "individual-in-relation-to-God" (Troeltsch) was perhaps the main consequence of the Reformation, and obviously its consequences were not originally secular. Now not only monks but everyone was called upon to be in the world but not of it, to attain a Grace that transcended this-worldly concerns.

Here we pick up again the threads of the Puritan movement, which failed to purify English society but had another chance in the New England across the sea. Calvinism broke down the traditional solidarities of a corporate Christianity by emphasizing a new kind of tie among people that replaced blood with religious belief. In place of kinship and localized identities, social solidarity became based on shared ideological commitment to the Reformation—literally, to the task of reforming society. It was formalized in covenants that created a "community of saints," with "each standing in unmediated relation to the source of transcendent power and authority." This implied a new type of authority: ministry was based on consent, mutual agreement, and the equality of believers and ministers before God (Seligman 69).

Far from liberating individuals to pursue their own self-interest, this new moral authority involved increased personal responsibility to pursue a state of spiritual perfection within this-worldly institutions. And the inner grace shared by covenanted members must be spread outside, in order to construct a Holy Commonwealth that would realize God's grace within the world. In place of ecclesiastical rule, however, the

New England Puritans distinguished civil from religious institutions, each helping the other for the mutual welfare of both. Only in this way could a pure social order be maintained, uncorrupted by history.

The law of nature was common to all societies, but the law of grace was now taken to be the special promise of New England, which had an "errand in the wilderness": to realize God's Kingdom in the Promised Land. This presupposed a community of *saints* who had experienced regeneration and the infusion of Grace. Again, however, it didn't work out as they hoped. Instead of converting the rest of the New World, after 1633 there was a decline in conversion experiences within the communities themselves. The second generation, which came of age in the 1650s, did not seem to have the same experience of saving grace as its fathers had. Economic growth around that time also contributed to breaking down the group solidarities of the founders. As communal life fragmented, there was a noticeable decline in commitment to the original values.

This led to a crisis that could maintain the old model of social order only by radically redefining its spiritual ideals. By the end of the seventeenth century the normative order, which before had been collectively determined by the covenanted churches of regenerate saints, was seen to reside *within each individual soul,* and this allowed a larger but looser group sense of *national* identity to develop. "The Puritan sect as an instance of the 'particularism of grace,' defining membership in the 'Holy Commonwealth,' gave way to a secularized form of civic virtue embracing the whole of the collective" (Seligman 77). Grace was interiorized into individual conscience. The old distinction between Nature and Grace, the World and the Church, the unregenerate and the regenerate, became a distinction within each individual, which meant that the moral order now rested not on the collective Grace of the community but on the moral behavior of each person, who carried within the sources of salvation as well as damnation. The communal approach to overcoming lack, in a church of covenanted saints, had not worked, so responsibility devolved upon each person to deal with his or her own lack in an inner moral struggle between good and evil. Grace and lack became privatized.

In practice, this meant that criteria for church membership in New England came to rest less on an avowed experience of saving grace and more on the moral uprightness of each individual. The secular consequences of this turned out to be immense, for this invested the individual with an absolute moral foundation unknown in Europe, where personal liberty was traditionally limited by the common good. For the first time in history, the individual as autonomous moral agent became the fundamental component of civil society and the political order.

This implied a new type of community. Early in the eighteenth century this new moral order was modified by adding the more secular principles of reason based on natural law. By the middle of the century politics and government were founded on a new trinity: God, Nature (natural law), and Reason. Together these transformed the "Holy Commonwealth" into a civil millennial tradition that defined the "Children of Israel" not in terms of a covenanted church but in terms of civic membership in the nation.

Again, this new consciousness was not really secular; rather, it *sacralized the nation*. "Enthusiasm," earlier an abusive term associated with evangelical millennialism, became "enthusiasm of liberty," a "noble infirmity," and a source of national pride, part of the developing discourse of civic virtue. "It is this unique interweaving of religious and civil traditions that characterized the civil society tradition in the United States, setting it off from those of other nation-states" and leading to Americans' sense of their exceptionalism. John Adams declared: "I have always considered the settlement of America with reverence and wonder, as the opening of a grand scene and design in Providence for the illumination of the ignorant and the emancipation of the slavish part of mankind all over the earth" (1977, 2). America's pristine wilderness allowed a new vision of man and nature woven with Biblical images: the New Canaan, the promised land, a new paradigm of a paradise "emancipated from history" (Seligman 79–84).

By the end of the eighteenth century American settlers agreed that they were a chosen people, and the destiny of their republic was identified with the course of redemptive history. As the main agent of God's activity in history, "America had become both the locus and the instrument of the great consummation. The equation of the Kingdom of God with the American nation . . . substituted the nation for the Church" (Seligman 85–86). The United States would show the rest of the world how to overcome lack. In place of the Puritans' Christian story, there was now the foundational myth of the sacred American nation to which Herman Melville (like many others, including Abraham Lincoln and Ralph Waldo Emerson) assigned the task of redemption:

> We Americans are the peculiar, chosen people—the Israel of our time; we bear the arc of the Liberties of the world. . . .

> God has given to us, for future inheritance, the broad do-
> mains of the political pagans, that shall yet come and lie
> down under the shade of our ark, without bloody hands
> being lifted . . . And let us always remember that with our-
> selves, almost for the first time in the history of the earth,
> national selfishness is unbounded philanthropy; for we can
> not do a good to America but we give alms to the world.
> (Melville)[14]

How blessed must America be, for even its selfishness to benefit the
whole world! Of course, less religious versions of this attitude are not
hard to find today—e.g., in the fervor with which we promote economic globalization, which is really in everyone's best interests, even if
some other countries do not realize it yet. We still see it as our duty
to export to the rest of the world our model of how to end lack: not
only democracy and free trade but our consumerist lifestyle.

This new national identity was based upon a new personal identity: the individual's freedom to pursue his own self-interest. Originally
this was understood in moral terms, as we saw, but growing emphasis
on reason and natural law tranformed the grace of a universal God
(already internalized as an inner light) into the still-transcendental qualities
of a universal Reason, which was able to realize our fundamental and
inalienable rights to life, liberty, and the pursuit of happiness. This too
was quite new, for English laws had recognized only inherited rights.

> In the closest connection with the great religious political
> movement out of which the American democracy was born,
> there arose the conviction that there exists a right not con-
> ferred upon the citizen but inherent in man, that acts of
> conscience and expressions of religious conviction stand
> inviolable over against the state as the exercise of a higher
> right. This right so long suppressed is not "inheritance," is
> nothing handed down from their fathers, as the rights and
> liberties of Magna Charta and of the other English enact-
> ments—not the State but the Gospel proclaimed it. (Jellinek
> 74–75)

If the individual were to be truly autonomous, the source of all moral
value, he required a firmer foundation in natural law and in the rationality that discovers that law. That individual became secularized when

"Reason replaced the Deity as locus of universalist values and injunctions in both the ethical and the social (interpersonal) sphere." To review, the sequence was as follows: God became internalized as an inner light of grace; that inner light became understood in moral terms as conscience; and then that moral conscience became Reason, originally that which enables us to apprehend God, the source of our natural goodness. The individual became secular when that reason became calculative and instrumental. The result was "a new idea of the universal no longer rooted in a transcendent and otherworldly sphere but in the immanent this-worldly workings of Reason" (Seligman 92–94).

But what has that development done to society? "Society itself is no longer a universal but exists only as a derivative of the individual as subject" (Seligman 95). As Margaret Thatcher famously expressed it in a different context, there is no such thing as society. And that, in a nutshell, is our problem. How can we have a social whole that would *be* a whole, that would overcome the particularity of its members without negating that particularity (as, for example, fascism does)? What binding ties are there on a society of individuals whose relationships and contracts emphasize their autonomy and independence over their fundamental communality? In short, how does one get a truly civil society out of a collection of independent self-interested individuals?

> We have seen that as long as this attempt was carried out in transcendent terms, either with John Locke or in the natural law philosophy of eighteenth-century America (which was uniquely tied to a secularized virtue and the traditions of ascetic-Protestantism), such a synthesis was possible. With the loss of the transcendent dimension and its replacement solely by Reason (and thus, in the civil sphere the ties of market exchange and strategic or instrumental action), the moorings of a unified social vision broke loose (Seligman 99).

The loss of a transcendent religious dimension means there is nothing left that binds us together. *Our individuality means that we now view civil society as largely irrelevant to our lack, also understood solely in individual terms.* Hence the overweening importance of my personal success in an increasingly competitive social environment. If my lack is now only my own problem, there is no reason for me to cooperate with others, except insofar as that helps me get the things I want. Morality, reason, and value reside within me. This voids all shared public spaces and events of any value in themselves. "More than anywhere else, America is characterized by a community of absolute subjects, each 'ontologically' self-contained, existing in a state of 'metaphysical equality' and united only by the logic of rational exchange" (Seligman 135). De Tocqueville noticed this even during his 1830–1831 visit:

> The first thing that strikes the observation is an innumerable multitude of men all equal and alike, incessantly endeavouring to procure the petty and paltry pleasures with which they glut their lives. Each of them, living apart, is as a stranger to the fate of the rest—his children and his private friends constitute to him the whole of mankind; as for the rest of his fellow-citizens, he is close to them, but he sees them not; he touches them, but he feels them not; he exists but in himself and for himself alone; and if his kindred still remain to him, he may be said at any rate to have lost his country. (*Tocqueville* II 338)

Of course, this type of civil society and market exchange was not what Adam Ferguson had in mind when he referred to human sociability, or even what Adam Smith meant when he wrote about our need for others' attention and approbation. For them, the arena of civil society is where we are morally constituted and validated; in lack terms, *our participation in civil society is important for resolving our* lack. But de Tocqueville's society of strangers follows inexorably from Hume's distinction between value and reason: reason in the public sphere is seen as value neutral and instrumental, while value is restricted to the individual and therefore the private sphere. This works against the very concept of a civil society. "The whole force of the civil society tradition is in fact aimed against any restriction of reason to what we would now call, following Weber, instrumental rationality" (Seligman 34). The victory of that calculative rationality has been the slow disintegration of civil society.

As God faded away, the path was cleared for the United States to conduct its grand social experiment in self-interested "free enterprise." But today the question becomes ever more pressing for us: How can such a collection of individuals constitute a civil society?

Seligman's own solution to this quandry involves a new appreciation of social trust as essential. Modern societies have universalized trust in terms of citizenship, welfare entitlements, etc., but these tend to vitiate the mutuality and communality of the interpersonal trust he has in mind: people networks based on ethnic relations, local communities, shared religious faith, and other traditions. He realizes that they will not be easy to revive, for they are premodern and precontractual (171–172).[15]

Such networks of trust continue to be eroded by our tendency to commodify everything, including human relationships. What social forces remain today to resist this commodification? We can answer that question by asking another: Historically, what institution has done the most to encourage interpersonal trust?

## A "NEW" CIVIL SOCIETY?

There is another important strand of thinking about civil society, one not yet discussed but usually the first to come to mind today: civil society as an intermediate sphere of voluntary associations standing between the individual and the state. According to de Tocqueville's conception, these voluntary associations focus on the pursuit of private matters and are not generally concerned with political or economic affairs. Nevertheless, they are essential for the ways they fuse personal interest with the common good. They protect individuals from the state because they are based upon localism and particularism; they also overcome the tendency of self-interested individuals to produce a society of strangers disconnected from one another.

The contemporary version of this is communitarianism,[16] which Ehrenberg subjects to a scathing critique for ignoring economic issues. He focuses on the negative effects of major changes in work and income. Declining involvement in the political process is caused by increasing income disparity; political participation continues to be heavily biased toward the top. The replacement of secure government and unionized manufacturing labor with nonunion, low-wage service and retail jobs has had a profoundly destructive effect. "Perhaps the 'unravelling of civic America' is due to changes in the nature of work rather than peoples' television habits or their individualism." Many people are too exhausted or busy or frustrated to engage in traditional comunity activities. Many of the intractable problems in inner-city neighborhoods— crime, drugs, family dissolution, welfare dependence—are fundamentally a consequence of the disappearance of work. Ehrenberg points at widening material disparities caused by "the largest transfer of wealth from the poor to the rich in human history." In 1999 nearly half of American families had a lower real income than in 1973 (245–59).

Tocqueville is not particularly helpful in these conditions. Categories derived from the face-to-face democracy of early nineteenth-century New England towns cannot furnish a credible model for public life in a highly commodified mass society marked by unprecedented levels of economic inequality. . . . [But de Tocqueville's] notion of civil society performs a normalizing function by making it difficult to see the economic roots of contemporary problems and blinding us to the political avenues for their resolution (Ehrenberg 234).

"In one of the most thoroughly commercialized social orders in human history, civil society is supposed to limit the intrusive state, attenuate the ravages of the market, reinvigorate a moribund public sphere, rescue beleaguered families, and revitalize community life." That is just too much to ask. In place of communitarianism's "nostalgic and moralizing infatuation with localism," only collective political action can address the deepening inequality caused by gigantic concentrations of private wealth and power (Ehrenberg 200, 250).

Ehrenberg's critique is persuasive, but his own political solution less so. Our problem today is not simply that civil society is under attack; more precisely, it is that we have at least three incompatible visions of civil society that seem to be engaged in a life-or-death struggle. One of them is intermediate voluntary associations, which, as Ehrenberg points out, have been suffering from the radical economic changes of the last few decades. The second is more difficult to see, because it has become so naturalized that we are often unaware it assumes a particular vision of how we should live together: the Locke/ Hume/Smith understanding of society as bound together by markets, which (for Locke and Hume) are in themselves morally neutral. Because we think of this as an *economic* system, we tend to overlook its profound social consequences.

The third is leftist or progressive visions derived from socialism, which seek to replace capitalist exploitation and commodification with more just and equal social arrangements. Despite personal sympathies with this third view, I am concerned that the need to reduce income disparities—which certainly needs to be done—may cause us to go to the other extreme and focus too much on an economic understanding of civil society. The usual leftist suspicion of entrenched religious institutions is well deserved, given their dismal record of complicity with oppressive economic and political elites. But civil society cannot be healthy unless there is something that binds us together, and, as we have seen, historically that unifying force in the West has been rooted in a religious vision. That particular Christian understanding of the world may no longer be persuasive to us, yet contemporary accounts of society that ignore or deprecate all religious perspectives do so at the risk of not being able to account for the spiritual (or ultimate existential) concerns that still motivate people.

Does that suggest another alternative to these three conceptions of civil society? I have argued that Anglo-American civil society and social thought have religious roots because they originated when our sense of lack came to be understood in a radically different way. A transcendent, otherworldly solution to lack was replaced by a covenanted project to reform this world. This new project was not secular, but its failure eventually led to a more secular understanding of the "inner light," which transformed from grace to conscience and then to a rationality that our self-interest could employ instrumentally. In this process, the transcendent social glue dissolved. Where are new bonds to be found today? To what extent do those religious origins survive as unacknowledged foundations that need to be revivified if civil society is to be revived?

The point is not merely that Anglo-American civil society has theological origins; our society remains theological in the sense that its values and institutions cannot help being based upon some ultimate view about our human nature—in my terms, about the nature of our lack and how that is to be overcome. This bedrock view may be taken for granted, but our self-understanding and life projects are nonetheless determined by it. Seventeenth-century discussions of the Bible produced the basic alternatives we still debate today in more secularized terms: Is human nature evil, in need of restraint? Or does an oppressive society deform our natural goodness? If we want to break out of the stultifying standoff between them, we need to return to the basic existential issues and rethink them afresh. The most fundamental one, I suggest, is our sense of lack. In order to know what to do about our lack, we need to come to some social understanding of what it is and what causes it. The question is not whether or not to do "theology," but whether our ultimate commitments are conscious or unconscious. Do we understand our deepest motivations, or are we their victims?

Seligman concludes that the problem of civil society is (re)constituting interpersonal trust, but he has no illusions about this being easy. "It is, finally, the intractable difficulties in theorizing any concrete and meaningful criteria of trust in modern, rationalized, and highly differentiated societies that make all contemporary (Western) attempts to reconstitute civil society as idea, or, more pointedly, as ideal, so difficult" (13). What does trust inhere in? What motivates us to commit ourselves to something greater than our own individual self-interest? English civil society originated in the seventeenth century, out a collective spiritual/moral purpose. The Puritans were willing to sacrifice themselves for His cause because they did not doubt that they were God's agents on earth.

This suggests that, for civil society to thrive, it must be based on something more than the pursuit of individual self-interest, on something more than intermediate associations that work to limit state power. The widespread assumption that civil society is a morally indifferent sphere of self-interested cooperation, and that the common good is merely a sum of our private goods, must be questioned. This is something religions are well-placed to do, for it is their role to offer alternative explanations of what our lack is and how to address it. Ferguson and Smith understood that the social sphere is an ethical arena where we become who we are through others' perceptions of us; the Puritan version of this emphasized our spiritual and moral responsibility for others. In my contemporary Buddhist terms, civil society must again be recognized as that dimension of our lives where we work together to reform society so that it does not objectify greed, ill will, and ignorance in institutions, but instead empowers us to understand and address our lack.

These hopes may be utopian, but without the nourishment of such "millennialist" roots, perhaps we cannot expect civil society to revive.[17]

SIX

# PREPARING FOR SOMETHING
# THAT NEVER HAPPENS

When I think of all the books I have read, wise words heard,
anxieties given to parents, . . . of hopes I have had, all life weighed
in the balance of my own life seems to me a preparation for
something that never happens.

—William Butler Yeats

Yeats died in 1939. Today in Japan, where I write this book, toddlers
take entrance exams to get into the "best" kindergartens, because the
best kindergartens help you get into the best primary schools, which
help you get into the best middle schools, which help you get into the
best high schools, which help you get into the best universities, which
help you get hired by the best corporations, where assuredly your
difficulties are far from over. . . .

Some of the obvious problems with these practices have been
publicized—e.g., teenage suicides owing to academic pressure, an increasing number of students so traumatized they refuse to attend school—
but the greater tragedy is whole generations of young people so burned
out preparing for "examination hell" that many of them are brain dead
by the ripe age of nineteen. Since the sole reason for studying is to pass
university entrance exams (your university, not your academic performance while there, determines your employment prospects), there is

171

little incentive to study once you are in—and, of course, any personal motivation for an education, any joy in learning, has been eliminated in the process.

Needless to say, this is only one example of a more widespread problem with education today. Those of us who teach humanities soon realize that our role is not Socratic: among other problems, the structure of higher education makes that almost impossible. The system of grading, credits, and degrees is a prime example of what can be called *means-ends reversal.* Inevitably one learns to study in order to pass exams, get credit, earn degrees, win fellowships, and so forth, rather than understanding the process as encouraging an *e-ducere* "leading forth" imperfectly (if at all) measurable in those terms. We readily acknowledge the intrinsic value of lifelong learning, yet this inversion is now so deeply rooted that it is taken for granted and one mentions it at the risk of being dismissed as naïve. Bertrand Russell already noticed the problem many decades ago: education today has become one of the main obstacles to intelligence and freedom of thought.

This chapter, however, is not another polemic on what is wrong with our educational systems. I want to reflect more generally on the duality between means and ends—not the usual problem of eggs and omelette, but their divergence. My concern is with the ways contemporary culture has become so preoccupied with means that it loses ends—or, more precisely, they become inverted, in that means, because they never culminate in an ends, in effect have come to constitute our ends.

Heidegger does not use the same vocabulary but this way of formulating our problem is consistent with his later thinking about technology, which for him too is a means that has become more than a means. *Technik* is the particular "way of revealing" whereby Being manifests itself today. "Everywhere everything is ordered to stand by, to be immediately at hand, indeed to stand there just so that it may be on call for a further ordering." He calls this *Bestand,* "the standing reserve." *Technik* discloses all beings as raw material to be exploited by the human subject; the subject also becomes raw material for exploitation, as we too become objectified by our own objectifications. The point of *Bestand* is not so much that our activities require such a "standing reserve" as that, for reasons we do not necessarily understand clearly, we want to have such a standing reserve always available. That is, we desire limitless convertible means that may be directed to any ends, even as—or all the more because—we no longer know what goals to seek, what values to value. In this way *Bestand* too loses ends, for *Technik,* being unable to provide an answer to our ultimate questions about what is valuable and meaningful, has itself become our answer.

If if it is true that today "endless means" have become our common goal, the taken-for-granted value, how important is that? What are its causes, and are there really any alternatives today? We begin by considering what Max Weber (1864-1920) wrote about the rationalization and disenchantment of the modern world. Weber himself noted that the "formal rationality" preeminent today deals only with means and cannot answer our ultimate questions about goals and values. This aspect of his thought is familiar, yet just as important is another, lesser known side of his social theory: his analysis of our reactive flights into subjectivity—innerworldly responses to the rationalization of the world that do not escape the problem but aggravate it. Weber's study of the origins of capitalism suggests not only that it had religious roots but that it may still retain a religious character. Then must any "solution" to the rationalization and disenchantment of the world also have something of a religious character?

Part two turns to Weber's colleague Georg Simmel (1858–1918) in order to contemplate the example par excellence of means-ends inversion: money. Simmel's magnum opus *The Philosophy of Money* contains, appropriately, the most profound reflections on the means-ends split in modern culture. It also challenges our understanding of their bifurcation by arguing that the distinction between them, including our quest for the meaning of life, is quite a recent cultural development. Our yearning for an ultimate is a product of our dissatisfaction with the possibilities contemporary life provides, because of its sacrifice of substantial values for instrumental rationality. But is there any way out of this "iron cage"?

This chapter concludes with some Buddhist-related reflections on how one might respond to this problem. For Mahayana Buddhism our contemporary bifurcation between means and ends is another version of dualistic (and delusive) thinking that should be related to the more fundamental duality between subject and object. Seeing the situation in this manner will enable us to appreciate how the Buddhist deconstruction of subject-object duality points toward a way to resolve the means-ends split.

## MAX WEBER

Precisely the ultimate and most sublime values have retreated from public life either into the transcendental realm of mystic life or into the brotherliness of direct and personal human

> relations. It is not accidental that our greatest art is intimate
> and not monumental, nor is it accidental that today only
> within the smallest and most intimate circles, in personal
> human situations, in *pianissimo,* that something is pulsating
> that corresponds to the prophetic *pneuma,* which in former
> times swept through the great communities like a firebrand,
> welding them together. (Weber 155)

Today the distinction between public and private has become so absolute that we have difficulty comprehending how anything could weld
whole civilizations together. What has taken the place of prophetic
*pneuma* for us? "The fate of our times is characterized by rationalization
and intellectualization and, above all, by the 'disenchantment of the
world'" (155). *Zweckrationalitat* is better translated as a purposive-rational
or instrumental-rational orientation; its complement is *Entzauberung,*
the "de-magic-ing" of the world. *Zweckrationalitat* is a fine example of
what Ludwig Wittgenstein called family resemblances: no single characteristic is common to all the types Weber analyzed. Instrumental
rationalization is a family of separable although interrelated processes
that have different historical roots, develop in different ways and occur
at different rates, and tend to promote different interests and groups.
Examples include an increasing emphasis on calculability in various
institutions; rule-determined bureaucratic administration; the specialization and compartmentalization of knowledge; and most generally, more
impersonal control over the ways we live and the decisions we make.

Weber distinguished such formal rationality from what he called
substantive rationality. Our problem today may be described in terms
of the conflict between them. "Formal rationality refers primarily to the
*calculability of means and procedures,* substantive rationality to the *value*
(from some explicitly defined standpoint) *of ends or results*" (Brubaker
36, his italics). From the perspective of a substantive rationality whose
concern is to actualize particular goals and values, instrumental rationality can be profoundly irrational. This irreducible antagonism between the rationality of our modern social and economic order and its
irrationality from the value perspectives of equality, fraternity, love, etc.,
is for Weber "one of the most important sources of all 'social' problems."
Weber explicitly describes capitalism, his most famous example of rationalization, as involving the "domination of the end (supply meeting
demand) by the means." The purely formal nature of instrumental
rationality, its indifference to all substantive ends and values, defines

what is unique about our modern world and demonstrates what is morally and politically problematic about it (Brubaker 10).

What allows instrumental rationality to become so problematic is that today we obviously do not agree about what goals and pursuits most deserve be valued; and in this matter—which is of course the most important matter—instrumental rationality, no matter how sophisticated, cannot help us. Weber knew his Nietzsche: The fate of our culture, which has "tasted the fruit of the tree of knowledge," is "to have to know that we cannot read the meaning of the world in the results of its investigation, no matter how perfect, but must instead be in a position to create that meaning ourselves." Yet such creation tends to be frustrated by the increasingly incomprehensible complexity of the modern world, whose organization escapes questions about value and morality by objectifying human activities into more impersonal processes. The "disenchantment of the world" means not so much the debunking of magic and superstition as the tendency to devalue all mysterious and incalculable forces in favor of the knowledge "that one can, in principle, *master* all things by *calculation*." Yet this proven calculability conceals what Lawrence Scaff calls a Simmelian paradox, for

> its extension throughout culture as a possibility to be applied only "in principle" is accompanied by the *individual's* diminishing knowledge and control over all the conditions of life. We can interpret this to mean that each of us comes to be surrounded by and dependent on myriad complex "processes," from economic transactions to nuclear fission, affecting the immediate experienced world and the prospects for continuation and transformation of that world, which we individually cannot possibly comprehend, much less control. (Scaff 227)

Consider, for example, that complex of rationalized economic forces known as the equities (stock) market. If we ignore such ineliminable abuses as insider trading, it functions according to an impersonal rationality that bypasses all the ethical dimensions to the issues of how people earn their livelihood. The leveraged buyouts popular in the 1980s were often justified as beneficial to the economy, but those decisions were made according to equations that determined how much debt could be borne, not its effect on people and their communities. Economics is a moral science because the problem of who gets what is inevitably a moral issue, yet economists and their clients strive to quantify economic processes into mathematical formulae that can be calculated and manipulated as if they were as impersonally valid as Euclidean geometry. The belief that an "invisible hand" will beneficently regulate the economy, if only government intervention were removed, is an almost perfect example of formal-instrumental rationality swallowing substantive rationality; and the never-ending controversy this belief generates demonstrates Weber's point about the irresolvable antagonism between such rationality and the more substantive rationality for which such a belief is deeply irrational.

The economic example is appropriate because Weber is best known for his controversial theory that locates the origins of capitalism in the "this-worldly asceticism" of Puritan, especially Calvinist, ethics. Qualifying rather than rejecting materialistic determinism, *The Protestant Ethic and the Spirit of Capitalism* argued that "idealist" factors sometimes affect the direction of historical development. Calvinism believed in the predestination of a select number for heaven, which encouraged what became an irresistible need to determine whether one was among the chosen; such predestination made sacraments unnecessary and led to devaluation of the sacred; in its place, economic success in this world came to be accepted as the demonstration of God's favor; which created the psychological and sociological conditions for importing ascetic values from the monastery, where they had been the prerogative of religious orders, into one's worldly vocation, as one labored to prove oneself by reinvesting any surplus rather than consuming it. The crux of Weber's essay reflects on how, in this complex interweaving of materialist and idealist factors, the original intention behind an activity may eventually be transformed into something quite different:

> The Puritan *wanted* to work in a vocation; we *must* do so. For when asceticism was carried out of monastic cells into vocational life and began to dominate inner-worldly morality, it helped to build the tremendous cosmos of the modern economic order. This order is now bound to the technical and economic presuppositions of mechanical, machinelike production, which today determines with irresistible force the life-style of all individuals born into this mechanism, *not* only those directly engaged in economic enterprise, and perhaps will determine it until the last ton of fossil fuel is burned. In [Richard] Baxter's view the care for external

goods should only lie on the shoulders of the saint like "a light cloak, which can be thrown aside at any moment." But fate decreed that the cloak should become an iron cage. (trans. Scaff, 88; Weber's italics)

We are a long way from Adam Smith's invisible hand. Weber's metaphor is less sanguine: the original Calvinist vocational ethos now "prowls about in our lives like the ghost of dead religious beliefs," conquered by a rationalized civilization of large-scale production and ravenous consumption that today rests on merely mechanical foundations (in Scaff 89). In lack terms: now that our lack has been objectified into these rationalized economic and technological systems, those lack systems dominate us, rather than vice versa.

One important implication of this has already been noticed in previous chapters. Weber's sociology of religion distinguishes more legalistic religions, which adapt themselves to the world, from salvation religions more hostile to it, which obey sacred conviction rather than sacred law. The latter are often revolutionary owing to the prophecy and charisma that motivate them, and missionary because they seek to inject a new message or promise into everyday life. Their efforts to ensure the perpetuation of grace in the world require reordering the social and economic system. Weber noticed that adherents of this type of religion usually "do not enjoy inner repose because they are in the grip of inner tensions."

All this serves just as well to describe the Puritans discussed in *The Protestant Ethic,* which supports the lack claim that capitalism began as, and may still be understood as, a type of salvation religion: one that seeks to inject a new promise into an unsatisfactory world, motivated by faith in the grace of profit and with a missionary zeal to expand and "rationalize" the economic system. Weber's argument suggests that although we think of the modern world as secularized, its values (e.g., economic rationalization) are not only derived from religious ones (salvation from injecting a revolutionary new promise into daily life), they are largely the same values, albeit transformed by the loss of reference to an otherwordly dimension. Or, more precisely, these values have been distorted because our motivation is no longer otherworldly yet still future-oriented; it has become unconscious, which implies, according to psychoanalytic theory, that those values will be projected. The routinization of our lives challenges religion because our new values constitute an alternative to its traditional forms. But then the rationalization and disenchantment of the world is not so much an alternative to religion as what might be considered a heretical—and perhaps demonic—form of it.

I shall not presume to evaluate the scholarly debate that Weber's thesis continues to provoke,[1] but *if true it is a paradigm of means swallowing ends.* Puritanism initially bifurcated the means (capital accumulation) from the goal (assurance of salvation); in its preoccupation with this means the original goal became attenuated, yet inner-worldly asceticism did not disappear as God became more distant and heaven less relevant; in our modern world the original motivation has evaporated but our preoccupation with capital and profit has not disappeared with it. On the contrary, it has become our main obsession, because it remains our main hope for ending our lack. As Weber emphasizes, the ascetic vocational ethos may have lost its original meaning yet that does not make it any the less powerful. Our type of salvation still requires a future-orientation.

The psychic toll of such a perpetual future-orientation, of this means which never reaches fulfillment in an ends, is not difficult to imagine. So it is no surprise that modernity is also characterized by compensations for the increasing rationalization of the world. In reaction to its objectivity and impersonality, there has developed what Weber called a "subjectivist culture" that attempts to redeem us by cultivating an *Innerlichkeit* inwardness. Traditionally religion has offered whatever salvation has been necessary, but the loss of belief in a "higher" world has removed that avenue of escape without eliminating our psychological need for a redemption from this world. The nineteenth century found a temporary alternative in the Hegelian and Spenglerian creeds of social evolution, yet by Weber's day liberal historicist belief in progress was being discredited and replaced by "value spheres" that sought an inner-worldly redemption. A new place of refuge was discovered or invented: what might be called "hypertrophied subjectivity." In various essays Weber focused on three such spheres whose "irrationality" (or nonrationality) we seize upon as a relief from the world's seemingly inexorable rationalization: an absolute ethics of "brotherliness," which for many of his contemporaries would be embodied in socialism; aestheticism; and eroticism.

The problem with brotherliness as an absolutist ethics is that, unless still rooted in religious, otherworldly imperatives, it is plagued by a dilemma. One must choose between idealistically hoping to end all forms of domination or accepting the expediencies necessary for effective political action. "If the former, then one must be prepared to live with the maddening incongruities between ideal and real. If the latter, then one must be prepared to live with the diabolic uncertainties of responsibility for consequences of action" (Scaff 98–99). Concern for results entails the loss of redemptive purity, but purity can be preserved only by withdrawing into a subjectivity that becomes that much more inner-worldly as it becomes more alienated from an impure world increasingly preoccupied with results and efficiency.

Like ethics, the other two value spheres, art and eros, originally were closely associated with religion, but today they too have become autonomous. The more we self-consciously elevate them into absolutes, and the more we understand them to preserve "the most irrational and thereby real kernel of life," the more aesthetic and erotic pursuits have taken over "the function of a this-worldly *salvation* from the routines of everyday life and, above all, from the increasing pressures of theoretical and practical rationalism." Chapter Three has already discussed the importance of romantic love for our lack today. Weber, like Simmel, had some contact with the aesthetic circle of Stefan George and he observed with disapproval how George developed into a "prophet" of aestheticism. Simmel, himself somewhat of an aestheticist, noticed that one who lives in more direct contact with nature may enjoy its charms yet "lacks that distance from nature that is the basis for aesthetic contemplation and the root of that quiet sorrow, that feeling of yearning estrangement and of a lost paradise that characterizes the romantic response to nature."

Simmel's insight becomes even more penetrating when we extrapolate it, to consider not only whether our valuation of aesthetic experience but whether our very notion of aesthetic experience might be modernist—that is, historically conditioned by the same social forces that have disenchanted the world. The implication is that *our aesthetic sensitivity to music, poetry, painting, etc., has developed in response to (and reciprocally encouraged) the de-aestheticization of the rationalized everyday world.* We appreciate various types of art in the way we do because certain types of "bracketed" sensory experience have been privileged, and our responsiveness to them has hypertrophied, at the same time as the rest of our sensory experience has been devalued. Kant's famous definition characterizes aesthetic experience as nonintentional and disinterested, in sharp contrast with the utilitarian, means-ends preoccupations of daily life; is this less a definition than a description of our modern construction of aesthetic experience?

Such a possibility suggests a similarly disturbing question about brotherliness: has our preoccupation with a purist personal ethics also developed in reaction to (and in its turn encouraged) the "de-ethicization" of our more rationalized and bureaucratized social world—e.g., the loss of community that has accompanied modernity?

Our third escape from the disenchanted everyday is eroticism, which we now experience as closest of all to the real and natural because we understand it as the ultimate font of life, for

> only in the secret, inward sphere of the irrational, far beyond the banalities of routine existence in the everyday, can one directly sense life's pulsating forces. To assume its fullest meaning, "life" in this world, the only world there is, must be lived "beyond good and evil." Only under such conditions can its irrational core—eroticism—ever be imagined to offer an avenue of eternal renewal and escape. (Scaff 109)

To express the dualism this way, by dialectically opposing "life" to the rational, makes us wonder whether such eroticism is another historically conditioned conception. Insofar as the parallel with aestheticism and brotherliness continues to hold, we may also ask whether eroticism in the modern world has been exaggerated in reaction to the de-eroticization of the rest of everyday life. The question is awkward because it is difficult to gain a sense of what other alternatives there might be to the banalities of rationalized everyday life today. Does our contemporary preoccupation with sex as that which frees us from the routinized utilitarian world reflect a commensurate lack of sensitivity to a larger "erotic" dimension—for example, a playfulness now almost completely lacking in the more "serious" economic and political spheres? Has the same thing happened to our bodies, whose erogenous zones have been hypereroticized at the price of de-eroticizing the rest? To try to evaluate these suppositions is not easy, yet some psychologists have reached similar conclusions about eros. For example, this is one of Norman Brown's main points in *Life Against Death*.

With all three value spheres the flight into subjectivity appears to be a dialectical reaction to the rationalization of the objective world. *Rather than providing an innerworldly salvation, however, each seems to aggravate the problem it flees.* An absolute ethic of brotherliness can maintain its purity only by becoming irresponsible (in the literal sense: unable to respond) and therefore more alienated from increasingly rationalized social forces. By developing an acute sensitivity to art, music, literature, etc., we may have acceded to the de-aestheticization—part of the disenchantment—of everyday life. And by becoming preoccupied with the erotic as the "most real kernel of life," we seem to have become desensitized to the routinization of the "less real." If so, what we have pursued as the solutions to our lack are actually parts of the problem. In this way modern culture has ended up deeply divided against itself, with the impersonal objectivist tendency toward rationalization at war with the subjectivist value spheres that develop in hostility to it—yet each dialectically reinforcing the other. The deceptive possibility of a private escape encourages us to yield to the degradation of the public realm, which in turn encourages the hypertrophy of subjectivist culture.

For Weber "the spheres of the irrational, the only spheres that intellectualism has not yet touched, are now raised into consciousness and put under its lense. This modern intellectualist form of romantic irrationalism . . . may well bring about the very opposite of its intended goal" (Weber 143). How might that happen? Scaff points to a paradox that emerges from the dependence of subjectivist culture on its objectivist enemy: "the blossoming of an inwardness of cultural redemption was scarcely imaginable without the new technologies of publication and communication, the cultural hothouse of the modern city, new possibilities for economically independent urban existence—or, in short, the complete intellectualization of even the most sacred value-sphere of subjectivity" (Scaff 112).[2]

Yet such a sociological explanation can be supplemented by a lack perspective, for which the basic problem may be understood more simply as our sense of lack aggravated by the bifurcation between an increasing sense of self-consciousness that by definition feels alienated from an increasingly objectified rationalized world. Since for Buddhism such a Cartesianlike subject is a delusion—an incorrect understanding of ourselves that is in fact the very source of our *dukkha* "suffering"— any salvation from modern *Zweckrationalitat* that involves a subjectivist withdrawal from it, thus granting instrumental rationality free reign within the objectified world, will only increase the anxiety and instability—the sense of lack—of such a groundless sense-of-self.

From his Weberian perspective, Scaff agrees that the sense "of an increasingly radical tension between this world and the thought-to-be-inviolable self seems to be at the basis of our most serious and austere responses to a disenchanted fate." He concludes that "[w]hat we now need is not so much seductive 'grand narratives' and enticing routes of

escape, but rather temporally bounded, self-restrained, and specific in-
quiries that bring our history back into view and retrieve the concrete
and particular, the locally expressed, the individually experienced, the
detailed" (Scaff 241, 240). He does not elaborate on what these might
be. Weber was pessimistic about our escaping the iron cage while finding his own personal solution in an "ethic of responsibility." That seems
to have been his attempt to integrate substantial rationality with instrumental rationality by combining a passionate committment to ultimate
values with a dispassionate analysis of the best ways to pursue them (see
Brubaker 108).

As a modernist ethics this is admirable and perhaps necessary, yet
it cannot be a sufficient response to the problem of modernity, if our
dilemma is rooted in subjectivist alienation from a disenchanted world.
If even capitalism has religious origins, as Weber argued, and still retains
a religious character, as I have suggested, perhaps the solution must also
have a religious character—religious in the sense that it addresses more
directly the fundamental and increasingly radical tension between an
objectified world and a subjectified, lack-driven self.

## GEORG SIMMEL

> Modern times, particularly the most recent, are permeated
> by a feeling of tension, expectation and unreleased intense
> desires—as if in anticipation of what is essential, of the
> definitive meaning and central point of life and things. This
> is obviously connected with the overemphasis that the means
> often gain over the ends of life in mature cultures. . . . the
> growing significance of the means goes hand in hand with
> a corresponding increase in the rejection and negation of
> the end. (Simmel 1907, 481)[3]

Simmel's most sustained meditations on the problem of means and ends
are found in what he considered his magnum opus, *The Philosophy of
Money*. Perhaps only the chapter on "Filthy Lucre" in Norman Brown's
*Life Against Death* equals its wealth of insight into the role of money
in our lives—a role that, it hardly needs to be pointed out, continues
to increase in modern life along with instrumental rationalization and
subjectification generally.

Higher concepts in philosophy are able to embrace an increasing
number of particulars only by a corresponding loss of content. Money

for Simmel is an exact sociological counterpart, "a form of being whose qualities are generality and lack of content" (221). For Brown too, money can be the purest symbol of all "because there is nothing in reality that corresponds to it" (Brown 271). Hence its nonpareil usefulness as a measure of everything else, and the inevitability by which such a perfect means becomes *the* end:

> Never has an object that owes its value exclusively to its quality as a means, to its convertibility into more definite values, so thoroughly and unreservedly developed into a psychological value absolute, into a completely engrossing final purpose governing our practical consciousness. This ultimate craving for money must increase to the extent that money takes on the quality of a pure means. . . . Money's value as a *means* increases with its *value* as a means right up to the point at which it is valid as an absolute value and the consciousness of purpose in it comes to an end. (Simmel 232)

Money has become most important in those times when other value pursuits (and lack solutions) such as religion, which encourage satisfaction with more modest circumstances, lose their attraction. Simmel compares our present situation with the decline of Greece and Rome, a period when life came to be deeply colored by monetary interests. He calls it an irony of history that, as the intrinsically satisfying purposes of life become atrophied, precisely that value which is nothing but a means assumes their place (236). More recently Brown and Becker have used psychoanalytic theory to relate money's hypertrophy to unconscious guilt and fear of death.

However, money's increasing importance for us is only part of a more general transformation of all the elements of life into means, as sequences that had previously terminated in autonomous purposes have become mutually connected into more complex teleological chains and structures. Today, in place of earlier, relatively self-satisfying ends Simmel like Weber sees "objectively and subjectively calculable rational relationships" that "progressively eliminate the emotional reactions and decisions which only attach themselves to the turning points of life, to the final purposes." Among the many examples he discusses is the English landed gentry, whose transformation into a class based on more portable wealth has been held responsible for much of England's economic development but also for a decline in their communal social responsibilities.

Rural self-governance had been based on the personal participation of this class, which has now yielded its paternalistic role to the more impersonal state (431, 343).

This is not to deny the advantages of money. It has also enabled people to join groups without needing to sacrifice any personal freedom. This is an exemplary difference from medieval types of association, which tended not to distinguish between people as such and people as members of a group. Medieval associations encompassed all one's interests—economic, political, familial, and religious alike. This is consistent with Weber's point about the modern development of subjectivist value-spheres, but Simmel's response to them is more positive. Money should be given its due:

> Thus money, as an intermediate link between man and thing, enables man to have, as it were, an abstract existence, a freedom from direct concern with things and from a direct relationship with them, without which our inner nature would not have the same chances of development. If modern man can, under favourable circumstances, secure an island of subjectivity, a secret, closed-off sphere of privacy—not in the social but in a deeper metaphysical sense—for his most personal existence, *which to some extent compensates for the religious style of life of former times,* then this is due to the fact that money relieves us to an ever-increasing extent of direct contact with things, while at the same time making it infinitely easier for us to dominate them and select from them what we require. (469, my emphasis)

Simmel had stronger ties with fin-de-siècle aestheticist culture than Weber did and was less inclined to critique it as part of a dialectical problem. However, this quotation suggests that he was also less sensitive to the intrinsic connection between the modern "feeling of tension, expectation and unreleased intense desires" he noticed and our modernist subjectivity alienated from an increasingly disenchanted objectivity.

Yet their differences are not as important as what they have in common. Just as Weber traces capitalism back, in part, to a vocational ethos imported from Puritanism into the economic sphere, Simmel also reflects on the religious origins and significance of money. He notices that all Greek money was originally sacred, for it emanated from the priesthood, along with other standard concepts of measure (weight, size, time, etc.); money bore the symbol of the common god because the priesthood at that time represented the unity of the various regions (187). Brown's *Life Against Death* supplements this sociological explanation with a psychoanalytic one that accounts for why money continues to be sacred for us: "the money complex, archaic or modern, is inseparable from symbolism; and symbolism is not, as Simmel thought, the mark of rationality but the mark of the sacred" (246).

Simmel is not unaware of symbolism's relationship with the sacred, for he notices a profound parallel between money and God:

> In reality, money in its psychological form, as the absolute means and thus as a unifying point of innumerable sequences of purposes, possesses a significant relationship to the notion of God . . . The essence of the notion of God is that all diversities and contradictions in the world achieve a unity in him, that he is the coincidentia oppositorum. Out of this idea, that in him all estrangments and all irreconcilables of existence find their unity and equalization, there arises the peace, the security, the all-embracing wealth of feeling that reverberates with the notion of God which we hold.
>
> There is no doubt that, in their realm, the feelings that money excite possess a psychological similarity with this. In so far as money becomes the absolutely commensurate expression and equivalance of all values, it rises to abstract heights way above the whole broad diversity of objects; it becomes the centre in which the most opposed, the most estranged and the most distant things find their common denominator and come into contact with one another. (236)[4]

So it is no coincidence that money exhibits the same duality in function as religion: it is one in the series of human concerns, yet also transcends the others as an integrative force that supports and infuses all other concerns (485).

Then do God and money suffer from similar problems? The difficulty with God, as usually conceived, is that in order to encompass all things He must become so attenuated that his Being becomes difficult to distinguish from nonbeing—which has made it easy for him to disappear altogether, or (as Simmel's analogy suggests) for his role to be assumed by money. We have noticed that money too is a perfect symbol because it has no content of its own, yet that is also what allows its means to become the end, what encourages us to take its no-thing-ness as more real than anything else. Preoccupation with either type of nonbeing devalues, and encourages a withdrawal from, our sensory world of more impermanent phenomena. Insofar as we attain a sterilized Being apparently immune to its impermanence, we, like Midas, become less able to appreciate its charms.

The Philosophy of Money concludes by relating the domination of monetary relationships today with the way that the relativistic character of existence finds increasing expression in our lives, for "money is nothing other than a special form of the embodied relativity of economic goods that signifies their value" (512). To a Buddhist this suggests a rather different analogy between money and sunyata, the concept of "emptiness" emphasized in Mahayana Buddhism. Sunyata has sometimes been reified into an Absolute or a Buddha-nature understood to constitute the essential nature of all things, but for Nagarjuna (whose Mulamadhyamikakarikas is the most important text of Mahayana philosophy) sunyata is a heuristic term used to describe the relativity, and therefore the lack of self-existence, of all phenomena. Nagarjuna took pains to emphasize that there is no such thing as sunyata: "Sunyata is a guiding, not a cognitive, notion" employed to "exhaust all theories and views; those for whom sunyata is itself a theory they [Buddhas] declared to be incurable" (Mulamadhyamikakarika 24:18, 12:8). If we misunderstand this the cure becomes more dangerous than the disease, for "the feeble-minded are destroyed by the misunderstood doctrine of sunyata, as by a snake ineptly seized" by the tail rather than by the neck (24:12).

Simmel's concern with means-ends teleology derives from a more fundamental paradox or unresolvable conflict that he believed to characterize all developing cultures. Life always produces cultural forms in which it expresses and realizes itself: these include technologies, institutions, and other social patterns as well as religions and works of art. Such forms provide the flow of life with content and order. Yet, although arising out of the life process, once objectified these forms no longer participate so directly in life's ceaseless rhythm of decay and renewal. They become cages (we are reminded of Weber's iron cage) for the life force that creates them but then transcends them; they remain fixated into identities whose own law and logic inevitably distance them from the creative process that produced them in the first place.[5]

As a culture evolves, more such forms are produced and take on an objectified life of their own, which entails a developing relationship between them and the creative impulse that produces them. Teleological series lengthen and ramify. A rudimentary example is basic tools. A knife is very useful but it already complicates things. As well as learning how to use it efficiently and safely we must learn how to make it, which requires further teleological chains to locate and work the right kind of bone or stone. So a developing culture constructs increasingly complex mechanisms of interlocking preconditions that become necessary to fulfill each step of the means.

A more intellectual example is the difference between Socrates and academic professors of philosophy today. Socrates wrote nothing, and as far as I know he may have read nothing. In fact, he didn't "do philosophy" at all; he talked with people in the marketplace and at dinner parties. How far would he get in a modern philosophy department? In order to become a professional philosopher today, aspirants must read hundreds of books and scholarly papers, write scores of essays, pass dozens of tests, obtain three degrees, publish in reputable journals . . . by which time one has been thoroughly socialized into focusing on certain types of questions using peer-approved methodologies.

Simmel was so impressed by this tendency that he considered it the tragedy of culture: once cultural forms exist, they become the unavoidable objects by whose assimilation we become acculturated—and with whose acculturation we necessarily become preoccupied, at the cost of a more direct relationship with the creative impulse. For prehistoric societies the *terminus a quo* as well as the *terminus ad quem* of cultural forms usually remained within the lifetime of their creator; the invention of writing systems constituted evidently the greatest quantum leap outside that boundedness. Today we are all technicians of teleologies whose *termini* are not only unknown but unimaginable. The incalculable abundance of modern artifacts and the continual ramification of modern teleologies means that in order to play whatever role we may within our own culture, we must subordinate ourselves more and more to them. Scholars need only reflect on the changes within their own disciplines during the past generation or two. The flood of noteworthy books and papers threatens to become a tidal wave that will submerge those who try to keep up with all the developments in their increasingly narrowly defined fields. A theoretical physicist once told me that specialists whose researches are interrupted for a year may never be able to catch up afterward.

A consequence of this heightened teleological consciousness, and of our own diminishing role within it, is the peculiar frustration of a life impelled to seek beyond itself for what it suspects will never be found and never be fulfilling.

> A developing culture not only increases the demands and tasks of men, but also leads the construction of means for each of these individual ends even higher, and already often demands merely for the means a manifold mechanism of interlocking preconditions. Because of this relationship, *the abstract notion of ends and means develops only at a higher cultural level.* Only at that level, and because of the numerous purposive sequences striving for some kind of unification, because of the continuous removal of the specific purpose by a larger and larger chain of means—only then does the question of ultimate purpose, that lends reason and dignity to the whole effort, and the question of why emerge. The idea of an ultimate purpose in which everything is again reconciled, but which is dispensable to undifferentiated conditions and men, stands as peace and salvation in the disunited and fragmentary character of our culture. (Simmel 1907, 360, my italics)

This is one of those insights that encourages us to rethink the way we understand the means-ends problematic—and view it more clearly in terms of lack. Lengthening teleological chains are what lead us to ask about *the* end, the ultimate purpose of life. What is distinctive about our situation today, then, is less means-ends inversion than our sense that they are increasingly divorced. Modernity is better defined as the aggravated awareness of a split between them. Then our need for absolute ends and goals reflects our future-driven tendency to make everything into a means to something else. A yearning for meaning and ultimate purpose is the other side of our inability to be satisfied with the possibilities our culture offers us, a dissatisfaction caused by our sense of lack, itself aggravated by our sacrifice of substantial values for instrumental rationality.

When the problem is viewed from this perspective, what "solution" is possible? The answer, I think, is *none whatsoever* so long as we understand any alternative as a particular goal that can be gained *by means of* instrumental rationality. Any such means-ends approach is revealed to be itself the problem. Then no seductive grand narrative or enticing mode of escape, as Scaff puts it, and no political or metaphysical end of history can be expected to fulfill us. What other alternative can there be? I think Wittgenstein points us in the right direction: If the abstract notion of ends and means develops only at a higher cultural level, "the solution to the problem of life is seen in the vanishing of the problem." But now that the problem of our rationalized, bureaucratized, instrumentalized life weighs so heavily upon us, how can it ever disappear?

## THE NONDUALITY OF MEANS AND ENDS

> The perplexity of utilitarianism is that it gets caught in the unending chain of means and ends without ever arriving at some principle which could justify the category of means and end, that is, of utility itself. The "in order to" has become the content of the "for the sake of"; in other words, utility established as meaning generates meaninglessness. (Arendt 154)

> It is by no means an objective truth that nothing is important unless it goes on forever or eventually leads to something else that persists forever. *Certainly there are ends that are complete unto themselves* without requiring an endless series of justifications outside themselves. . . . If no means were complete unto themselves, if everything had to be justified by something else outside of itself which must in its turn also be justified, then there is infinite regress: the chain of justification can never end. (Yalom 466)

> We, at the present day, can hardly understand the keenness with which a fur coat, a good fire on the hearth, a soft bed, a glass of wine, were formerly enjoyed. (Huizinga 9)

We have seen that Weber's modern world is characterized not only by instrumental rationality and disenchantment but also by compensatory emphasis on a private inner-worldly salvation for the self. Increasing objectification correlates with increasing subjectification, and although one could argue about which preceded which, the more important point is that each aggravates the other. Extrapolating a hint of Simmel's, I have suggested that Weber's subjectivist refuges themselves contribute to the world's disenchantment. Circumscribing our aesthetic sensibilities within narrowly defined limits works to to de-aestheticize the everyday world; the hypertrophy of sexuality today contributes to de-eroticizing the rest of our bureaucratized lives; and preoccupation with living a morally pure life within our own circle encourages us to reject the rest of the world as irredeemably corrupt—which can become a self-fulfilling prophecy.

I mentioned that this way of formulating our situation is especially meaningful for Buddhism, since the sense of dualism between subjectified self and objectified world is understood as the crucial delusion that causes us to suffer, as we try to secure a sense of self that because it is illusory can never quite ground itself. Contrary to the other-worldly salvations sought by most religions, Nagarjuna claims that the goal of Buddhist practice is another way of experiencing this world. "The ontic range of nirvana is the ontic range of the everyday world; there is not even the subtlest difference between the two" (*Mulamadhyamikakarika* 25:20). In Weber's terms, Buddhism may be understood to promote the reenchantment of our everyday world by reducing our dualistic sense of alienation from it until we realize that we are not other than it. In this concluding section we need to see what such a reenchantment has to do with teleology and the split between means and ends.

For Simmel, modern culture is characterized by a widening divergence between means and ends. Lengthening and ramifying teleological chains lead to means drowning out goals, a process best exemplified by the role of money in contemporary life. As money becomes the absolute value, in which our consciousness of purpose reaches its end, the other activities of life become demoted into our methods to attain it.

Simmel observes that only in more ramified cultures does the question of ultimate purpose emerge. As teleological chains multiply, we begin to wonder *why?* and yearn for some reconciliation that can unify our fragmented lives. For Buddhism, however, this modern sense of a growing bifurcation between means and ends is another example of our more general problem with dualistic thinking. Usually we dualize (e.g., good vs. evil, success vs. failure) in order to affirm one term at the price of its opposite. In this case we *use* the means to *get* some ends, yet the same paradox bedevils us: the opposites are so dependent upon each other that each gains its meaning only by negating the other. A life self-consciously "good" is preoccupied with avoiding evil; my desire for success is equaled by my fear of failure; and when ends disappear into the future they reappear the only place they can. The further our goals and purposes are projected into an indefinite future, the more inexorably our means take over their role. Weber characterized modernity as emphasizing instrumental rationality at the price of more substantive rationality, yet a better way to express it is that instrumental rationality has itself become our substantive rationality. In reaction to our confusion about what to value, we have come to value *Zweckrationalitat* itself.

Unfortunately, such instrumental rationality grants us no peace, no end to our lack. Being a means (to end our lack), *Zweckrationalitat* is always going somewhere, but, being a means that never actually ends our lack, it can never rest anywhere. Hence the peculiarly modern feeling of tension, expectation, and unreleased desires that Simmel notices: our perpetual anticipation of something essential yet to occur, Yeats's sense of a whole lifetime preparing for something that never happens. No wonder, then, that we cannot understand the keenness with which a good fire and a glass of wine were enjoyed in medieval times; today they do not satisfy us, with our stronger sense of self and therefore our stronger sense of lack. The intensified psychological *dukkha* of modern life corresponds to our intensified subjectivity.

This shows us the relationship between Simmel's increasingly ramified and frustrating teleological chains, and Weber's dualism between the rationalized objectification of a disenchanted world and the subjectification necessary for an inner-worldly escape from it. *If the modern, more subjectified ego-self is a delusion whose lack is never satisfied, it will understand its dissatisfaction as being caused by not having attained its goals; and since the more modest goals of the past (e.g., a glass of wine before the fire) bring little satisfaction, the need develops to project more ambitious goals at the end of lengthening teleological chains. . . .*

For Buddhism, the only solution to this situation is a spiritual one: to deconstruct the delusive sense of a duality between such an alienated self and its objectified, disenchanted world. To conclude, we need to see how Buddhism relates this deconstruction of self to the deconstruction of causality, since the problem of means and ends depends upon our more basic notion of cause and effect.[6] What happens to the self when the causal relation it elaborates to make itself real turns out to be problematical? Nietzsche (whom Weber and Simmel read) traced the fiction of self back to the fiction of intentionality, the supposed need for an agent to *cause* the action. His critique of the self follows from his critique of causality, which led him to conclude that "everything of which we become conscious is a terminal phenomenon, an end—and causes nothing" (Nietzsche 1968, 265, no. 478). Mahayana Buddhism reached similar conclusions by a different route, which offers a more practical path to overcome our subject-object, means-ends dualities. For this our point of reference is again Nagarjuna's *Mulamadhyamikakarika*.

The relationship between cause and effect was one of the main issues of classical Indian philosophy. Nagarjuna's own approach, however, seems paradoxical. On the one hand, causality is the main weapon he uses to demonstrate the interdependent relativity of things and therefore their lack of self-existence. On the other hand, probably the most important verse in the *Mulamadhyamikakarikas* seems to deny causality and interdependence from what is evidently a "higher" point of view: "That which, taken as causal or dependent, is the process of being born and passing on, is, taken non-causally and beyond all dependence, declared to be *nirvana*" (25:9). Chapter 25 argues that if there is no self-existence, then the enlightenment of *nirvana,* the Buddhist goal, must also be *sunya*—that is, even *nirvana* cannot be said to exist. Nagarjuna turns traditional Buddhism upside down by asserting there is no specifiable difference between *samsara* (our everyday world of *dukkha,* in which things are born, change, and disappear) and *nirvana*. There is, however, a change in perspective, or a difference in the way things are "taken"—a difference that is important if we want to avoid always preparing for something that never happens.

The irony of Nagarjuna's approach to the interdependent relativity of things is that his use of causation also denies causation. Having deconstructed the self-existence of things (including us) into interdependent conditions, causality itself disappears, because without any*thing* to cause or be effected, the world will not be experienced in terms of cause and effect. Once causality has been used to refute the apparent self-existence of objective things, the lack of things to relate together also refutes causality. If things originate (and change, cease to exist, etc.) there are no self-existing things; but if there are no such things then there is nothing to originate and therefore no origination. It is because we see the world as a collection of discrete things that we need to superimpose causal relationships, to glue them together. Without the former, there can be no latter.

This transforms the Buddhist doctrine of dependent origination into an account of nondependent nonorigination. It describes not the interaction of things but a sequence and juxtaposition of appearances—or what could be called appearances if there were some nonappearance to be contrasted with. Without any self or essential "thing-ness" *behind* appearances, however, no such contrast is possible. Origination, duration, and cessation become "like an illusion, a dream, or an imaginary city in the sky" (*Mulamadhyamikakarika* 7:34). This is not self-causation, for the category of causality is eliminated altogether. It is *tathata,* the thusness or just *this!*-ness that describes the way an enlightened being lives, according to Buddhism.[7]

This, of course, does not eliminate causality experienced "as if" in everyday life (Nagarjuna ends up with a two-tiered concept of truth), but it does enable us to experience the everyday world in a fresh, noncausal way. The crucial difference from our usual understanding becomes clear if we translate Nagarjuna's dialectic into Simmel's (and our) problematic: *if there are only means, then there are no means, for every event becomes an end in itself.* Ultimately, events are not to be justified by their reference to some other events, e.g., by their effectiveness in producing another event. According to Kant (1985, 90), people should never be used as means unless they are also ends. What if we lived in such a way that that were true for each of our *actions?* To live only in a means-causing-ends world is to overlook the most obvious thing about ourselves and this world we are "in." The challenge, for a Buddhist, is to realize this and then to live it—a task that soon exposes our inability to dwell in the present, the sense of self's need to flee its present sense-of-lack by projecting itself into the future and identifying itself with its goals, which we hope will make us feel more secure, more *real.* In this way the deconstruction of the cause-effect duality also leads to deconstructing the duality between the objectified world and subjectified self.

Here is not the place to describe how meditation practices can lead to "forgetting the self," but the result of that conflation is less sense of an alienated self that needs to use instrumental rationality to try to get something *from* the world. This breaks the vicious circle between the increasing objectification of the world and the increasing subjectification of an internalized self. It would also transform our utilitarian, bureaucratized world, for we would become less tolerant of many of the "means" we accept today once we realized that they are also ends. For example, we would insist on working less, and change the quality of our work, if we stopped thinking of work as merely a means to buying all those commodities that are supposed to satisfy us. We would not tolerate the ugly, functionalist architecture that now plagues most urban environments, but expect buildings to be beautiful to look at as well as practical to work in.

Needless to say, such a critique of instrumental rationality is not confined to Buddhism,[8] yet the Buddhist understanding of this process, which emphasizes deconstructing both causality and subject-object duality, presents our problem and its solution in a manner clearly related to what Weber and Simmel have noticed about modern culture. In place of end-less means, this gives us something that might be described as means-ful ends or end-full means. Another way to describe it is that life becomes more playful.

Something is play when nothing needs to be gained from it. For an ego-self haunted by its lack, there can be no such thing. From the broadest perspective, however, we are always playing; the question is not whether we are playing but how. Do we suffer our games as if they were life-or-death struggles, because they are the means by which the self hopes to end its lack sometime in the future (by qualifying for heaven, becoming rich and famous, etc.), or do we dance with the light feet that Nietzsche called the first attribute of divinity? In Derrida's terms, it is the difference between dreaming of deciphering a truth that will end play by restoring self-presence, and affirming a play that no longer seeks to ground itself. For Buddhism the latter is possible only insofar as the self is not alienated from its world, for the alienated ego-self is haunted by a sense of lack that makes us preoccupied with grounding ourselves. The loss of such self-preoccupation makes true play possible.

> To be playful is not to be trivial or frivolous, or to act as though nothing of consequence will happen. On the contrary, when we are playful with each other we relate as free persons, and the relationship is open to surprise; everything that happens is of consequence. It is, in fact, seriousness that closes itself to consequence, for seriousness is a dread of the unpredictable outcome of open possibility. To be serious is to press for a specified conclusion. To be playful is to allow for possibility whatever the cost to oneself. (Carse 15)

The problem with instrumental rationality is, finally, its seriousness, which presses for results and therefore is not open to the unpredictable. When everything that happens is of consequence—not because of its causal consequences, but because we are open to possibility—the world becomes reenchanted. According to Buddhism, however, our sense of lack can be ended only by resolving the problem of our dualistic sense of self.

> *End and Goal.*—Not every end is a goal. The end of a melody is not its goal; but nonetheless, if the melody had not reached its end it would not have reached its goal either. A parable. (Nietzsche 1986, 360, no. 204)

# Seven

# The Religion of the Market

Religion is notoriously difficult to define. If, however, we adopt a functionalist view and understand religion as what grounds us by teaching us what this world is, and what our role in the world is, then it becomes evident that traditional religions are fulfilling this role less and less, because that function is being supplanted by other belief systems and value systems. Today the most powerful alternative explanation of the world is science, and the most attractive value system has become consumerism. Their academic offspring is economics, probably the most influential of the "social sciences."

In response, this concluding chapter will argue that our present economic system should also be understood as our religion, because it has come to fulfill a religious function for us. The discipline of economics is less a science than the theology of this new religion, and its god, the Market, has become a vicious circle of ever-increasing production and consumption by pretending to offer a secular salvation. The eclipse of Communism makes it more apparent that the market is the first truly world religion, binding all corners of the globe into a worldview and set of values whose religious role we overlook only because we insist on seeing them as secular.

So it is no coincidence that our time of economic globalization and ecological catastrophe also happens to be a time of extraordinary challenge to more traditional religions. Unfortunately, it is somewhat ludicrous to think of conventional religious institutions as we know them today serving a significant role in resolving either crisis. Their more immediate problem is whether they, like the rainforests we anxiously monitor, will survive in any recognizable form the on-slaught of this new religion. The major religions are not yet moribund but, on those few occasions when they are not in bed with the economic and political powers that be, they tend to be so preoccu-pied with past problems and outmoded perspectives (e.g., pronatalism) that they are irrelevant to what is really happening (e.g., fundamen-talism) or trivialized (e.g., television evangelism). The result is that they have been unable to offer what is most needed, a meaningful challenge to the aggressive proselytizing of market capitalism, which has already become the most successful religion of all time, winning more converts more quickly than any previous belief system or value system in human history.

This situation is becoming so critical that the environmental crisis may actually turn out to be a positive thing for religion, for ecological catastrophe is awakening us not only to our need for a deeper source of values and meaning than market capitalism can provide, but also to the realization that contemporary religious institutions are not meeting this need either.

## ECONOMICS AS THEOLOGY

It is intolerable that the most important issues about human livelihood will be decided solely on the basis of profit for transnational corporations. (Daly and Cobb 178)[1]

According to the United Nations Development Report for 1999, three-fifths of the 4.4 billion people in developing countries lack basic sani-tation, a third have no access to clean water, a quarter do not have adequate housing, while a fifth do not have enough food or access to modern health services. Today the richest 20 percent of the world's population now accounts for 86 percent of private consumption, the poorest 20 percent only 1.3 percent—a gap that continues to grow. As a result, a quarter million children die of malnutrition or infection every week, while hundreds of millions more survive in a limbo of hunger and deteriorating health. . . .

Why do we acquiesce in this social injustice? What rationalization allows us to sleep peacefully at night?

[T]he explanation lies largely in our embrace of a peculiarly European or Western [but now global] religion, an individualistic religion of economics and markets, which explains all of these outcomes as the inevitable results of an objective system in which . . . intervention is counterproductive. Employment is simply a cost of doing business, and Nature is merely a pool of resources for use in production. In this calculus, the world of business is so fundamental and so separate from the environment . . . that intervention in the ongoing economic system is a threat to the natural order of things, and hence to future human welfare. In this way of thinking, that outcome is just (or at least inevitable) which emerges from the natural workings of this economic system, and the "wisdom of the market" on which it is based. The hegemony achieved by this particular intellectual construct— a "European religion" or economic religion—is remarkable; it has become a dogma of almost universal application, the dominant religion of our time, shoring up and justifying what would appear to be a patently inequitable status quo. It has achieved an immense influence which dominates contemporary human activity. (Dobell 232)

According to Rodney Dobell, this theology is based on two counterintuitive but widely accepted propositions: that *it is right and just* (which is why "the market made me do it" is acceptable as a defense of many morally questionable activities); and that *value can be adequately signaled by prices*. Since natural resources are unpriced, harvesting techniques such as drift nets and clearcuts are acceptable and often necessary in order to be competitive, even though "more or less everybody now knows that market systems are profoundly flawed, in the sense that, left on their own with present pricing and practices, they will lead inevitably to environmental damage and destruction of irreplaceable ecological systems" (237).

The basic assumption of both propositions is that such a system is natural. If market capitalism did operate according to economic laws as natural as those of physics or chemistry—if economics were a genuine science—such consequences would seem unavoidable, even though they are leading to extreme social inequity and environmental catastrophe. Yet there is nothing inevitable about our economic relationships. That misunderstanding is precisely what needs to be addressed—and this is also where religion comes in, since, with the increasing prostitution of the media and now universities to these same market forces, there seems to be no other moral perspective left from which to challenge them. Fortunately, the alternative worldviews that religions offer are still able to help us realize that the global victory of market capitalism is something other than the simple attainment of economic freedom. Rather, globalizing capitalism is the ascendancy of one particular way of understanding and valuing the world that need not be taken for granted. Far from being inevitable, our economic system is one historically conditioned way of organizing and reorganizing the world; it is a worldview, with an ontology and ethics, in competition with other understandings of what the world is and how we should live in it.

What is most impressive about market values, from a more traditional religious perspective, is not their "naturalness" but how extraordinarily persuasive their conversion techniques are. As a professor of philosophy and religion, I know that whatever I can do with my students a few hours a week is practically useless against the proselytizing influences that assail them outside class: the attractive (often hypnotic) advertising messages on television and radio and in magazines and buses, etc., that constantly urge them to "buy *me* if you want to be happy." If we are not blinded by the distinction usually made between secular and sacred, we can see that advertising promises another kind of salvation, i.e., another way to solve our lack. Insofar as this strikes at the heart of the truly religious perspective—which offers an alternative explanation for our inability to be happy and a very different path to become happy—religions are not fulfilling their responsibility if they ignore this religious dimension of capitalism, if they do not emphasize that this seduction is deceptive because this solution to our unhappiness leads only to greater dissatisfaction.

Instead of demonstrating their inevitability, the history of economic systems reveals the contingency of the market relationships we now take for granted. Although we tend to view the profit motive as universal and rational (the benevolent "invisible hand" of Adam Smith), anthropologists have discovered that it is not traditional to most traditional societies. Insofar as it is found among them it tends to play a very circumscribed role, viewed warily because of its tendency to disrupt social relations. Most premodern societies make no clear distinction between economic activities and social activities, subsuming economic roles into more general social relationships. Precapitalist man "does not act so as to safeguard his individual interest in the possession of material goods; he acts so as to safeguard his social standing, his social claims, his social assets. He values material goods only in so far as they serve this end." But in capitalist society "instead of economy being embedded in social relations, social relations are embedded in the economic system" (Polanyi, 46, 57).

Tawney discovered the same perspective on market forces in the pre-Renaissance West: "There is no place in medieval theory for economic activity which is not related to a moral end, and to found a science of society upon the assumption that the appetite for economic gain is a constant and measurable force, to be accepted like other natural forces, as an inevitable and self-evident datum, would have appeared to the medieval thinker as hardly less irrational and less immoral than to make the premise of social philosophy the unrestrained operation of such necessary human attributes as pugnacity and the sexual instinct" (31).

We have seen that the crucial transformation began in the late Middle Ages—which, by no coincidence, is when the prevailing religious interpretation of the world began to lose its grip on people's lives. As profit gradually became the engine of the economic process, the tendency was for gradual reorganization of the entire social system and not just of the economic element, since *there is no natural distinction between them.*[2] "Capital had ceased to be a servant and had become a master. Assuming a separate and independent vitality it claimed the right of a predominant partner to dictate economic organization in accordance with its own exacting requirements" (Tawney 86). It is another example of the technological paradox: We create complex systems to make our lives more comfortable, only to find ourselves trapped within the inexorable logic of their own development. The monster in Mary Wollstonecraft Shelley's *Frankenstein* expresses it more brutally: "You are my creator, but I am your master."

The scholar who did the most to uncover the religious roots of market capitalism was Max Weber. As the previous chapter discusses, his controversial theory not only locates the origins of capitalism in the "this-worldly asceticism" of Puritan ethics but suggests that capitalism remains essentially religious in its psychological structure. According to *The Protestant Ethic and the Spirit of Capitalism,* Calvinist belief in predestination encouraged what became an irresistible need to determine whether one was among the chosen; economic success in this world came to be accepted as demonstrating God's favor; which created the psychological and sociological conditions for importing ascetic values from the monastery into worldly vocations as one labored to prove oneself saved by reinvesting any surplus rather than consuming it.

Gradually this original goal became attenuated, yet inner-worldly asceticism did not disappear as God became more distant and heaven less relevant. In our modern world the original motivation has evaporated but our preoccupation with capital and profit has not disappeared with it; on the contrary, it has become our main obsession. Since we no longer have any other goal, there being no other final salvation to believe in, we allow the means to be, in effect, our end. Weber's arguments imply that although we think of the modern world as secularized, its values (e.g., economic rationalization) are not only derived from religious ones (salvation by injecting a revolutionary new promise into daily life), they are largely the same values, although transformed by the loss of reference to an otherwordly dimension.

Our type of salvation still requires a future-orientation. "We no longer give our surplus to God; the process of producing an ever-expanding surplus is in itself our God" (Brown 261). In contrast to the cyclic time of premodern and nonmodern societies, with their seasonal rituals of atonement, our economic time is linear and future-directed, since it reaches for an atonement that can no longer be achieved because it has disappeared as a conscious motivation. As an unconscious incentive, however, it still functions, for we continue to reach for an end that is perpetually postponed. So our collective reaction has become the need for growth: the never satisfied desire for an ever higher "standard of living" (because once we define ourselves as consumers we can never have too much) and the gospel of sustained economic expansion (because corporations and the GNP are never big enough).

## THE GREAT TRANSFORMATION

> Engels tells the story of remarking to a Manchester manufacturer that he had never seen so ill-built and filthy a city: "The man listened quietly to the end, and said at the corner where we parted: 'And yet there is a great deal of money made here; good morning, sir.'" (Sale 58)

The critical stage in the development of market capitalism occurred during the industrial revolution of the late eighteenth century, when new technology created an unprecedented improvement in the tools of production. This led to the "liberation" of a critical mass of land, labor, and capital, which most people experienced as an unprecedented catastrophe because it destroyed the community fabric—a catastrophe recurring today throughout much of the "developing" world.

Karl Polanyi's *The Great Transformation* (1944) is an expression of outrage at these social consequences as well as an insightful explanation of the basis of this disfiguration: the way that the world became converted into exchangeable market commodities in order for market forces to interact freely and productively. Earlier the commercialization of English agriculture had led to enclosure of the common pasturage land that traditionally had been shared by the community. The plague of industrial commodification proved to be much worse. The earth (our mother as well as our home) became commodified into a collection of resources to be exploited. Human life became commodified into labor, or work time, also valued according to supply and demand. Social patrimony, the cherished inheritance laboriously accumulated and preserved for one's descendants, became commodified into capital for investment, a source of unearned income for the lucky few and a source of crushing debt for many more.

The interaction among these commodifications led to an almost miraculous accumulation of capital and an equally amazing collapse of traditional community life, as villagers were driven off their land by these new economic forces. "To separate labor from other activities of life and to subject it to the laws of the market was to annihilate all organic forms of existence and to replace them by a different type of organization, an atomistic and individualistic one," emphasizes Polanyi. Such a system "could not exist for any length of time without annihilating the human and natural substance of society." The laissez-faire principle, that government should not interfere with the operations of the economic system, was applied quite selectively: although government was admonished not to get in the way of industry, its laws and policies were needed to help reduce labor to a commodity. What was called noninterference was actually interference to "destroy noncontractual relations between individuals and prevent their spontaneous reformation" (Polanyi 163, 3).

Is it a coincidence that the same doublespeak continues today? While so-called conservatives preach about liberating the free enterprise system from the restraining hand of government, federal subsidies are sought to support uneconomic industries (e.g., nuclear power) and underwrite economic failures (the savings-and-loan scandal), while international policies are designed to make the world safe for our multinational corporations (GATT, the WTO, and the Gulf War). The traditionally cozy relationship between church and state, between sacred authority and secular power, continues today: far from maintaining an effective regulatory or even neutral position, the U.S. government has become the most powerful proponent of the religion of market capitalism as the way to live, and indeed it may have little choice insofar as it is now dependent upon skimming some of the cream off market profits (although the percentage of taxes paid by corporations has dropped dramatically in recent years).

A direct line runs from the commodification of land, life, and patrimony during the eighteenth century to the ozone holes and global warming of today, and those commodifications have also led to another kind of environmental destruction that, in a different way, is just as problematic: the depletion of "moral capital," a horrible term that could only have been devised by economists to describe another horrific social consequence of market forces. As Adam Smith emphasized in his *Theory of Moral Sentiments,* the market is a dangerous system because it corrodes the very shared community values it needs to restrain its excesses. "However much driven by self-interest, the market still depends absolutely on a community that shares such values as honesty, freedom, initiative, thrift, and other virtues whose authority will not long withstand the reduction to the level of personal tastes that is explicit in the positivistic, individualistic philosophy of value on which modern economic theory is based" (Daly and Cobb 50). A basic contradiction of the market is that it requires character traits such as trust in order to work efficiently, but its own workings tend to erode such personal responsibility for others. This conflict tends toward a breakdown that is already quite advanced in many corporations. Massive "downsizing" and a shift to part-time workers demonstrate diminishing corporate concern for employees, while at the top astronomical salary increases (with lucrative stock options), and other unsavory practices such as management buyouts, reveal that the executives entrusted with managing corporations are becoming more adept at exploiting or cannibalizing them for their own personal benefit. Between 1980 and 1993 Fortune 500 firms increased their assets 2.3 times but shed 4.4 million jobs, while CEO compensation increased more than sixfold, so that the average CEO of a large corporation in 1994 received a compensation package over $3.7 million a year (Korten 218)—*much* more today, of course.

In such ways the market shows that it does not accumulate "moral capital"; it "depletes" it and therefore depends upon the community to regenerate it, in much the same way it depends upon the biosphere to regenerate natural capital. Unsurprisingly, long-range consequences have been much the same. Even as we have reached the point where the ability of the biosphere to recover has been damaged, our collective moral capital has become so exhausted that our communities (or rather, our collections of now-atomized individuals each looking out for "number one") are less able to regenerate it, with disturbing social consequences apparent all around us.

This point bears repetition because the economic support system that was created to correct the failures of capitalism is now blamed for the failures of capitalism. The social rot affecting so many "developed" societies is not something that can be corrected by a more efficient application of market values (such as getting unmarried mothers off welfare so their work will contribute to society); rather, it is a direct consequence of those market values. The commodification that is destroying the biosphere, the value of human life, and the inheritance we should leave for future generations also continues to destroy the local communities that maintain the moral fiber of their members. The degradation of the earth and the degradation of our own societies must both be seen as results of the same market process of commodification, which continues to rationalize its operation as natural and inevitable.

The cumulative depletion of "moral capital" reminds us that a community is greater than the sum of its parts, that the well-being of the whole is necessary for the well-being of each member. This, however, is not something that contemporary economic theory can factor into its equations. Why not? The answer brings us back to the origins of economic thought in the eighteenth century, origins embedded in the individualistic philosophy of utilitarianism prevalent at that time. Philosophy has become much more sophisticated since then, yet economic theory remains in thrall to utilitarian values, all the more for being ignorant of its debt.[3] According to utilitarianism, society is composed of discrete individuals seeking their own personal ends. Human values are reduced to a calculus that maximizes pleasures and minimizes discomfort. Rationality is defined as the intelligent pursuit of one's private gain.

According to this utilitarian understanding, individuals are "capable of relating themselves to others in diverse ways, basically either in benevolence or in self-love, but they are not constituted by these relationships or by any others. They exist in fundamental separation from one another, and from this position of separateness they relate. Their relations are external to their own identities" (Daly and Cobb, 160). Inasmuch as the discipline of economics seems to have attained some priority among the social sciences, this view of our humanity has come to prevail at the same time that its presuppositions have been thoroughly discredited by contemporary philosophy, psychology, and sociology—not to mention religion, which has always offered a very different understanding of what it means to be a human being. Nonetheless, as market values lead to a decline in the quality of our social relationships, "[s]ociety becomes more like the aggregate of individuals that economic theory pictures it as being. The 'positive' model inevitably begins to function as a norm to which reality is made to conform by the very policies derived from the model" (Daly and Cobb 162). We have learned to play the roles that fit the jobs we now have to do, and dutifully consume in response to the commercial images that constantly assail us.

Given the influence today of Neo-Malthusian thinking about population, it is important to notice that Thomas Malthus stands within this tradition. His *Essay on the Principle of Population* (1798) argued for an iron law of wages: a subsistence wage is the just wage, because higher wages lead only to rapid population growth until that growth is checked by poverty. It follows that poverty is not a product of human institutions but the natural condition of life for most people. The influence of this way of thinking has been in inverse proportion to the (lack of) empirical evidence for it, for world demographic trends have provided little. The rapid population increase that occurred in nineteenth-century England, which happened after many people had been driven off their land and into factory work, supports the contrary conclusion, that people are not poor because they have large families, but require large families because they are poor (there was a great demand for child labor). Morally, Malthusianism tends to gloss over the issue of who is actually consuming the earth's resources. Theoretically, its major propositions—that population grows geometrically while food increases arithmetically—arbitrarily isolate two causal variables from the complexity of historical factors, while assuming as constant perhaps the most important variables of all: the "naturalness" of an unfettered market and the competitive, self-seeking "rational" individual that neoclassical economics still presupposes.[4]

Our humanity reduced to a source of labor and a collection of insatiable desires, as our communities disintegrate into aggregates of individuals competing to attain their own private ends . . . the earth and all its creatures commodified into a pool of resources to be exploited to satisfy those desires . . . does this radical dualism leave any place for the sacred? for wonder and awe before the mysteries of creation? Whether or not we believe in God, we may suspect that something is missing. Here we are reminded of the crucial role that religions can serve: to raise fundamental questions about this diminished understanding of what the world is and what our life can be.

## THE ENDLESS HUNGER

It is not the proletariat today whose transformation of consciousness would liberate the world, but the consumer. (Miller 19)

From a religious perspective, the problem with market capitalism and its values is twofold: greed and delusion. On the one hand, the unrestrained market emphasizes and even requires greed in at least two ways. Desire for profit is necessary to fuel the engine of the economic system, and an insatiable desire to consume ever more must be generated to create markets for what can be produced. Within economic theory and the market it promotes, the moral dimension of greed is inevitably lost; today it seems left to religion to preserve what is problematic about a human trait that is unsavory at best and unambiguously evil at its worst.

Religious understandings of the world have tended to perceive greed as natural to some extent, yet, rather than use that as an excuse to liberate it, they have seen a need to control it. The spiritual problem with greed—both the greed for profit and the greed to consume—is caused not only by the consequent maldistribution of worldly goods (although a more equitable distribution is of course necessary) or to its effect on the biosphere, but even more fundamentally because greed is based on a delusion: the delusion that happiness is to be found by satisfying one's greed.

In other words, greed is part of a defective value system (the way to live in this world) based on an erroneous belief system (what the world is). The atomistic individualism of utilitarianism, which "naturalizes" such greed, must be challenged both intellectually and in the way we actually live our lives. The great sensitivity to social justice in the Abrahamic religions (for whom sin is a moral failure of will) needs to be supplemented by the emphasis that the Asian enlightenment traditions place upon seeing through and dispelling delusion (ignorance as a failure to understand). Moreover, I suspect that the former without the latter is doomed to be ineffective in our cynical age. We are unlikely ever to solve the problem of distributive social justice without also overcoming the delusion of happiness through individualistic accumulation and consumption, if only because of the ability of those who control the world's resources to manipulate things to their own perceived advantage.

According to the French historian Fernand Braudel, the Industrial Revolution was "in the end a revolution in demand," or more precisely "a transformation of desires" (183). Since we have come to look upon our own insatiable desires as natural, it is necessary to remember how much our present mode of desiring is also one particular, historically conditioned system of values—a set of habits as manufactured as the goods supplied to satisfy it. According to the U.N. Development Report for 1999, the world spent at least $435 billion the previous year for advertising, and according to the Worldwatch Institute almost half that was spent in the United States alone. That does not include related industries affecting consumer taste and spending, such as promotion, public relations, marketing, design, and fashion, which in 1994 already amounted to another $100 billion a year (Durning 122).

Put together, this constitutes the greatest effort in mental manipulation that humanity has ever experienced—all of it to no other end than creating consumerist needs for the sake of corporate profit. No wonder a child in the developed countries consumes and pollutes thirty to fifty times as much as a child in the Third World, according to the UNDR 1999. While 270 million "global teens" inhabit a single pop-culture world, consuming the same designer clothes, music, and soft drinks, almost a billion people in seventy countries consume *less* today than twenty-five years ago.

If the market is simply the most efficient way to meet our economic needs, why are such enormous industries necessary? Economic theory, like the market itself, makes no distinction between genuine needs and the most questionable manufactured desires. Both are treated as normative. It makes no difference why one wants something. The consequences of this approach, however, continue to make a great difference. The pattern of consumption that now seems natural to us provides a sobering context to the rapid deterioration of ecological systems over the last half century: according to the Worldwatch Institute, more goods and services have been consumed by the people living between 1950 and 1990 (measured in constant dollars) than by all the previous generations in human history (Durning 38).

If that is not disturbing enough, add to it the social consequences of our shift to consumption values, which, in the United States at least, have revolutionized the way we relate to one another. "With the breakdown of community at all levels, human beings have become more like what the traditional model of *Homo economicus* described. Shopping has become the great national pastime. . . . On the basis of massive borrowing and massive sales of national assets, Americans have been squandering their heritage and impoverishing their children" (Daly and Cobb 373). So much for patrimony. Our extraordinary wealth has not been enough for us, so we have supplemented it by accumulating extraordinary amounts of debt. How ingenious we have been to devise an economic system that allows us to steal even from the assets of our descendants! Our commodifications have enabled us to achieve something usually believed impossible, time-travel: we now have ways to colonize and exploit even the future.

The final irony in this near-complete commodification of the world is no shock to anyone familiar with what has become addictive behavior for so many millions of people. According to the 1999 UNDR, the percentage of Americans who considered themselves happy peaked in 1957, although consumption has more than doubled since then; meanwhile, studies of U.S. households have found that the income desired to fulfil their consumption aspirations doubled between 1986 and 1994. The fact that we in the developed world are now consuming so much more does not seem to be having much effect on our level of contentment.

This information comes as no surprise to those with a more spiritual orientation to the world. The best critique of this greed for consumption continues to be provided by traditional religious teachings, which not only serve to ground us functionally but show us how our lives can be transformed. Buddhism, for example, emphasizes renunciation and generosity. As Shunryu Suzuki-roshi put it, renunciation does not mean giving up the things of this world but accepting that they go away. To see and accept that everything goes away—including ourselves—is necessary in order to live serenely. Only someone whose identity is not tied to acquisition and consumption can truly renounce the world. The sign of renunciation is generosity, which is deeply honored in Buddhism as in all the major religions (Jeffrey 12). True generosity demonstrates not only moral development but insight. "As the need to define and present ourselves diminishes, so do possessiveness and acquisitiveness. Eventually we may come to see that the experience of possessiveness itself rests on delusion. Something is mine only if it is not yours. Yet if we can see that there is no me apart from you, as well as no us apart from the phenomena of the world, the idea of ownership begins to lose its meaning. Fundamentally there can be no acquisitiveness, for nothing is lacking" (Jeffrey 12). Consumerism not only overlooks the superior joy of giving to others, it forecloses the ontological realization of nonduality between me and others, which resolves our sense of lack. Such a realization leads to the transformative insight that there is no need to be acquisitive if nothing is lacking.

Other religions find other ways to express the importance of generosity, but it seems to me that their different paths work toward a similar realization of our interconnectedness. If we contrast spiritual approaches with market indoctrination about the importance of acquisition and consumption—an indoctrination that is necessary for the market to thrive—the battle lines become clear. All genuine religions are natural allies against what amounts to an idolatry that undermines their most important teachings.

In conclusion, the market is not just an economic system but a religion—yet not a very good one—for it can thrive only by promising a secular salvation that it never quite supplies. Its academic discipline, the "social science" of economics, is better understood as a theology pretending to be a science.

This suggests that any solution to the problems that acquisition and consumption have created must also have a religious dimension. That solution is not a simple matter of turning from secular to sacred values, but involves discovering how our secular obsessions have become symptomatic of a spiritual need they cannot meet. This book has explored how, as we have turned away from a religious understanding of the world, we have come to pursue this-worldly goals with a religious zeal all the greater because they can never be attained. The solution to the environmental catastrophes that have begun, and to the social deterioration we are suffering from, will occur when we redirect this repressed spiritual urge back onto its true path, a path that more consciously addresses the problem and the opportunity provided by our sense of lack. For the time being, that path includes struggling against the false religion of our age.

# AFTERWORD: THE FUTURE OF LACK

> No people can live without faith in the ultimate victory of
> something.
>
> —Rosenstock-Huessy

What general conclusions can be drawn from these studies of lack in Western history?

Freedom, progress, fame, romance, money, the nation-state, corporate capitalism, mechanistic science, civil society, consumerism: hardly new themes, but this inquiry into the origins of our preoccupation with them casts them in a different light. My lack approach has not attempted a "balanced" evaluation that weighs the positive against the negative consequences for our historical development—whatever that might mean. Instead, the argument has been that each of them is problematical in a way that has been little noticed, if at all.

If the argument is valid, what does it mean for us today? Our ever-growing technological powers imply that it is increasingly dangerous for us to be motivated by an unconscious drive for *being*, for a grounding that can never be attained in the way we seek it.

From a traditional religious perspective, the most important characteristic of the modern world is its secularity, more precisely our understanding of ourselves as motivated by solely this-worldly possibilities. After lack itself, therefore, the most important thread that winds its way through all the chapters is the notion that a lack perspective vitiates our usual distinction between sacred and secular. If the problem provided by our sense of lack cannot be avoided, the difference between sacred and secular is reduced to where we think our lack can be resolved. This leaves us, finally, with an urgent question: What does this critique mean for those of us now reluctant to believe in mythological notions of transcendence? If our "secular" responses are not working to assuage our lack, as I have argued, then what solutions are possible for those agnostic of other "higher" worlds? We conclude with a few reflections on this, which amplify some hints scattered here and there in the chapters.

Half a century ago, Karl Jaspers (1953) noticed an important spiritual development that occurred almost simultaneously (but apparently independently) in Greece, the Middle East, India and China between 800 and 200 B.C. He believed it to be so important that he named this period "the Axial Age." There are various ways to describe what this transformation involved, but for our purposes the most relevant is that it involved a new understanding of transcendence. The transcendental world or dimension became more important, and its existence was now understood to challenge us to transform ourselves individually (strive for religious salvation) and collectively (restructure society according to the transcendental vision). This meant a greater awareness of our lack as well as the elaboration of a transcendental solution to it. Chapter One points out that such transcendence has three main aspects: a sacred otherworldly realm or dimension; an ethical demand involving universal values that must be followed; and (what is often overlooked) a critical perspective that involves "rising above" (L., *trans+scendere*, to rise above) the given world, therefore providing the intellectual leverage necessary to evaluate and change that world. Each of these aspects involves the determination that something is lacking in this world, and each allows for a way to resolve that lack. Something is wrong, but it can be fixed.

It is no coincidence that all major players on the world stage today are the descendants of those four original Axial cultures—with one striking exception, Japan. I think that is why Japanese culture is so fascinating to the rest of the developed world, but it may also be why Japan finds it so difficult to assume a leadership role in the developed world (see Eisenstadt 1996).

The modern history of the West is a story of how the first two aspects of this Axial transcendence have lost their hold over us as the solution to our lack. Our loss of belief in a transcendental dimension, and a transcendentally grounded morality, does not of course mean that we have escaped the problem that transcendence purported to solve, for we now try to resolve our sense of lack in various this-worldly ways. This book examines why those ways have been unsuccessful.

From that perspective, the challenge of a new millennium is whether we will be able to understand our lack in a better way—that is, more consciously—and whether that understanding will enable us to address it more directly, both individually and collectively. Most of the chapters have made the point that since our lack is basically a spiritual problem, any solution must also have a spiritual dimension. But what does spirituality mean today, when myths of another and better reality can no longer be taken literally? If lack vitiates our usual distinction between sacred and secular, mustn't any solution to our lack also conflate that dualism?

The history of Buddhism suggests such a third alternative, which some chapters touch upon. As Nietzsche pointed out, the discovery or projection of a transcendental dimension is also the construction of our secular one: this world, not as it is in itself, but as devalued by the comparison. Then what happens to this world if it is revaluated? Just how transcendental is *nirvana* "awakening," Zen enlightenment, Amida Buddha's Pure Land? Significantly, the Buddhist tradition is ambivalent in its understanding of salvation. There is scriptural support for the idea of attaining some higher spiritual realm, but also for the alternative notion that enlightenment is better demythologized as experiencing the true nature of this world, hitherto unnoticed owing to the blindness caused by our greed, ill will, and delusions. The second possibility offers the option of a here-and-now liberation from our lack. The Buddhist denial of a substantial self opens up the possibility of a *this-worldly* transcendence of self, in realizing the nondual interdependence of a no longer alienated subject with a no longer objectified world. The "interpermeation" of all phenomena is what Nagarjuna describes as their *sunyata* "emptiness," and is also the point of the Hua-yen analogy of Indra's Net:

> Far away in the heavenly abode of the great god Indra, there is a wonderful net that has been hung by some cunning artificer in such a manner that it stretches out infinitely in all directions. In accordance with the extravagant tastes of deities, the artificer has hung a single glittering

jewel in each "eye" of the net, and since the net itself is infinite in all dimensions, the jewels are infinite in number. . . . If we now arbitrarily select one of these jewels for inspection and look closely at it, we will discover that in its polished surface there are reflected all the other jewels in the net, infinite in number. Not only that, but each of the jewels reflected in this one jewel is also reflecting all the other jewels, so that there is an infinite reflecting process occurring. (Cook 2)

Buddhist awakening occurs when I realize that I am not other than the world: I am what the world is doing right here, right now. This is liberation because it frees me from the self-preoccupation of always trying to ground myself. If "I" am not inside "my" body, looking out at the world outside, then "I" do not need to secure myself. Once "I" have truly realized this by letting-go of myself, there is nothing to lose, *nothing that needs to be made "real."* Since my sense-of-lack is the shadow of my sense of self, transforming the latter also transforms the former. And if each jewel in Indra's Net mutually conditions and is conditioned by all the others, to become completely groundless is to become completely grounded in the whole web of interpermeating phenomena.

Then the final irony of our struggles to ground ourselves—to make ourselves feel real by filling up our sense of lack—is that they cannot succeed because we are already grounded in the totality. I am groundless and ungroundable insofar as delusively feeling myself to be separate from the world; but I have always been fully grounded insofar as I am nondual with the world. It turns out that my lack is a lack only as long as I dread it and attempt to fill it up. When I cease doing that, it can be experienced as the source of my creative energy, which wells up from a fathomless source.

According to Buddhism, such awakening is spontaneously accompanied by compassion for all beings, now perceived as part of myself. To awaken from preoccupation with my own sense of lack is to become aware of the suffering of other beings, who are not separate from me. This points to the Buddhist solution to the problem of the meaning of life. Ironically (but as the law of *karma* implies), a life devoted to helping others turns out to be more joyful than a life devoted to helping oneself.

All the joy the world contains
Has come through wishing happiness for others
All the misery the world contains
Has come through wanting pleasure for oneself

—Shantideva, *The Way of the Bodhisattva*

To sum up, this demythologized vision finds the solution to lack in a this-worldly liberation from our usual dualistic sense of self into an awareness of interdependence that awakens our empathy with, and hence our responsibility for, all beings.[1]

That such a liberation might become widespread is too much to hope for, but if this possibility were to become socially acknowledged, more widely appreciated and encouraged, the consequences would undoubtedly be immense. Whether or not even that is a collective possibility for humanity at this point in our cultural development is another question. It would require a social reformation perhaps as great as the Axial revolution that Jaspers describes . . . but the cusp of a new millennium encourages such speculations. A Papal revolution at the dawn of the previous millennium initiated what became the West. Another religious reformation five hundred years later sparked the development of modernity. If our need is any indication, it is time for another and perhaps equally radical transformation.

# NOTES

<hr>

## ONE: THE Lack OF FREEDOM

1. "The loss of freedom is often dismissed on the grounds that because of cultural differences, authoritarian policies that would not be tolerated in the West are acceptable to Asians. While we often hear references to 'despotic' Oriental traditions, such arguments are no more convincing than a claim that compulsion in the West is justified by the traditions of the Spanish Inquisition or of the Nazi concentration camps. Frequent references are often made to the emphasis on discipline in the 'Confucian tradition'; but that is not the only tradition in the 'East,' nor is it easy to assess the implications of that tradition for modern Asia (even if we were able to show that discipline is more important for Confucius than it is for, say, Plato or Saint Augustine)" (Amartya Sen, *New York Review of Books*, 22 September 1994: 69).

2. This does not mean that slavery was an integral part of many social economies. According to M. I. Finley (1980, 9), there have been only two genuine slave societies outside the Americas, classical Greece and classical Italy. If Finley is correct, it carries the uncomfortable implication that the world's first democracy generated the world's first slave economy: the slave economy of Athens was a consequence of Solon's reforms, which gave political and economic rights to the *demos*. The loss of such a large source of involuntary labor was compensated by the decision to import large numbers of slaves from outside Athens, a solution welcomed by the *demos*. Perhaps this helps to explain the Greek understanding of freedom and slavery as opposites that require each other.

3. *History of the Peloponnesian War* I.10. Thucydides' main concern in this book was to demonstrate the vulnerability of Athenian democracy; Pericles' rule was a golden age before the populace deteriorated into private ambition and interest. "Thucydides' *History* is the greatest text ever written on the powerful, ultimately self-destructive, impulses toward greed and domination . . . Ironically, in his obsessive attempt to prove how rationally the Athenians could behave in the jungle world of international politics, he demonstrates just how mad they were" (Patterson 364).

4. "In discarding the Inherited Conglomerate [traditional worldview], many people discarded with it the religious restraints that had held human egotism on the leash. To men of strong moral principle—a Protagoras or a Democritus—that did not

matter: their conscience was adult enough to stand up without props. It was otherwise with most of their pupils. To them, the liberation of the individual meant an unlimited freedom of self-assertion; it meant rights without duties, unless self-assertion is a duty" (Dodds, 191).

5. See Sagan (1991) ch. 11 and *passim*.

6. The emphasis that Euripides put on human irrationality (in *Medea, Iphigenia in Aulis,* etc.) reminds us that the discovery of reason is also the discovery of unreason. This gave his tragedies a nihilistic undertone that rationality thereafter has never escaped, because nihilism becomes reason's alter ego, the *other* that reason can never subdue. For Euripides "the gain which has accrued to man from his newly-found independence" is that "he has no firm ground to stand on, and is helplessly exposed to the hazards of life" (Snell 130).

7. "Plato is almost the last Greek intellectual who seems to have real social roots; his successors, with very few exceptions, make the impression of existing beside society rather than in it. They are 'sapientes' first, citizens afterwards or not at all, and their touch upon social realities is correspondingly uncertain" (Dodds 192).

8. "[I]t is one of the more wonderful ironies of late medieval and early modern Europe that the more independent and absolute the European state became, the more it acquired the trappings and thought processes of the church it sought to separate from and dominate. And at the same time, the more the church came to look like an absolutist state" (Patterson 377).

## Two: The Lack of Progress

1. "It is one of the most amazing facts of Western cultural history that the striking acceleration of technological development in post-Carolingian Europe emanated from contemplative monasticism" (Ernest Benz, in Noble 13).

2. "What he [the prophet of a millenarian revolt] offered them was not simply a chance to improve their material lot. It was also, and above all, the prospect of carrying out a divinely ordained mission of stupendous, unique importance" (Cohn, in Strozier and Flynn, 36).

## Three: The Renaissance of Lack

1. The phrase is from Dr. Samuel Johnson's poem "The Vanity of Human Wishes."

2. See, for example, his *Mulamadhyamikakarika* 1:13.

3. Associated Press, 12 February 1978.

4. "When in the twelfth century unsatisfied desire was placed by the troubadours of Provence in the center of the poetic conception of love, an important turn in the history of civilization was effected. Antiquity, too, had sung the sufferings of love, but it had never conceived them save as the expectation of happiness or as its pitiful frustration. . . . Courtly poetry . . . makes desire itself the essential motif, and so creates a conception of love with a negative ground note" (Huizinga 104).

5. "There exists a condition which with me at least is not all that rare in which the presence and the absence of a beloved person are equally hard to endure; or at least in which

the pleasure derived from their presence is not that which, to judge from the intolerableness of their absence, one would have expected it to be" (Lichtenberg 107 [1780]).

6. James Hillman generalizes this point into a critique of our preoccupation with "interpersonal relationships": "By our use of them to keep ourselves alive, other persons begin to assume the place of fetishes and totems, becoming keepers of our lives. Through this worship of the personal, personal relationships have become the place where the divine is to be found, so the new theology asserts. The very condition that modern rational consciousness would dissuade us from—personifying—returns in our relationships, creating an animistic world of personified idols. Of course these archetypally loaded relationships break down, of course they require constant proprietary attention, of course we must turn to priests of this cult (therapists and counselors) for instruction concerning the right ritual for relation to persons. . . . We seek salvation in personal encounters, personal relations, personal solutions. Human persons are the contemporary shrines and statues where personifying is lodged" (47).

## FOUR: THE LACK OF MODERNITY

1. This two-stage process is reflected in the word *state*, a contraction from *estate*. *L'etat* was originally ambiguous, referring both to the state and to the king's estate. The same ambiguity made it unclear whether the community contained principles that limited the king's office, to which appeal could be made against the ruler, or whether justice inhered in that office, which made the right of resistance a logical impossibility. See Dyson (1980) 28.

2. Attributed to Josef Pilsudski.

3. This account is a generalization, of course, since every instance of nation building was unique. For example, Britain experienced a more gradual development from feudalism to parliamentary politics (the Commonwealth and Glorious Revolution were "preemptive strikes" more than revolutions), while France's political development was more characterized by the leading role of the state, from a strongly theocratic medieval polity to the centralized state of postrevolutionary regimes.

4. Cf. the concept of "the King's two bodies," which distinguished the monarch's mortal incarnation from his eternal essence or "godhead." All the old christological problems of the early church regarding the two natures of Christ were resuscitated in the juridical controversies that used this doctrine to rationalize the development of absolute sovereignty. But this approach could be problematic for rulers, as when the Puritans "fought the king to defend the King." See Kantorowicz 1957.

5. "Nazism, part and parcel of a deep-seated and genuine rebellion against an increasingly demythologised world, provides us with a disturbing example of how the coldest of modern technological devices and services could be utilised by political mystics, individuals who sincerely believed that they were providing those conditions necessary for the emergence of that natural man in whom the highest of life's forces would be actualised" (Pois 133).

6. See Dyson 35–36. The wars of religion "were essentially about attempts to base civil society on a religious foundation. When the protagonists fought each other to exhaustion, they at last realized this was no longer possible. Consequently, they had to find another reason for the existence of the State, and what they found was its function in securing the rights of private property" (Kingston 385).

7. Although corporations are not mentioned in the U.S. Constitution, legal decisions gave them the civil, political, and property rights of enfranchised natural persons in 1886, well before the majority of human beings in the U.S. gained them.

8. As this implies, a large proportion of the early scientists were Protestant.

9. "Bacon's scientist [in his *New Atlantis*] not only looked but behaved like a priest who had the power of absolving all human misery through science." He "had an aspect as if he pitied men"; "he held up his bare hand as he went, as blessing the people, but in silence" (Merchant 181).

10. From Newton's *The Mathematical Principles of Natural Philosophy,* quoted in Mason 86. Rabb speculates on why Newton was so idolized, and concludes "that it was the need he and his colleagues filled, rather than the compelling force of their insights, that prompted such serene and total adoration" (115).

11. For example, trading "pollution rights": our economic system can commodify anything!

## Five: The Lack of Civil Society

1. In addition to the other works cited in this chapter, see for example Robert Bellah et al. (1985), John Keane (1988), and Jean L. Cohen and Andrew Arato (1992).

2. "When we ask whether those who advocated war with Spain [a major political issue during the same period] were motivated by religious or economic considerations, our question is unanswerable. Contemporaries could not have answered it, would not indeed have asked it. It is an anachronistic question" (Hill 1994, 35).

3. This section draws mainly on Ehrenberg chapters 1 and 2, and Seligman chapter 1.

4. Hill 1988, 68–69. According to Hill, this despair reached its height in the middle of the seventeenth century, when the Bible too became questioned.

5. According to Hill (1994, 335), the century from the 1580s to the 1680s is also the greatest age in English literature. This section draws heavily on his *The English Bible* and *The World Turned Upside Down.*

6. Clement Walker quoted in Hill.

7. Predestination has become an alien and repugnant doctrine to us, but Haller makes it, if not plausible, at least more understandable: "As in later times men were taught to follow with patient observation the least workings of natural law in the external universe, men in the Puritan age were taught to follow by intense introspection the working of the law of predestination within their own souls. Theoretically, there was nothing they could do but watch, nothing they could of their own will do to induce or further the process of regeneration. They were only the witnesses of a drama they could do no more than marvel at. But the theatre of that drama was the human breast, and their own fate right up to the deathbed scene hung upon its outcome. They watched its unfolding, therefore, with the most absorbed attention. With the most anxious curiosity, they looked into their own most secret thoughts for signs that the grace of God was at its work of regeneration, and what they so urgently looked for they naturally saw. Seen by the light of the word, as they read it in the holy book and heard it expounded from the pulpit, their own lives fell under their gaze into the pattern set by Paul" (91). The Puritans kept diaries, and a growing literature of spiritual biographies became popular for its account of internal struggle. The test of true con-

version was active and continual perseverance. Does that help to explain our distaste? "Perhaps the desire of later generations to escape from Puritanism has been at least in part a desire to do business with less hindrance from a scheme of life so insistent upon keeping the individual forever in mind of his moral responsibilities" (119).

8. There were also local attempts to reform particular communities. One of them is described in David Underdown's *The Fire from Heaven: Life in an English Town in the Seventeenth Century* (1992). After a disastrous fire that was interpreted as a providential sign, the largely Puritan gentry of Dorchester, in Dorset, reorganized the town according to Biblical principles of collective welfare.

9. *Leviathan* 161. Is Hobbes's understanding of our human nature valid, or was he misled by the particularly chaotic times in which he lived? For a well-known debate on this topic, see Michael Oakeshott's introduction to *Leviathan* (1946) and C. B. Macpherson's *The Political Theory of Possessive Individualism* (1962). From my Buddhist perspective, the basic issue is the source of our lack. Rather than takes sides in a debate about whether our nature is originally good or bad, Buddhism emphasizes that all of us have both unwholesome traits (which should be reduced and eliminated) and wholesome ones (which should be encouraged and developed).

10. I am grateful to Will Adams for coining this term.

11. Today this fits well with the computerization of mind, for such a metaphor is appropriate if reasoning is a kind of data processing.

12. Notice where the "always" and "frequently" are placed.

13. As quoted in Lasch 55.

14. As quoted in Lapham's "Notebook," *Harper's Magazine*, March 2000, 15.

15. Against Habermas's idea of "free and unrestrained communication" to solve our disagreements, Seligman points out (195) that it is precisely these shared affective aspects of the world that cannot be subsumed into the workings of some rational formula for linguistic pragmatics.

16. See, for example, Amitai Etzioni, *The Spirit of Community: Rights, Responsibilities and the Communitarian Agenda* (London: Fontana, 1995).

17. There is an obvious and powerful objection to this line of thought. The modern distinction between state and church was hard-won, and many unsavory "premodern" examples of religious influence on politics still survive: the Taliban in Afghanistan, Brahmin sectarians in India, the Catholic church in fascist Spain, etc. Common to them is a "fundamentalism" that *knows* the truth and therefore seeks to impose its moral code on the rest. This has been perhaps the main reaction of religious institutions to the challenge of "secular" modernity, but if so it just highlights the importance of a different response: the need for interreligious dialogue. Such dialogue is necessary to help religions gain the perspective on themselves they need to distinguish what is still essential in their messages from what is historically dated. Those perspectives will also be vital for our developing understanding of what civil society is and what it can be.

## SIX: PREPARING FOR SOMETHING THAT NEVER HAPPENS

1. For an early overview, see *The Protestant Ethic and Modernization: A Comparative View*, ed. Eisenstadt (1968), especially 67–86.

2. Weber wrote in the earliest decades of the last century. Since then, the subjective value spheres that were supposed to be refuges from the instrumentalized

public sphere have themselves been colonized by the forces they were supposed to protect us from. A good example is the corporate commercialization of youth culture, profitably selling sex and rebellion.

3. Translated altered. Weber was a friend of Simmel's and benefited from his writings, including the *Philosophy of Money,* yet this influence, although no doubt considerable, is not well understood. See, for example, Scaff chapter 4 "The Sociology of Culture and Simmel."

4. Simmel also notices a very different parallel: "The indifference as to its use, the lack of attachment to any individual because it is unrelated to any of them, the objectivity inherent in money as a mere means which excludes any emotional relationship—all this produces an ominous analogy between money and prostitution" (77).

5. See, for example, Simmel 1968, 11.

6. Simmel notes that "the whole structure of means is one of causal connection viewed from the front" (1907, 431).

7. The *aporia* of causality are well known in Western philosophy, mainly because of Hume's critique. Nagarjuna's version points to the contradiction necessary for a cause-and-effect relationship: the effect can be neither the same as the cause nor different from it. If the effect is the same as the cause, nothing has been caused; if it is different, then any cause should be able to bring about any effect (*Mulamadhyamikakarika* 10:19, 22). Weber too abandoned the one-dimensional causal model, ordered from the foundation upward (e.g., Marxist materialism) in favor of what may be understood as a network model of causality. For more on this, see Scaff 48–49, and *Nonduality* chapter six.

8. In *The Dialectic of Enlightenment,* Max Horkheimer and Theodor Adorno argue that the Enlightenment has subverted its own emancipatory project. The triumph of the market and its commodification of everyday life have turned instrumental rationality against all normative concerns, heralding bureaucratic forms of domination and what they describe as a "totally administered society."

## SEVEN: THE RELIGION OF THE MARKET

1. This chapter is much indebted to Herman Daly and John Cobb's excellent book *For the Common Good,* which presents a detailed critique of modern economic theory and goes far to demonstrate how our environmental and social problems might be solved if we had the will to do so.

2. This implies that an alternative to our market religion would not require eliminating the market (and the failure of twentieth century socialism suggests that it should not be eliminated), but limiting market forces to a circumscribed place within society.

3. "Economics sprang at least half-grown from the head of Adam Smith, who may very properly be regarded as the founder of economics as a unified abstract realm of discourse, and it still, almost without knowing it, breathes a good deal of the air of the eighteenth-century rationalism and Deism" (Boulding 1968, 187).

4. For an incisive critique of Malthusianism, see Rao 1994.

## AFTERWORD: THE FUTURE OF LACK

1. For more on this approach, see Loy 1996.

# BIBLIOGRAPHY

Adams, John. 1977. *The Papers of John Adams.* Edited by R. Taylor. Cambridge, Mass.: Belknap Press.

Arendt, Hannah. 1958. *The Human Condition.* Chicago: University of Chicago Press.

Aries, Philippe. 1981. *The Hour of Our Death.* Harmondsworth, Eng.: Penguin.

Aristotle. *Politics.* 1958. Translated by Ernest Barker. Oxford University Press.

Auerbach, Erich. 1963. *Mimesis.* Princeton, N.J.: Princeton University Press.

Aurelius, Marcus. 1952. *The Meditations of Marcus Aurelius.* Translated by George Long. In *Great Books of the Western World,* Vol. 12. Edited by Robert Maynard Hutchins. Chicago: Encyclopaedia Britannica.

Aveni, Anthony. 1995. *Empires of Time.* New York: Kodansha.

Becker, Ernest.. 1975. *Escape from Evil.* New York: The Free Press.

———. 1973. *The Denial of Death.* New York: Free Press.

———. 1971. *The Birth and Death of Meaning.* Second ed. New York: The Free Press.

———. 1964. *The Revolution in Psychiatry.* New York: The Free Press.

Bellah, Robert, et al. 1985. *Habits of the Heart: Individualism and Commitment in American Life.* Berkeley: University of California Press.

Benjamin, Jessica. 1988. *The Bonds of Love.* New York: Pantheon Books.

Berman, Harold J. 1983. *Law and Revolution: The Formation of the Western Legal Tradition.* Cambridge, Mass.: Harvard University Press.

Boulding, Kenneth E. 1968. *Beyond Economics.* Ann Arbor, Mich.: University of Michigan Press.

Bouwsma, William. 1968. *Venice and the Defense of Republican Liberty.* Berekley: University of California Press.

Braudel, Fernand. 1982. *The Wheels of Commerce.* Translated by Sian Reynolds. New York: Harper and Row.

Braudy, Leo. 1986. *The Frenzy of Renown: Fame and its History.* New York: Oxford University Press.

Brown, Norman O. 1961. *Life Against Death: The Psychoanalytic Meaning of History.* New York: Vintage.

Brown, Peter. 1969. *Augustine of Hippo.* Berkeley: University of California Press.

Brubaker, Rogers. 1991. *The Limits of Rationality: An Essay on the Social and Moral Thought of Max Weber.* London: Routledge.

Burckhardt, Jacob. 1921. *The Civilization of the Renaissance in Italy.* New York: Macmillan.

Camilleri, Joseph. 1994. "Human Rights, Cultural Diversity and Conflict Resolution," *Pacifica Review* 6, no. 2.

Carse, James P. 1987. *Finite and Infinite Games.* New York: Free Press.

Cohen, Jean L., and Andrew Arato. 1992. *Civil Society and Political Theory.* Cambridge, Mass.: MIT Press.

Cohn, Norman. 1997. "Medieval Millenarianism: Its Bearing on the Comparative Study of Millenarian Movements," in *The Year 2000: essays on the end.* Edited by Charles B. Strozier and Michael Flynn. New York: New York University.

————. 1970. *The Pursuit of the Millennium.* Oxford, Eng.: Oxford University Press, 1970.

Cook, Francis H. 1977. *Hua-yen Buddhism: The Jewel Net of Indra.* University Park, Penn.: Pennsylvania State University Press.

Cordella, J. Peter. 1991. "Reconciliation and the Mutualist Model of Community," in *Criminology as Peacemaking.* Edited by Harold Pepinsky and Richard Quinney. Bloomington, Ind.: Indiana University Press.

Daly, Herman E., and John B. Cobb, Jr. 1994. *For the Common Good.* Boston: Beacon Press.

Dobell, A. Rodney. 1995. "Environmental Degradation and the Religion of the Market," in *Population, Consumption, and the Environment.* Edited by Harold Coward. Albany, New York: State University of New York Press.

Dodds, E. R. 1951. *The Greeks and the Irrational.* Berkeley: University of California Press.

Dogen. 1985. *Moon in a Dewdrop: Writings of Zen Master Dogen.* Edited by Kazuaki Tanahashi. Translated by Dan Welch and Kazuaki Tanahashi. San Francisco: North Point Press.

Duby, George, ed. 1987. *A History of Private Life,* Vol. 2: *Revelations of the Medieval World.* Cambridge, Mass.: Harvard University Press.

Dumont, Louis. 1975. "On the Comparative Understanding of Non-Modern Civilizations," *Daedalus* Spring.

Durning, Alan. 1992. *How Much is Enough?* New York: Norton.

Dyson, Kenneth H. F. 1980. *The State Tradition in Western Europe: A Study of an Idea and Institution.* Oxford, Eng.: Martin Robertson.

Ehrenberg, John. 1999. *Civil Society: The Critical History of an Idea.* New York: New York University Press.

Eisenstadt, S. N. 1968. *The Protestant Ethic and Modernization: A Comparative View.* New York: Basic Books.

Eisenstadt, S. N. 1996. *Japanese Civilization: a comparative view.* Chicago: University of Chicago Press.

Epictetus, *The Discourses of Epictetus.* 1952. Translated by George Long. In *Great Books of the Western World,* Vol. 12. Edited by Robert Maynard Hutchins. Chicago: Encyclopaedia Britannica.

Etzioni, Amitai. 1995. *The Spirit of Community: Rights, Responsibilities and the Communitarian Agenda.* London: Fontana.

Ferguson, Adam. 1995. *An Essay on the History of Civil Society.* New Brunswick, N.J.: Transaction Publishers.

Finley, M. I. 1980. *Ancient Slavery and Modern Ideology.* New York: Viking Press.

Fish, Stanley. 1999. *The Trouble with Principle.* Cambridge, Mass.: Harvard University Press.

Freud, Sigmund. 1964. *The Origins of Psycho-analysis*. Edited by Marie Bonaparte et. al. New York: Basic Books.

Gierke, Otto. 1934. *Natural Law and the Theory of Society 500–1800*. Cambridge, Eng.: Cambridge University Press.

Grossman, Richard. n.d. "Corporations' Accountability and Responsibility." Unpublished paper.

Haller, William. 1938. *The Rise of Puritanism*. New York: Columbia University Press.

Hamburg, Dan. 1997. "Inside the Money Chase," *The Nation*. 5 May.

Harrington, Alan. 1977. *The Immortalist*. Millbrae, California: Celestial Arts.

Herz, John. 1976. *The Nation State and the Rise of World Politics*. New York: McKay.

Hill, Christopher. 1994. *The English Bible and the Seventeenth-Century Revolution*. Harmondsworth, Eng.: Penguin.

———. 1972. *God's Englishman: Oliver Cromwell and the English Revolution*. Harmondsworth, Eng.: Penguin.

———. 1997. *Liberty Against the Law: Some Seventeenth-Century Controversies*. Harmondsworth, Eng.: Penguin.

———. 1988. *A Tinker and a Poor Man: John Bunyan and His Church, 1628–1688*. New York: Norton.

———. 1975. *The World Turned Upside Down*. Harmondsworth: Penguin.

Hillesum, Etty. 1986. *Etty: A Diary, 1941–43*. Translated by Arnold J. Pomerans. London: Triad Grafton. Also published under the title *An Interrupted Life*.

Hillman, James. 1975. *Re-Visioning Psychology*. New York: Harper.

Hobbes, Thomas. 1946. *Leviathan*. Edited by Michael Oakeshott. Oxford, Eng.: Blackwell.

Huang Po. 1958. *The Zen Teaching of Huang Po*. Translated by John Blofeld. London: Buddhist Society.

Huizinga, Johann. 1987. *The Waning of the Middle Ages*. Translated by F. Hopman. Harmondsworth, Eng.: Penguin.

Hume, David. 1948. *A Treatise of Human Nature*. Edited by H. D. Aitken. New York: Macmillan.

Humphreys, S. C. 1975. "'Transcendence' and Intellectual Roles: The Ancient Greek Case," *Daedalus*, Spring.

Jaspers, Karl. 1953. *The Origin and Goal of History*. Translated by Michael Bullock. London: Routledge and Kegan Paul.

Jeffrey, Meg. 1995. "Consumerism in the Monastery," *Turning Wheel*, Summer.

Jellinek, Georg. 1979. *The Declaration of the Rights of Man and of Citizens: A Contribution to Modern Constitutional History*. Westport, Conn.: Hyperion Press.

Kant, Emanuel. 1985. *Critique of Practical Reason*. Translated by L. W. Beck. New York: Macmillan.

Kantorowicz, Ernst H. 1957. *The King's Two Bodies: a study in medieval political theology*. Princeton, N.J.: Princeton University Press.

Keane, John. 1988. *Democracy and Civil Society*. London: Verso.

———. 1989. "Despotism and Democracy," in *Civil Society and the State: New European Perspectives*. Edited by John Keane. London: Verso.

Keen, Maurice. 1968. *A History of Medieval Europe*. London: Routledge.

Kennedy, Paul. 1988. *The Rise and Fall of the Great Powers*. New York: Random House.

Kingston, William. 1992. "Property Rights and the Making of Christendom," *The Journal of Law and Religion* 9, no. 2.

Korten, David C. 1995. *When Corporations Rule the World*. West Hartford, Conn.: Kumarian Press.

LaBarre, Weston. 1954. *The Human Animal*. Chicago: University of Chicago Press.

Landes, David S. 1983. *Revolution in Time*. Cambridge, Mass.: Harvard University Press.

Landes, Richard. 1997. "The Apocalyptic Year 1000: Millennial Fever and the Origins of the Modern West," in *The Year 2000: essays on the end*. Edited by Charles B. Strozier and Michael Flynn. New York: New York University Press.

———. "While God Tarried: Modernity as Frankenstein's Millennium." Center for Millennium Studies at Boston University, at internet website www.mille.org.

Lapham, Lewis H. 1988. *Money and Class in America*. New York: Ballantine.

Lasch, Christopher. 1991. *The True and Only Heaven: progress and its critics*. New York: W. W. Norton.

Le Goff, Jacques. 1988. *Your Money or Your Life*. New York: Zone Books.

Lerner, Michael. 1996. *The Politics of Meaning*. Reading, Mass.: Addison-Wesley.

Lichtenberg, Georg Christoph. 1990. *Aphorisms*. Translated by R. J. Hollingdale. Harmondsworth, Eng.: Penguin.

Liechty, Daniel. n.d. *Abstracts of the Complete Writings of Ernest Becker*. Privately distributed.

Loy, David. [1996] 1999. *Lack and Transcendence: The Problem of Death and Life in Psychotherapy, Existentialism, and Buddhism*. Atlantic Highlands, N.J.: Humanities Press, 1996; Amherst, N.Y.: Humanity Books.

———. 1988. *Nonduality: A Study in Comparative Philosophy*. New Haven, Conn: Yale University Press.

Macpherson, C. B. 1962. *The Political Theory of Possessive Individualism*. Oxford, Eng.: Oxford Univerity Press.

Maguire, Daniel C. 1998. "More People: Less Earth." In *Ethics for a Small Planet*. Edited by Daniel C. Maguire and Larry Rasmussen. Albany, N.Y.: State University of New York Press.

Mason, S. 1994. "The Scientific Revolution and the Protestant Reformation—I," *Annals of Science* 9, no. 1.

May, Rollo. 1997. *The Meaning of Anxiety*. New York: Norton.

Merchant, Carolyn. 1980. *The Death of Nature*. New York: Harper & Row.

Miller, Daniel. 1995. "Consumption as the Vanguard of History." In *Acknowledging Consumption*. Edited by Daniel Miller. London: Routledge.

Montaigne. 1960. *The Complete Essays*, Vol. 3. Translated by Donald M. Frame. Garden City, N.Y., p. 164.

Muller, Herbert J. 1961. *Freedom in the Ancient World*. New York: Harper & Row.

Muller, Jerry Z. 1993. *Adam Smith in His Time and Ours: Designing the Decent Society*. Princeton, N.J.: Princeton University Press.

Mumford, Lewis. 1970. *The Culture of Cities*. New York: Harcourt, Brace, Jovanovich.

Murray, Oswyn. 1989. *Times Literary Supplement*. 16 June: 656.

Nagarjuna. 1979. *Mulamadhyamikakarika*. In Candrakirti, *Lucid Exposition of the Middle Way*. Translated by Mervyn Sprung. Boulder, Colo.: Prajna Press.

Nandy, Ashis. 1996. "State." In *The Development Dictionary*. Edited by Wolfgang Sachs. London: Zed.

Nietzsche, Friedrich. 1986. *Human, All Too Human*. Translated by R. J. Hollingdale. Cambridge, Eng.: Cambridge University Press.

———. 1968. *The Will to Power*. Translated by Walter Kaufmann and R. J. Hollingdale. New York: Random House.

Noble, David F. 1998. *The Religion of Technology.* New York: Knopf.

Pande, G. C. 1991. "Two Dimensions of Religion." In *Culture and Modernity: East-West Philosophical Perspectives.* Edited by Eliot Deutsch. Honolulu: University of Hawaii Press.

Patterson, Orlando. 1991. *Freedom in the Western World.* New York: Basic Books.

Plato. 1973. *Collected Dialogues.* Edited by Edith Hamilton and Cairns. Princeton, N.J.: Princeton University Press.

Poggi, Gianfranco. 1978. *The Development of the Modern State: a sociological introduction.* London: Hutchinson.

Pois, Robert A. 1986. *National Socialism and the Religion of Nature.* New York: St. Martin's Press.

Polanyi, Karl. 1957. *The Great Transformation.* Boston: Beacon.

Rabb, Theodore K. 1975. *The Struggle for Stability in Early Modern Europe.* New York: Oxford University Press.

Rank, Otto. 1958. *Beyond Psychology.* New York: Dover.

Rao, Mohan. 1994. "An Imagined Reality: Malthusianism, Neo-Malthusianism and Population Myth," *Economic and Political Weekly.* 29 January.

Rosenstock-Huessy, Eugen. 1993. *Out of Revolution.* Providence, R.I.: Berg.

Rougemont, Denis de. 1956. *Love in the Western World.* Translated by Montgomery Belgion. New York: Pantheon Books.

Sagan, Eli. 1991. *The Honey and the Hemlock: Democracy and Paranoia in Ancient Athens and Modern America.* New York: Basic Books.

Sale, Kirkpatrick. 1995. *Rebels Against the Future.* Reading, Mass.: Addison-Wellesley.

Sampson, Leo. 1974. "Americanism as Surrogate Socialism." In *Failure of a Dream.* Edited by J. Laslett and S. M. Lipset. New York: Anchor.

Scaff, Lawrence A. 1989. *Fleeing the Iron Cage: Culture, Politics, and Modernity in the Thought of Max Weber.* Berkeley: University of California Press.

Seligman, Adam B. 1992. *The Idea of Civil Society.* Princeton, N.J.: Princeton University Press.

Simmel, Georg. 1968. *Conflict in Modern Culture and other essays.* Translated by K. Peter Etzkorn. New York: New York Teachers College Press.

———. [1970] 1978. *The Philosophy of Money.* 2d ed. Edited by David Frisby. Translated by Tom Bottomore and David Frisby. London: Routledge and Kegan Paul.

Smith, Adam. 1993. *An Inquiry into the Nature and Causes of the Wealth of Nations.* Edited by Kathryn Sutherland. Oxford, Eng.: Oxford University Press.

———. 1982. *The Theory of Moral Sentiments.* Indianapolis, Ind.: Liberty Classics.

Snell, Bruno. 1960. *The Discovery of the Mind in Greek Philosophy and Literature.* Translated by T. G. Rosenmeyer. New York: Dover.

Southern, R. W. 1990. *Saint Anselm: A Portrait in a Landscape.* Cambridge, Eng.: Cambridge University Press.

Tawney, R. H. 1926. *Religion and the Rise of Capitalism.* New York: Harcourt, Brace.

Thompson, Damian. 1996. *The End of Time.* London: Minerva.

Tilly, Charles. 1975. *The Foundation of the National States in Western Europe.* Princeton, N.J.: Princeton University Press.

Tocqueville, Alexis de. 1945. *Democracy in America.* New York: Vintage.

Toulmin, Stephen. 1990. *Cosmopolis: the hidden agenda of modernity.* New York: The Free Press.

Toynbee, Arnold. 1957. *A Study of History.* Abridged by D. C. Somervell. New York: Oxford University Press.

Unamuno, Miguel de. 1921. *Tragic Sense of Life.* Translated by J. E. Crawford Flitch. London: Macmillan.

Underdown, David. 1992. *The Fire from Heaven: Life in an English Town in the Seventeenth Century.* New Haven, Conn.: Yale University Press.

Weber, Max. 1946. *From Max Weber: Essays in Sociology.* Edited and translated by Hans Gerth and C. Wright Mills. New York: Oxford University Press.

West, Delno C., and Sandra Zimdars-Swartz. 1983. *Joachim of Fiore.* Bloomington, Indiana: Ind. University Press.

Winstanley, Gerrard. 1973. *The Law of Freedom in a Platform or, True Magistracy Restored.* Edited by Robert Kenney. New York: Schocken.

Yalom, Irvin. 1980. *Existential Psychotherapy.* New York: Basic Books.

# INDEX

Abraham, 34

Absolutism, 98; royal, 144

Acontius, Jacobus, 140

Acts of contrition, 49

Adam: original sin and, 90

Adams, John, 163

Adam's Fall, 14, 24, 127, 130, 145, 147

Advertising, 88, 200, 208

Aeschylus, 29

Aestheticism, 15, 178

Afterlife: belief in, 11; decline of sacred, 69; importance to theology, 69; secular, 69

Aggression: institutionalization of, 88; military, 90, 108; motivation for, 109; as response to anxiety, 109

Altruism, 29, 155

Americanism, 160

Amish, 101

Amos, 26, 34

Anabaptists, 101, 103, 140

Anarchy: feudal, 96

*Anatta,* 3, 4

Anaxagoras, 28

*An Essay on the History of Civil Society* (Ferguson), 155

Anselm (Archbishop of Canterbury), 46, 48, 49, 50, 51, 130

Antichrist, 135

Antinomianism, 139, 150, 151

Anti-semitism, 43, 134

Antisthenes, 33

Anxiety, 5; accumulation of, 23; aggression and, 109; death, 5, 66, 84; fears in, 22; freedom and, 22; Greek, 27, 28; growth of, 28; of guilt-culture, 29; increase in, 29, 31; of inwardness, 24; lack and, 23, 106, 109; "liberation" of, 90; social, 12, 89; stranger, 29

*Apatheia,* 33

Apocalypse, 62

Apocalypticism, 60

"The Apocalyptic Year 1000" (Landes), 64

Apollo, 29

Aquinas, Thomas, 130, 156

Arendt, Hannah, 189

Aries, Philippe, 66, 68, 73, 79, 92

Aristotle, 28, 29, 30, 83, 89, 113, 114, 128, 129

Art, 179

Associations: medieval, 184; voluntary, 168

Astrology, 32

*Ataraxia,* 33

Atonement: Anselm's theory of, 48, 49, 50; unconscious, 12

Auerbach, Erich, 56

Augustine, 9, 34, 35, 36, 38, 61, 62, 129

Aurelius, Marcus, 24, 67

*Autarkeia,* 33

Authoritarianism, 18, 20–23

Authority: of antiquity, 89; attacks on, 90; biblical, 140; civil, 89, 103; derived from God, 96, 153; of the law, 42, 43; moral, 89, 98, 106, 110, 161;

*Authority (continued)*: need to make
   effective, 97; of Papacy, 44, 51; of
   priests, 131; of rule of law, 48; sacred,
   37, 38, 204; search for, 43; secular,
   36–37, 38; sovereign, 95; spiritual, 94,
   95, 98; of temporal power, 43;
   worldly, 94
Autonomy: attaining, 4; individual, 38,
   164; of self-consciousness, 5, 65; of
   sense of self, 20
Aveni, 54, 55
*Avidya,* 19
Awareness: of death, 4, 73; guilt and, 7;
   of impermanence, 2; "liberation" of,
   7; meditation and, 7; of sin, 35
Axial Age, 212
Aztec civilization: time and, 55

Babylon, 27
Bacon, Francis, 59, 89, 98, 112, 115, 116
Bacon, Roger, 59
Banking: origin of, 109
Barebones Parliament (1653), 136, 143
Bauthumley, Jacob, 140
Baxter, Richard, 176
Becker, Ernest, 4, 5, 78, 79, 80, 88, 95,
   103, 121, 123, 183
Being, 24; accumulating through money,
   79; of beloved, 11; dependent, 67;
   nonbeing duality, 7; reason and, 24;
   self, 67; unconscious drive for, 211
Belief: in belief, 119; in sin, 81
Bellah, Robert, 160
Berman, Harold, 10, 42, 43, 44, 46, 47,
   48, 49, 50, 51, 53, 57, 58
*Bestand,* 172
Bible, 14; availability in English, 132;
   centrality to intellectual life, 131;
   heresy and, 133; infallibility of, 140;
   metaphorical understandings of, 147;
   New Testament, 57, 134; Old
   Testament, 57, 134; as only source of
   wisdom, 132; proliferation of
   interpretations of, 93, 141; quoting
   for one's own purpose, 133, 134;
   revolutionary, 131–144; solutions for
   urgent problems in, 131–132; as
   source of religious truth, 92; theological controversy and, 133; toleration and, 140
Boniface VII (Pope), 52
*Book of Prophecy* (Columbus), 59
Boyle, Robert, 59
Brahe, Tycho, 135
Braudel, Fernand, 208
Braudy, Leo, 68, 69, 70, 71
Brotherliness, 179, 180
Brown, Norman, 4, 77, 78, 80, 81, 82,
   83, 122, 179, 180, 182, 183, 185, 202
Brown, Peter, 6, 35, 36, 45, 80
Brubaker, Rogers, 174, 175
Buddhism: adaptability of, 2; compassion
   and, 2; deconstruction of self and,
   191; doctrine of dependent origination, 190, 191; ennobling truths in, 3;
   generosity and, 2, 209; impermanence
   in, 2, 3; Mahayana, 84, 91, 173, 186,
   191; means-ends bifurcation and, 190;
   no-self doctrine in, 19–20; as personal
   path to transform evils, 151–152;
   psychology and, 2; reenchantment of
   everyday world in, 190; refutation of
   self-existing individuality in, 155;
   renunciation in, 209; roots of evil in,
   87; sense-of-self and, 4; social control
   in, 47; Tibetan, 2; wisdom and, 2
Buddhist perspective: being/nonbeing, 7;
   of ego-self, 19; of fame, 70; of freedom,
   18; of lack, 8, 35, 61, 143; on money,
   79; self/nonself, 7; on spirituality, 123
Bunyan, John, 135, 138
Burckhardt, Jacob, 27, 66, 68, 73
Burke, Edmund, 18
Burnham, Walter Dean, 160
Byron, Lord, 68

Calvin, John, 12, 14, 91, 93, 112, 113,
   116, 127, 150
Calvinism, 138, 139
Camilleri, Joseph, 101
Canon law: belief in lawful universe in,
   51; criteria for, 49; development of,
   10; as first legal system, 48; influence
   of, 57; as response to new attitudes
   toward death, 48–49; sin and, 10;
   systemization of, 46

Capital, 157; accumulation, 178, 203; development of nation-states and, 108; domestic, 108; "liberation" of, 16, 202; as master, 81, 201; moral, 204, 205; preoccupation with, 178

Capitalism: corporate, 12, 15, 89, 105–111, 123; defining, 174; domination by, 104, 123; failures of, 205; lack and, 105; market, 15–16, 107, 108, 198, 200, 201, 207; mode of production and, 101; as objectified form of collective lack, 112; origins of, 105, 173, 176, 184; predestination and, 106; Protestant ethic and, 80; as rationalization, 174; religious dimension of, 200; religious roots of, 173; rise of, 80

Carse, James, 71

Causality, 190, 191, 193, 222n7

Censorship, 133, 146

Change: apocalyptic, 57; social, 143

Chaos, 97; creation of order out of, 54; fear of, 90; political, 100; social, 99, 103; subduing, 109, 116

Charity, 92

Charlemagne, 46

Charles I (King of England), 13, 114, 126, 136

Charles II (King of England), 136, 142

Charles VIII (King of France), 108

Christ, 34; rejection of, 134; resurrection of, 50; return of, 45, 57, 58, 147

Christianity: apocalyptic, 48, 61; decline of, 11; Neoplatonic thought and, 24, 38; overcoming lack and, 68; subordination of, 95; understanding of lack in, 9

Church(es). See also Christianity; Religion; changes in, 43; delegalization of, 53; diminution of authority of, 126; Eastern, 43, 49, 50; Gregorian concept of, 51; independence of, 48; indulgences as source of income in, 52, 107; moral authority of, 89; Papal Reformation and, 48; separate from state, 152; understanding of sin, 90; Western, 43, 50, 4350

Cicero, 129

City of God (Augustine), 36, 37

Civil society: as alienated sphere, 160; Anglo-American, 13, 14, 127, 137, 154, 169; coercive state and, 149; common good and, 154; competition and, 159; as countervailing force to state coercion, 128; defining, 125; development of, 13, 14; disintegration of, 166; economic activity and, 157; interpersonal trust in, 169; as irrelevant, 165; lack of, 13–14, 125–170; loss of religious dimension, 137; modern conception of, 157; nature of, 127; necessity of literacy for, 132; need for, 125, 128; need for mortal God in, 149; "new," 167–170; normalizing function of, 168; origins of, 127–131; participation in, 166; politically organized commonwealths and, 127; production and, 157; pursuit of personal goals in, 156; religious foundation of, 219n6; roots of, 155; secularization and, 126; shaping the state, 160; Stoic conception of, 129; theological origins of, 14; voluntary associations in, 167, 168

Clergy: appointment by kings, 46; law investiture, 46; oaths of fealty from, 46

Clocks, cathedral, 56

Cobb, John, 198, 204, 206, 209, 222n1

Cohn, Norman, 60, 61

Colonialism, 59; corporations and, 108

Columbus, Christopher, 59, 105

Commodification, 168; industrial, 203; of land, 204; of sin, 10, 49; of whole earth, 40

Commonwealth, 13, 14, 98, 126, 127, 140, 143

Communism, 197

Communitarianism, 167

Community: of all with all, 30; bonds of, 47, 154; breakdown of, 101, 209; bureaucracy and, 101; erosion of, 18; international, 103; lack and, 25; loss of, 179, 180; mutualist, 101; need for, 22; penitential law and, 47–48; protection from barbarism, 128; relationships in, 47; responsibility to, 110; of saints, 162; stability of, 103; substitution for, 103; values, 158, 204

Compassion, 2
Competition: among nations, 13, 102; economic, 102; Greek, 28; military, 102; natural, 148
Compulsions, 5
Concordat of Worms (1122), 46
Confession, 38, 43, 131
*Confessions* (Augustine), 35
Conscience: autonomous, 130; distinguishing from reason, 140; exploration of, 37–38; grace and, 162; higher law of, 144; individual, 162; inner light of grace as, 165; interpretation of Bible and, 133; moral, 165; outside state, 130; precedence of, 140; spiritual stress of, 137
Consciousness: automatized reflexivity of, 7; autonomous, 6; collective, 47; conditioned, 4; repression and, 4, 82; self-existing, 6, 19; self-sufficient, 4; of sin, 6
Consumerism, 16, 40, 124, 164, 197, 209, 210; antinomianism and, 150; creating, 208; ever-increasing, 197; need for, 87
Contracts: sanctification of, 53
Cook, Francis, 214
Copernicus, Nicolaus, 112, 114
Cordella, J. Peter, 101
Corporations, 220n7; colonial exploitation and, 108; early, 108; executive cannibalization of, 204; freedom of, 111; limited liability, 108, 110, 121; multinational, 204; shares in, 110; state and, 108; transnational, 110, 111, 124, 198
Cosmopolis, 118–121
Cosmos: creation by God, 12; harmony with self and, 33; hierarchical, 12, 89; integration into, 25; maintenance of, 25; mathematical structure of, 51; place in, 89
Crashaw, Richard, 145
Cromwell, Oliver, 13, 126, 135, 136, 138, 142
Cromwell, Thomas, 98
Crusades, 43, 52, 59

Culture: communal, 160; contemporary, 14–15, 172; feudal, 160; group-based, 160; guilt, 29; modern, 194; time and, 53, 54; Western, 41
*Cur Deus Homo* (Anselm), 49
Cynicism, 32
Cynics, 128

da Gama, Vasco, 108
Daly, Herman, 198, 204, 206, 209, 222n1
*Daniel,* 134, 135
Dante, 57, 68, 84
Darwin, Charles, 117
da Vinci, Leonardo, 68
Death: acceptance of, 92; anxiety, 5, 66, 84; attitudes toward, 48–49; awareness of, 4, 73; belief in, 69; conquering, 4; as end in itself, 92; fear of, 183; increase in preoccupation with, 66, 68, 91; love and, 74; meaning imparted to, 103; representations of, 92; resolution of lack in, 36; transition to eternal life, 92
Debt, 209
Delusion, 16, 87, 123, 151; consequences of, 2; dispelling, 208; greed and, 16; knowledge sought by Greece as, 24; possessiveness and, 210
Democracy, 164; Athenian, 27, 28, 217n3; condemnations of, 128; conditions for, 21; criticism of, 30; failure of, 31; Socrates dislike of, 29; weakness of, 30
Democritus, 27
Demosthenes, 31
Dennett, Daniel, 117
de Rougemont, Denis, 72, 73, 74, 75, 76
Derrida, Jacques, 67, 194
Descartes, René, 4, 53, 60, 98, 116, 118, 119, 120
Determinism: materialistic, 176
de Tocqueville, Alexis, 70, 166, 168
*Deuteronomy,* 134
Development: of canon law, 10; of civil society, 13, 14; economic, 12, 18, 82,

91, 159, 183; ethical, 129; of freedom, 17; human, 43; of humanism, 26; intellectual, 17; of law, 43; moral, 159, 209; of nation-states, 95; personal, 159; political, 219n3; of Purgatory, 43; religious, 161; of science, 51; of self, 9; social, 91, 159; sustained, 12, 82; technological, 218n1

d'Haenens, Albert, 56

*Dharma,* 90

Diagoras, 28

Dickens, Charles, 68

Diderot, Denis, 69

Diggers, 140, 146, 148

Diogenes the Cynic, 33

Dionysus, 29

Diotima, 73, 76

*Discourse on Method* (Descartes), 116

*Discourses* (Epictetus), 33

Dobell, Rodney, 199

Dodds, E.R., 29, 32

Dogen, 7, 8

Donne, John, 89

Dooms, German, 47

*Dosa,* 87

Dreams: power of, 65

Dualities: being/nonbeing, 7; internal/ external, 9; life/death, 7; means/ends, 172; otherwordly/thisworldly society, 91; public/private, 174; sacred/secular, 8, 25, 26, 46, 66, 75; subject/object, 9; supernatural/natural, 93

Duby, George, 38

*Dukkha,* 3, 4, 6, 9, 152, 181, 191

Durning, Alan, 208, 209

Dyson, Kenneth, 104

Eckhart, Meister, 36

Ecological degradation, 18, 39, 45, 87, 124, 197, 199, 204, 205, 208; economic globalization and, 87

Economic: activity, 80; competition, 102; development, 82, 91, 159, 183; equality, 79; expansion, 42; exploitation, 150; freedom, 200; globalization, 81, 87, 154, 197; growth, 82, 83, 87, 104, 162; organization, 108; processes, 176; rationalization, 177, 202; relationships, 199; religion, 199; theory, 107; thought, 106; values, 108

Economics, 197; laissez-faire principle in, 203; as theology, 197, 198–202

Economic system, 168; defect in, 83; desire for profit and, 207; history of, 200; as meaning system, 79; noninterference in, 203; profit motive and, 80, 81; promotion of greed in, 87; as religion, 15–16, 197–210; requirment for continual growth, 83

Economy: market, 13, 91; social relationships and, 80

Education, 172; means-ends reversal in, 172; as obstacle to freedom of thought, 172

Ego: lack and, 6

Egoism, 99

Ego-self, 4, 7, 194; Buddhist perspective, 19; conditioning of, 3; delusive nature of, 6; as mental construction, 5; need to feel real, 158; subjectified, 15, 191

Egypt, 27; early kings, 95; hierarchy of clientages in, 21; integration in social structure in, 25; as liturgy-state, 21

Ehrenberg, John, 130, 149, 152, 157, 160, 167, 168

Einstein, Albert, 117

Eisenstadt, S.N., 212

Eliade, Mircea, 54

Eliot, T.S., 144

Elizabeth I (Queen of England), 137

Emerson, Ralph Waldo, 163

Empathy, 29

Emptiness, 186, 213

Ends: domination by means, 174; growth as, 111; loss of, 14–15; means swallowing, 178

Engels, Friedrich, 150, 202

English civil war, 99, 126, 136

Enlightenment, 13; antagonism to religion and, 2

Epictetus, 24, 33

Epicureanism, 24, 32, 33, 128

Epicurus, 129

*Epistle of James,* 134

Eros, 179
Eroticism, 15, 178, 179, 180, 190
*Essay on the Principle of Population*
    (Malthus), 206
*Essays* (Montaigne), 119
Ethics, 179; of brotherliness, 15;
    personal, 179, 180; purist, 179, 180
Eucharist, 43
Euripides, 28, 29, 30, 218*n6*
Evil: civil war as, 99; free will and, 93;
    institutional roots of, 88; roots of, 87;
    universal, 146
Existence: material conditions of, 45
*Exodus,* 134

Fame, 65, 66–72; acceptability in, 69;
    anonymity and, 69–70; Buddhist
    perspective of, 70; as delusive craving,
    65; desire for, 10–11; disappointment
    with, 68, 71–72; dreams of, 66; good/
    bad, 69; as imitation of divinity
    before witnesses, 67; lack of satisfac-
    tion in, 11; for own sake, 84;
    posthumous, 69; preoccupation with,
    68; pursuit of, 11; reality and, 71; as
    replacement for afterlife, 67; Roman
    standards of public glory and, 68;
    secularization of, 69, 70; as trap, 66
Familists, 146
Fascism, 103, 104, 154
Fear: of death, 3, 22, 183; imagination
    and, 148; life, 22; of nothingness, 8; of
    Purgatory, 42; of the void, 3
Ferguson, Adam, 155, 156, 158, 166
Fetishism, 123
Fichte, Johann, 104
Filmer, Sir Robert, 145, 146
Finley, M.I., 31, 217*n2*
Fish, Stanley, 143
Foundationalism, 118, 119
Fourth Lateran Council (1215), 38
Freedom: anxiety and, 22; becoming
    libertinism, 30; Buddhist perspective
    of, 18; civic, 18; colonial, 17;
    common good and, 154; comparative
    approach, 18; complete, 40; of
    corporations, 111; defining, 18;
    development of, 17; development of

self and, 9; divine grace and, 93; to
    do good, 93; economic, 17, 200; from
    emotional bonds to external world,
    33; in enjoyment of the earth, 147;
    flaws in, 9; from freedom, 38–40;
    growth of, 17; healing and, 36;
    historical conditions for, 22; indi-
    vidual, 9, 34, 154; inner/outer, 33;
    internalized, 34; lack of, 9, 17–40; loss
    of, 217*n1;* misuse by Adam, 24;
    outer/inner, 31; personal, 18, 21, 23,
    30, 33, 34, 39, 184; political, 17;
    progress in, 40; racial, 17; reason and,
    9, 32; redefinition of, 31; religious, 17;
    resolution of lack and, 34; right to,
    152; sacrificing, 22; of self, 19; as self-
    determination, 20; self-interested, 154;
    social, 21; sovereignal, 18, 21, 23, 33–
    34, 37, 39–40; spiritual, 34; as
    supreme value, 18; technological, 18;
    of thought, 172; tyranny and, 20–23;
    value of, 34, 39; virtue of, 18;
    Western ideal of, 9, 18, 19
Free grace, 138
Freud, Sigmund, 4, 19, 81
Frondes, 98
Fundamentalism, 198

Galileo, 113, 114
Generosity, 2, 209–210
*Genesis,* 34, 55
*Genjo-koan* (Dogen), 7
George, Stefan, 179
Gierke, Otto, 102
Glorious Revolution, 143, 219*n3*
God: as abstract necessity, 123; alienation
    from, 10, 48, 49; authority derived
    from, 96; choosing for salvation, 93;
    creation of cosmos by, 12; internaliza-
    tion of, 165; as judge, 49; as law, 51;
    maintenance of cosmos by, 89; moral
    authority of, 106; mortality of, 100;
    obedience to, 34; omnipotence of, 93;
    omniscience of, 93; personal relation-
    ship with, 12; plan for humanity, 17,
    59; private relationship with, 93;
    reason and, 148; relationships with,
    14, 39, 49, 127; role of, 39; severance

of continuity with, 112; submission to will of, 34; time belonging to, 56; transcendence of, 44, 117, 161; transcendental validation and, 153; turning back to, 10; wealth as sign of approval from, 106; will of, 47, 113

Goethe, Johann Wolfgang von, 17

Goodwin, John, 140

Greece, 9; anxiety in, 27; colonialism of, 27; decline in, 128; drama in, 27; humanism in, 24; mob rule in, 28, 30; money in, 78, 184; romantic love in, 73; skepticism in, 27; slavery in, 217n2; transcendence in, 25

Greed, 87, 123, 151; consequences of, 2; for consumption, 209; delusion and, 16; individualism and, 18; institutionalization of, 88; market capitalism and, 16; as part of defective value system, 207; promotion of, 87; spiritual problem with, 207

Gregory VII (Pope), 46, 48

Grounding: in modern science, 118; organic paradigm and, 89; spiritual, 13

Groundlessness, 1; denial of, 4; dread of, 84; fear of, 3; modernity and, 89

Guilt: awareness and, 7; coping with, 6–7; culture, 29; expiation of, 6, 45; illusion of, 6; money and, 81, 82, 83, 183; neurotic, 7; ontological, 5, 6, 7; Protestantism and, 150; role of, 6; sense of self and, 7; unconscious, 183

Haberman, Jurgen, 221n15

Hades, 27–28

Hadrian, 46

Hall, Joseph, 133

Haller, William, 91, 131, 135, 137, 138, 139, 140–141, 144, 220n7

Hamburg, Dan, 104

Harrington, Alan, 67

Harvey, William, 114

Hatred, 123

Hawthorne, Nathaniel, 66

Hazlitt, William, 69

Hegel, G.W.F., 128, 160, 178

Heidegger, Martin, 83, 172

Henry IV (Holy Roman Emperor), 46

Henry VI (Holy Roman Emperor), 57

Henry VIII (King of England), 98, 137

Herder, Johann, 104

Heresy, 43

Herodotus, 27

Heroism, 67

Herz, John, 108

Hill, Christopher, 131, 132, 133, 134, 136, 138, 139, 140, 142, 144, 145, 146, 147, 148, 150, 220n4

Hillesum, Etty, 76–77

Hillman, James, 219n6

Hobbes, Thomas, 14, 99, 111, 127, 130, 132, 145, 146, 148, 149, 150, 152, 154, 156, 157

Hölderlin, Friedrich, 104

Holy Commonwealth, 163

Holy Roman Empire, 89; secular fissipation of, 43

Homer, 26

Horace, 66, 67

Huang-po, 8

Hugh of St. Victor, 58

Hugo, Victor, 68

Huizinga, Johann, 66, 68, 75, 92, 189, 218n4

Humanism, 24, 34; classical, 34; development of, 26; origins of, 28

Humboldt, Alexander von, 104

Hume, David, 150, 156, 157, 159, 166, 222n7

Humphreys, S.C., 26, 44

Hutterites, 101

Identity, national, 163, 164

Idolatry, 121–124

Imagination: covetous, 149; fear and, 148; selfish, 148, 151

Immaculate conception, 43

Immortality: obsession with, 68; sacred power and, 88; symbolic, 68

India, 19, 25, 26, 27, 90, 108

Individualism, 130; democratic, 18; extreme, 18; freedom and, 9; greed and, 18; Greek, 28; increase in, 31, 154; proliferation of, 93; secularity of, 65; self-interested, 160; of utilitarianism, 207

Indulgences, 52; as source of income in, 52, 107

Inherited Conglomerate, 217n4

Innocent III (Pope), 52

Inquisition, 43

Institutions: calculability in, 174; civil, 162; ecclesiastical, 50; impersonal, 110; legal, 50; modern, 91; need for new, 97; political, 96, 124; religious, 92, 162, 198; salvation through, 92; secular, 13, 50, 92, 121; social, 8, 140; state, 95; this-worldly, 161; trust in, 101

Intentionality, 191

Isaiah, 26, 34

Jainism, 26

James I (King of England), 97

Japan, 212

Jaspers, Karl, 212

Jeanne d'Arc, 68

Jeffrey, Meg, 209, 210

Jellinek, Georg, 164

Jeremiah, 26

Joachim of Fiore, 57, 59, 61, 62, 148

Joyce, James, 65

Kant, Immanuel, 104, 179, 193

Karma, 3

Keane, John, 126, 127

Keen, Maurice, 46, 47, 52

Kennedy, Paul, 109

Kenney, Robert, 146

Kepler, Johannes, 111, 113

Kings: as absolute rulers, 95, 99; as agents of God, 102; appointment of clergy by, 46; centralization of power in, 95, 98; distance from subjects, 95; divine right of, 46–47, 95, 142, 145, 149; as feudal landlords, 95; holding court, 47; influence on church affairs, 37; law of, 51, 53; loss of relevance of, 99; need for power by, 97; replacement by bureaucratic states, 117; as semireligious personages, 37; as stand-in for God, 97; sun, 98

Knowledge, 89; compartmentalization of, 174; grounding, 120; human, 118, 119; infallible, 140; as power, 112;

principles of, 118, 119; scientific, 117; specialization of, 174

Koestler, Arthur, 1, 8

Korten, Davud, 204

LaBarre, Weston, 82

Labor, 157; as commodity, 203; involuntary, 217n2; "liberation" of, 16, 202

Lack: anxiety and, 23, 106, 109; bifurcation of supernatural from natural and, 121; Buddhist perspective on, 35, 61; capitalism and, 105; causes of, 169; of civil society, 13–14, 125–170; communal approach to, 162; community and, 25; creation of future and, 61; defective myths of, 12; economic solution to, 111; ego and, 6; of enough money, 12; fame and, 66–72; feeling of "I don't yet have enough..," 65, 83; feeling of "something is wrong with me" and, 6, 39, 65; of freedom, 9, 17–40; future of, 211–215; individuality and, 36; ineradicable, 150; institutional, 13, 122; letting go of self in, 74; of modernity, 12–13, 87–124; New World and, 110; objectification of, 9, 13, 96, 122; as origin of the origin, 67; personal solutions to, 11; privatization of, 162; of progress, 9–10, 41–64; rationality and, 24; religious solution to, 45; Renaissance of, 10–11, 65–85; resolution of, 6, 10; sin and, 36; social relationships and, 61; social understanding of, 169; thriving on love, 73; in traditional societies, 25

Lack, sense of, 1, 4, 5, 8; acknowledgment of, 90; attempts to overcome, 122; Buddhist perspective of, 8, 143; collective, 89; coping with, 35; nation-states and, 103; overcoming, 138; predestination and, 94; religious explanation, 81; resolving, 8–9; scientific knowledge and, 117; secular alternatives to, 81; social behavior and, 8; as source of social domination, 88; strength of, 39; time and, 45

Laissez-faire, 203

Land, 157; as commodity, 135; enclosures, 146, 202; "liberation" of, 16, 202; profit and, 135

Landes, David, 56, 60, 63

Landes, Richard, 62

Language: vernacular, 43

Lapham, Lewis, 66

Last Days: belief in, 61

Last Judgment, 10, 42, 49, 50

Law: ancient, 47; authority of, 42, 43; civil, 140; codes, 43; development of, 43; divine, 50; focus on precedent, 53; folk, 47; God as, 51; of grace, 162; kings, 47; king's, 51; kings as guardians of, 47; medieval, 47; natural, 50, 88, 98, 116, 144, 162, 163, 164, 165, 220n7; need for new concepts of, 98; obedience to, 140; overarching, 101; penitential, 47–48; as product of rationality, 53; public, 99; rational codification of, 44; redemption and, 48; respect for, 101; of righteousness, 148; sacred, 177; science of, 46; secular, 53; spiritual foundations of, 44, 48–53; theology of, 49; transcendence and, 43; of wages, 206; Western, 42

The Laws (Plato), 30

Le Goff, Jacques, 106, 107

Leibniz, Gottfried, 104

Lennon, John, 70

Lerner, Michael, 123

Levellers, 146

Leviathan (Hobbes), 99, 100, 132, 145, 154, 221n9

Liberation: textual, 17

Lincoln, Abraham, 163

Literacy, 132

Lobha, 87

Localism, 167

Locke, John, 14, 127, 152, 153, 155, 156, 157, 165

Logic: deductive, 120

Longfellow, Henry Wadsworth, 66

Louis XIV (King of France), 102, 114

Love, 65, 72–77; absence and, 73; consummation of, 75; courtly, 75;

court of, 74; death and, 74; as delusive craving, 65; incompatibility with marriage, 74; love of, 10–11; as madness, 73; myths of, 76; narcissism and, 74; Platonic, 76; poetic conception of, 218n4; preoccupation with sex and, 11; reason and, 148; romantic, 11; spiritual character of, 74; from standpoint of self, 73, –74; thriving on lack, 73; transformational abilities of, 76

Luke, 134

Luther, Martin, 12, 39, 52, 53, 77, 91, 92, 93, 112, 130, 145, 161

Maguire, Daniel, 93

Mahavira, 26

Malthus, Thomas, 206

Manichaeism, 74

Mappo, 90

Market(s): arms, 87–88; capitalism, 15–16, 107, 108, 198, 200, 201, 207; commodification of human relations and, 156; economy, 91; equities, 175; exchange, 155, 158; free, 91; indoctrination, 210; invisible hand in, 176, 177, 200; laws of, 88; local, 110; moral, 155; moral neutrality of, 168; need for trust in, 204; relations, 154, 200; religion of, 15–16, 197–210; sacred, 78; self-regulating, 160; stock, 110, 121, 175; values, 200; wisdom of, 199

Marx, Karl, 104, 124, 135, 150, 160

Marxism, 59

Mason, S., 114

Materialism: spiritual, 107

Matthew, 134

Maya civilization, 54–55

Mead, George Herbert, 155

Meaning: of history, 59; of life, 13; "not yet enough" and, 13, 83; ultimate, 38

Means: of absolution, 65; becoming the ends, 15; calculability of, 174; domination of the end by, 174; endless, 173; money as, 15; over ends, 100; preoccupation with, 14–15; swallowing ends, 178

Means-ends: inversion, 173; nonduality of, 189–195; reversal, 172; widening divergence in, 190

Media: advertising in, 88; infotainment and, 88; prostitution of, 200

Medieval paradigm: overthrow of, 90, 91

Meditation: awareness and, 7; becoming nothing and, 7; de-reflection in, 7; forgetting the self in, 193

*Meditations* (Aurelius), 33, 67

*Meditations* (Descartes), 120

Melville, Herman, 163, 164

Mennonites, 101

Mersenne, Marin, 116

Messiah: return of, 48

Michelangelo, 66, 68

Middle Ages: economic activity in, 42, 43, 201; origin of West and, 41; situation of Popes in, 44

Military-industrial complex, 87, 88

Millenialism, 13, 59, 127, 135, 136, 137; discouragement of, 61; encouraged by the Bible, 144; popular importance of, 62, 136; Puritan, 14; role in Western history, 60

Miller, Daniel, 207

Milton, John, 68, 84, 132, 133, 135, 145

Modernity: groundlessness and, 89; idolatry of, 121–124; lack of, 12–13, 87–124; loss of community in, 179, 180; means/ends problem, 14–15; nihilism of, 13, 122; secular, 122; spiritual roots of, 89

*Moha,* 87

Money, 65, 77–84; accumulating Being through, 79; advantages of, 184; Buddhist perspective on, 79; complex, 15, 77, 81, 82, 185; as condensed wealth, 81; control of destiny and, 80; as delusive craving, 65; desire for, 78; domination of, 186; as embodied relativity of economic goods, 186; as fetishized symbol, 12; guilt and, 81, 82, 83, 183; as happiness *in abstracto,* 77; hypertrophy of, 183; importance of, 10–11; issued by priests, 78; as means, 15; origins of, 78, 184; profit motive and, 80; psychoanalytic theory

of, 77; as pure symbol, 183; pursuit of, 11; role of, 182; sacred nature of, 78, 185; as solace, 80; symbolism of, 185; as value, 11–12, 15, 77, 79, 107; value as means, 183

Montaigne, Michel, 119

Moral: accountability, 143; agents, 163; authority, 97, 98, 106, 110, 161; capital, 204, 205; confusion, 137; conscience, 165; development, 209; governance, 38; neutrality, 110; order, 161; principles, 39; responsibility, 96, 143; science, 175; value, 164

Morality: decline of, 44; minimalist, 44; religiously based, 44; transcendent, 156, 213

Mortality: acknowledgment of, 159

Mosaic Decalogue, 25, 26

Moses, 27

*Mukti,* 19

*Mulamadhyamikakarikas* (Nagarjuna), 186, 190, 192, 193

Muller, Herbert, 24

Muller, Jerry, 158

Mumford, Lewis, 87, 109, 150

Murray, Oswyn, 67

Mutuality, 101

Mysticism: personal, 68

Myth: creation, 54; Indian, 90; of love, 76; personal, 74; religious, 58

Nagarjuna, 67, 84, 186, 190, 191, 193, 213, 222n7

Nandy, Ashis, 102

Napier, John, 135

Narcissism, 74, 77

National interest, 121

Nationalism, 94; domination by, 123; as most popular religion, 94; sense of security and, 102

Nation-states, 12, 94–104. *See also* State; becoming real through, 104; birth of, 46; charismatic rulers of, 12–13; competition among, 13, 102; development of, 95; fissipation of Holy Roman Empire into, 43; instability of, 13; Lutheran/Calvinist accomodation with, 101; as most successful god, 94; noninterference in domestic affairs of other states, 97; as objectified form of collective lack, 112; Protestant Reformation and, 94; religious origins of, 96; rule by absolute sovereigns in, 97; secularity of, 89; self-aggrandizement and, 122; self-grounding, 95; self-justification of, 102; sense of lack and, 103; signification of, 116; spiritual role of, 107; stability of, 122; substitution for community, 103

Natural selection, 117

Nature: after the Fall, 150; description of, 115; domination of, 40, 134; human, 14, 92, 99, 146, 152; laws of, 116, 144, 162; man's, 14; of power, 37; prepolitical state of, 155; state of, 13, 97, 127, 149, 152, 153; totalitarian relationship with, 40

New England, 137, 161, 162

Newton, Isaac, 59, 60, 113, 116, 117, 135, 220n10

New World: civil utopia and, 110; colonization and, 109; religious projection and, 109–110; solving lack in, 110

Nicene Creed, 50

Nietzsche, Friedrich, 5, 8, 27, 76, 82, 96, 175, 191, 194, 195, 213

Nihilism, 218n6; of modernity, 13

Nirvana, 85, 190, 191, 213

Noble, David, 58, 59

No-self, 3

Nothingness: fear of, 8; sense-of-self and, 6, 19

Objectification: of disenchanted world, 191; of lack, 9, 13, 96, 122; lack of satisfaction and, 5; of self, 4

Occultism, 32

Oedipal project, 4, 122

Organic paradigm, 89–91; collapse of, 109, 110, 112

Origen, 61

Other: bifurcation of self from, 33

Pacifism, 142

Pande, G.C., 19

Papacy. See also individual Popes; authority of, 44, 51; power of, 52; as state, 52; supremacy of, 46; temporal entanglements of, 52; transformation of, 10; as ultimate spiritual authority, 51

Papal Reformation, 9–10, 42, 43, 46–48, 50

Parker, Henry, 144, 145

Parmenides' Being, 24

Particularism, 167

Patriotism, 94, 103

Patterson, Orlando, 18, 19, 20, 21, 28, 33, 37

Paul, 34

Pax Christi, 64

Paz, Octavio, 41

Peloponnesian War, 28

Penance, 92; meaning of, 10

Perfection: attainability of, 36; classical ideal of, 36; self, 35

Pericles, 27, 217n3

Persecution, 142

Philip Augustus (King of France), 57

Philosophy: Cartesian, 120; ethical, 31; founding, 118, 120; mechanical, 116; modern, 118, 119, 120; natural, 98, 112, 113; political, 145; social, 134

The Philosophy of Money (Simmel), 182, 186

Plato, 27, 28, 29, 31, 76, 128, 129, 218n7

Plotinus, 32

Plutarch, 73

Poggi, Gianfranco, 97, 99, 102, 104, 109

Polanyi, Karl, 80, 81, 201, 202

Political: action, 168; chaos, 100; development, 219n3; fragmentation, 96; institutions, 96, 124; order, 163; organization, 136; participation, 167; philosophy, 145; polytheism, 102; power, 95; reconstruction, 57; sovereignty, 97; thought, 97; traditions, 150

Political theory: biblical foundations of, 144–152; origin of, 144

Politics: as branch of theology, 96; as moral consummation of human activity, 128; as religion, 87; secular, 99; skepticism about, 128; war, 109

"Politics as a Vocation" (Weber), 103
Popes: divine right of, 145; as God's
    vicar, 44
Popper, Karl, 128
Poverty, 160, 206
Power: absolute, 152, 154; balance of,
    94; centralization of, 95; consolidation
    of, 125; of covetousness, 146; desire
    for, 99, 149; divine, 21; downward
    shifts of, 96; of emperors, 36; as end
    in itself, 13; as goal, 13; of monarch,
    97; nature of, 37; of nightmares, 65;
    of Papacy, 52; political, 95; protection
    of, 158; sacred, 88; secular, 142, 204;
    state, 99, 103, 152; sufficiency of, 122;
    technological, 117; temporal, 43;
    transcendent, 103; transfer of, 42
Prajna, 3
Predestination, 93, 94, 105, 106, 220n7;
    antinomianism and, 139; capitalism
    and, 105, 106; human depravity and,
    138; lack and, 94, 106; salvation and,
    138
Principia (Newton), 116
Production: capitalist means of, 101; civil
    society and, 157; ever-increasing, 197;
    for local markets, 110; medieval, 110
Profit, 157, 201; desire for, 207;
    preoccupation with, 178
Progress: cult of, 69; faith in, 57; lack
    of, 9–10, 41–64; preoccupation with,
    45; time for, 53–60; toward precondi-
    tions for salvation, 10
Projection: lack and, 1
Property: communal, 147; defense of,
    152; inequality and, 158; ownership
    of, 146; private, 14, 127, 152, 219n6;
    protection of, 147; relations, 155;
    sanctification of, 53, 153; sin and,
    147; socialist critiques of, 127
Protagoras, 28
The Protestant Ethic and the Spirit of
    Capitalism (Weber), 176, 201
Protestantism: guilt and, 150; lack of
    confession in, 131; salvational doctrine
    of, 154
Protestant Reformation, 12, 68, 90, 91–
    94, 143; consequences of, 161; denial

of need for intermediaries between
    God and world, 113; implications of,
    92, 93; nation-states and, 94; scientific
    attitude and, 114; shared ideological
    commitment to, 161
Psyche and Cupid, 76
Psychoanalysis: religion and, 2
Purgatory, 42, 49; development of, 43;
    duration of, 107; indulgences and, 107
Puritanism, 105, 116, 127, 137, 138,
    161, 162; capitalism and, 184; heresy
    and, 140; schism and, 140
Puritans, 14
Pym, John, 145, 146
Pythagoras, 27

Quakers, 142

Rabb, Theodore, 90, 94
Rank, Otto, 6, 22, 81
Ranters, 140, 146
Rationality, 45, 160; calculative, 166;
    capitalist, 82; deductive, 149; defining,
    205; formal, 173, 174, 176; Greek, 32;
    human, 119; instrumental, 15, 100,
    156, 166, 174, 175, 176, 189, 191,
    193, 194; law as product of, 53; self-
    grounding, 120; sense of lack and, 24;
    substantive, 174, 176, 191
Rationalization, 173; economic, 177,
    202; of objective world, 179, 180
Reagan, Ronald, 77
Reality: fame and, 71; sense of, 70;
    social, 30; true, 93
Realpolitik, 96
Reason, 147, 148; Being and, 24;
    classical emphasis on, 35; collective
    understanding of, 156; conscience
    and, 140; discovery of, 218n6;
    emancipation from myth, 17; as error,
    35; freedom and, 9, 32; God and, 148;
    human, 130; liberation from require-
    ments of faith, 130; love and, 148;
    myth and, 26; nihilism and, 218n6; in
    public sphere, 166; as supplement to
    faith, 53; theology of, 148; universal,
    164; as value neutral, 166; veneration
    of, 129

Redemption, 42, 163; crucifixion and, 50; efforts to learn truth and, 140; God's plan for, 130; law and, 48; as legal transaction, 49; participation in, 130

Reductionism: materialistic, 66; psychologistic, 66

Reformation, 17

Relativism, 34

Religion: Abrahamic, 207; American, 160–167; antagonism to, 2; defining, 197; deinstitutionalization of, 68; economic, 199; economic system as, 15–16; Enlightenment and, 2; expulsion of politics from, 130; grounding by, 1; immortality of soul and, 3; legalistic, 107, 177; of the market, 15–16, 197–210; of the masses, 94; nationalism as, 94; negation of, 77; as opiate, 160; personal, 11; as political force, 87; preoccupation with outmoded perspectives, 198; as private matter, 142; privatization of, 12, 53; psychoanalysis and, 2; replaced by technology, 58; ritualistic, 107; salvation, 107, 108, 177; secularization of, 32; of the self, 24–34; sociology of, 177; survival of, 198; symbols and, 81; time structures and, 53–54; wars of, 219n6

Renaissance: of lack, 10–11, 65–85; as revolution, 41; sense of self in, 11

Rent, 157

Repression, 3, 19–20; consciousness and, 4, 82; denial of self and, 4; return of, 5

The Republic (Plato), 30, 31, 128

Reputation, 67

Resistance: passive, 142

Responsibility: need for, 40

Restoration, 138, 142

Revelation, 59, 60, 61, 134, 135

Revolutions, 90; American, 17, 126; destruction of existing orders by, 52; English, 17; experience of, 10, 50; French, 17, 126, 127, 143; industrial, 202, 208; Papal, 9–10; religiopolitical, 127; religious, 143; Renaissance, 41; secular, 42; social, 25; spiritual, 10, 42

Richard I (King of England), 57

Rights: of appeal, 46; civil, 17; divine, 99; to freedom, 152; gay, 17; human, 28–29; individual, 14, 101, 127, 130, 152; to liberty, 164; of man, 126; pollution, 220n11; to pursuit of happiness, 164

Romans, 134

Rome, 9; disintegration of, 129; as expansionist war machine, 129; money in, 78; romantic love in, 73

Rosenstock-Huessy, Eugen, 52, 211

Rousseau, Jean-Jacques, 150

Russell, Bertrand, 172

Sacrifices, 55, 57

St. Anselm, 130

St. Bonaventura, 57

St. Francis, 57, 68, 84

Sale, Kirkpatrick, 202

Salvation, 57; assurance of, 178; being chosen for, 93; corporate orientation toward, 68; dealers in, 32; God's scheme of, 130; individual, 32; inner-worldly, 179, 180, 189; irrelevance of institutional mediation for, 92, 93; material success and, 106; preconditions for, 10, 50; predestination and, 138; profanation of, 69; religion, 107, 108, 177, 212; secular, 70, 197; from self-cultivation, 32; self-transformation and, 37; sexual, 75; spiritual, 58; through advertising, 200; through religious institutions, 92; through romance, 74; total, 60; yearning for, 60

Samadhi, 3

Sampson, Leo, 161

Samsara, 3, 19, 191

Samskaras, 3

Samuel, 134

Sartre, Jean Paul, 84

Satan, 140, 144

Scaff, Lawrence, 175, 177, 179, 180, 181

Schopenhaure, Artur, 77

Science: as alternative explanation of world, 197; development of, 51; moral, 175

Science, mechanistic, 12, 111–118; origins of, 89; theory of mechanics in, 113

Scottish Enlightenment, 154–155

Second Advent, 61

Second Coming, 51, 57, 135

*Second Treatise of Government* (Locke), 152, 153

Self: actualization, 7; alienated, 193; being, 67; bifurcation from other, 33; Cartesian, 39; deconstruction of, 191; denial of, 4; development of, 9; empowerment, 102, 111; existence, 9, 20, 155; experience of, 9; forgetting, 7; freedom of, 19, 20; fulfillment, 69; harmony with cosmos, 33; individuality of, 9, 20; internalized, 193; justification, 102, 111; liberation from, 36; non-Western concepts of, 20; objectification of, 4; perfection, 35; preoccupation, 36; realization, 11; reflection, 7, 31; religion of, 24–34; sanctity of, 29; self-governance of, 31; sinfulness of, 25; study of, 7; sufficiency, 129; valuation of freedom by, 21

Self, sense of, 6; autonomy of, 20; collective, 95–96; as construct, 1; experiencing, 2; forgetting, 7; formation of, 155; groundless, 35; guilt and, 7; illusory nature of, 190; internalization of, 11; need to realize, 66; nothingness and, 19; in Renaissance, 11; self-reflection and, 7; sense-of-lack and, 4; strength of, 39

Self-consciousness, 1; assumption of role of God by, 39; autonomy of, 5, 65; historical causes for, 26; illusion of, 4; increase in, 29

Self-destruction, 1

Self-esteem, 7

Self-grounding, 3

Self-interest, 157, 158; pursuit of, 157

Seligman,, 153, 154, 156, 158, 160, 161, 163, 165, 166, 169, 221n15

Seligman, Adam, 125

Serenity, 8

Servetus, Michael, 113–114

Sex: obsessive nature of, 11; preoccupation with, 11, 75; salvation from, 75; spiritual fulfillment from, 75

Shakespeare, William, 77

Shakyamuni, 2–3, 3, 4, 6, 26, 90, 159

Sieyes, Emmanuel Joseph, 94

Simmel, Georg, 15, 78, 173, 179, 182–189, 190, 191, 193, 194, 222n4

Sin: acts of contrition and, 10; ancient, 34–38; atonement for, 35; Augustinian construction of, 9, 34; awareness of, 35; belief in, 39, 81; canon law and, 10; Christian understanding of, 35; church's understanding of, 90; commodification of, 10, 49; as condition of alienation from God, 49; consciousness of, 6; coping with lack and, 36; God's scheme of, 130; intent and, 37; legalistic definitions of, 10; loss of belief in, 12, 83; objectified sense of, 49; as offense against God, 51; original, 6, 24, 35, 36, 90, 93, 129, 146; property and, 147; redemption from, 10, 140; religious conception of, 6; spiritual slavery of, 34; as state of alienation from God, 48; theological doctrine on, 42

Skepticism, 27, 119; about politics, 128

Slavery, 20, 21, 134, 217n2; spiritual, 34

Smith, Adam, 111, 150, 157, 158, 159, 166, 177, 200, 204, 222n3

Social: anxiety, 12, 89; attitudes, 144; behavior, 8; bonds, 155; change, 143; chaos, 99, 103; conditioning, 11; control, 47; crises, 45, 61; development, 91, 159; domination, 88; evolution, 41, 160, 178; ferment, 126–127; freedom, 21; injustice, 124, 198; institutions, 8, 140; justice, 34, 207, 208; norms, 140; order, 125, 130, 162; philosophy, 134; reality, 30; relationships, 21, 61, 80, 154, 201; responsibility, 183; revolution, 25; services, 87; solidarity, 161; stability, 100; standing,

201; strife, 30; structures, 39; system, 81; theory, 99, 173; thought, 169; transformation, 137; trust, 166

Social contract, 145; common good and, 156; deriving from Adam's Fall, 145; secular, 130

Socialism, 103, 150, 154, 160, 168, 178

Society. *See also* Civil society; archaic, 81; atomized, 154; censored, 133; commercialization of, 152–159; degradation of, 205; feudal, 89; human, 43, 99; integration into cosmos, 25; madness in, 8; as mechanical construct, 99; medieval, 42, 58; personal oaths of individuals and, 47; reform of, 13, 126, 161; religious, 91; reshaping, 45; restructuring, 146, 212; secular, 67, 91; threats from chaos, 97; time structures in, 53–54; transformation of, 50; unified, 89; Western, 67

Socrates, 27, 28, 29, 31, 73, 76, 187

Solon, 27

Soul: fallen state of, 49; harmony in, 31; immortality of, 3

Speier, Julius, 76

Spengler, Oswald, 53, 178

Spinoza, Baruch, 120

Stael, Madame de, 72

State: absolutizing, 95; bureaucracy in, 95, 98, 100, 101, 117; censorship, 133; coercive, 101, 147, 149; corporations and, 108; cultural mission of, 104; despotism, 126; existence of, 219n6; harmony in, 31; ideal, 128; impersonal evolution of, 95; institutions, 95; intrusive, 168; invention of concept of, 51; limits to sovereignty in, 102; national interest and, 121; of nature, 14, 97, 127, 149, 152, 153; objectification of power in, 99; origin, 219n1; Papacy as, 52; power, 99, 103, 152; protection against, 28–29; public law and, 99; reform, 137; role of, 219n3; secular, 53, 132, 142; security purpose of, 104; separate from church, 152; shaped by civil society, 160; socialism,

103, 154; sovereignty, 101; subordination of church to, 37; sympathetic, 158; theory of, 149; theory of justice as neutral, 53; war, 109

Stoicism, 24, 32, 33, 34, 128, 129

Strayer, Joseph, 51

Subjectivity: broadening of, 9; Cartesian thought and, 118; flight into, 179, 180; hypertrophied, 14–15, 178; intensification of, 191; of internalized self, 193; modern, 120; reactive flights into, 173; religious, 120–121; self-grounded, 118; self-sufficient, 37

Suffering, 3, 19, 90, 181, 190; salvation from, 60

*Sunya,* 123, 191

*Sunyata,* 84, 186, 213

*Svabhava,* 4

Syndicalism, 160

*Tathata,* 193

Tawney, R.H., 80, 81, 201

*Technik,* 172

Technology, 45; medieval attitude toward, 58; replacement for religion, 58

Temporality, 45; associative, 56; cause and effect continuum in, 56; cosmology/history and, 56, 57; modern, 55; space-time continuum in, 55, 56

Tenenti, Alberto, 92

Thales, 27

Thatcher, Margaret, 165

Theology: of law, 49; of reason, 148; Western, 50

*Theory of Moral Sentiments* (Smith), 158, 204

Thirty Years War, 135

Thompson, Damian, 54, 57, 58

Thought: abstract, 31; apocalyptic, 135; Cartesian, 118, 120; economic, 106; freedom of, 172; Neoplatonic, 24, 38; political, 97; social, 169

Thucydides, 27, 217n3

Tichonius, 61

Tilly, Charles, 109

Time. *See also* Temporality; absolute, 117;
    archaic civilizations and, 54–55;
    autonomous, 56; belonging to God, 56;
    clock, 56; culture and, 53; cyclic, 81;
    future-oriented, 81; individual, 56;
    linear, 81; measurement of, 55;
    medieval, 57; for progress, 53–60;
    redefining, 45; as renewable pattern, 54;
    secular, 54, 60; sense of lack and, 45
Tithes, 142
Tolerance, 134, 137, 140, 142, 143
Totalitarianism, 20–23, 30; of Plato, 128
Toulmin, Stephen, 97, 100, 118, 119, 120
Tower of the Winds (Athens), 56
Toynbee, Arnold, 94
Tranquillity, 33
Transcendence: Axial, 212, 213; in
    development of West, 38–40; as
    divine revelation, 43; of God, 44, 117,
    161; as higher reality, 25; Indian, 25,
    26; law and, 43; main aspects of, 212;
    new understanding of, 212; search for
    authority and, 25–26; spiritual, 75; as
    theoretical cosmology, 43; as universal
    ethic, 25
Transcendentalism, 32
Transference, 3
*Treatise of Human Nature* (Hume), 156
Treaty of Westphalia (1648), 97
Tristan and Iseult, 73, 74
Trust: breakdown of, 101; criteria of,
    170; diminution of, 101; in institu-
    tions, 101; interpersonal, 167, 169; in
    markets, 204; personal, 101; social,
    166; universalized, 166
Truth: criteria of, 156; objective, 189;
    propositional, 32; religious, 92; self-
    understanding of, 140
*Tyche,* 32

Unamuno, Miguel de, 70
Universe: absolute space/time in, 117;
    absolutist theory of governance of,
    113; Calvinist, 113; hierarchical, 129,
    130; maintenance of, 120; need for
    deity in, 120; role in, 117; role of
    angels in, 113; understanding of, 118
Urban II (Pope), 51

Usury, 56, 106, 107
Utilitarianism, 189, 205; individualism
    of, 207

Values: commitment to, 162; community,
    158, 204; consumption, 209; eco-
    nomic, 108; fact and, 156; future-
    oriented, 108; human, 205; moral,
    164; prices and, 199; secular, 108;
    shared, 158, 204; utilitarian, 205
Virgin Mary, 43, 49
Virtue: location of, 31
Void: charismatic rulers in, 12–13;
    falling into, 7; fear of, 3; as realm of
    real dharma, 7
Vulnerability, 7

Wages, 157; iron law of, 206; population
    growth and, 206; subsistence, 206
Walwyn, William, 145
War, 90; defensive, 108; gunpowder and,
    108; politics, 109; states, 109
*The Wealth of Nations* (Smith), 157
Weber, Max, 14, 15, 21, 80, 103, 105,
    106, 107, 166, 173–182, 184, 189,
    194, 201, 221*n2, 222n3*
the West: anomalous nature of, 41;
    dynamism of, 45; greed and, 2;
    historical eras of, 42; ideals of
    freedom in, 9, 18, 19; legal tradition
    in, 44; loss of confidence in, 44;
    origin of, 41, 42; secularization of, 1;
    transcendence in development of, 38–
    40
West, Delno, 57, 59, 61
"While God Tarried" (Landes), 63
Will: free, 35, 93; of God, 34, 47, 113;
    ill, 87, 151; primacy of, 35; sin as, 35;
    to sovereignty, 102
Winstanley, Gerrard, 140, 146, 147, 148,
    149, 150, 156
Wittgenstein, Ludwig, 174

Yalom, Irvin, 4, 189
Yates, Francis, 59
Yeats, William Butler, 171, 191

*Zweckrationalitat,* 14–15, 174, 181, 191

CPSIA information can be obtained at www.ICGtesting.com
Printed in the USA
LVOW081739150212

268859LV00001B/109/A